CW00339507

# PC Programmer's Pocket Book

# PC Programmer's Pocket Book

Stephen Morris

NEWNES

Newnes
An imprint of Butterworth-Heinemann Ltd
Linacre House, Jordan Hill, Oxford OX2 8DP

 A member of the Reed Elsevier plc group

OXFORD LONDON BOSTON
MUNICH NEW DELHI SINGAPORE SYDNEY
TOKYO TORONTO WELLINGTON

*First published under the title Newnes PC User's Pocket Book 1991*
*Reprinted 1993*
*This revised and updated edition, under the title Newnes PC Programmer's Pocket Book, first published 1993*
*Reprinted 1995*



**British Library Cataloguing in Publication Data**
A catalogue record for this book is available from the British Library

ISBN 0 7506 1386 6

Produced by Butford Technical Publishing
Butford Farm, Bodenham, Hereford
Printed and bound in Great Britain

# Contents


**Preface** 9

**1 Components of the System** **11**

The 80x86 family 11
80x87 maths co-processors 12
The system clock 12
Programmable Interval Timer (PIT) 13
Direct Memory Access (DMA) 14
Programmable Interrupt Controller (PIC) 15
Other components 15
Memory 16
User RAM 16
Video RAM 18
Expansion ROMs 18
The BIOS 19
Upper Memory Area (UMA) 19
High Memory Area (HMA) 20
The system RAM variables 20
The system board dip switches 23
Checking the configuration list 23
Detecting the RAM size 27
Real and protected modes 28
The main system board 29
The system bus 31
Ports 32

**2 Programming Principles** **37**

Binary 37
Hexadecimal 41
Binary operations 49
ASCII representations 52
Organisation of memory 57
The registers 59
The stack 65
Addressing modes 68
80x86 instructions 73
Assembler operation 75
Binary and executable files 76
DEBUG 77
The program segment prefix 78
Ending a program 84
Address interrupts 85
Calling other programs 86
Critical errors 91
Multi-tasking 93
Terminate and Stay Resident programs (TSRs) 96

**3 DOS** **99**

Versions of DOS 99
The DOS boot record 106

| | | |
|---|---|---|
| | The DOS BIOS | 108 |
| | The kernel | 109 |
| | The command interpreter | 109 |
| | The environment | 111 |
| | Country-dependent information | 112 |
| | Booting up the computer | 120 |
| | Loading the operating system | 124 |
| **4** | **Interrupts** | **125** |
| | Interrupt vectors | 125 |
| | Handling interrupts | 127 |
| | Hardware interrupts | 128 |
| | Software interrupts | 130 |
| | Interrupt replacements | 132 |
| | Compatibility | 134 |
| **5** | **The Clock** | **135** |
| | Timing processes | 135 |
| | The Real Time Clock | 139 |
| | The time functions | 146 |
| | The alarm | 150 |
| **6** | **The Keyboard** | **151** |
| | The keyboard hardware | 151 |
| | Operation of the keyboard | 152 |
| | The special keys | 158 |
| | The keyboard translation table | 161 |
| | The KEYB programs | 166 |
| | Duplicate keys | 168 |
| | Key repeats | 168 |
| | Keyboard functions | 169 |
| | Getting a character | 170 |
| | Reporting the next character | 174 |
| | Combining keyboard and screen operations | 175 |
| | Clearing the keyboard buffer | 176 |
| | String input | 177 |
| **7** | **Other Input Devices** | **179** |
| | The mouse | 179 |
| | Mouse movement | 181 |
| | The mouse cursor | 182 |
| | Mouse appearance | 185 |
| | The mouse buttons | 189 |
| | The user mouse interrupt | 191 |
| | The light pen | 192 |
| | The joystick | 193 |
| **8** | **The Video Display** | **195** |
| | Screen components | 195 |
| | The monitor | 195 |
| | Video RAM | 197 |
| | Adaptors and gate arrays | 197 |

The video ports 200
Pixel components 201
Video state 203
Text modes 203
Writing directly to memory 208
Graphics modes 212
Working with pixels 214
Palettes 216
Display modes 223
Display pages 225
Windows 226
Writing characters to the screen 229
The hardware cursor 237
Cursor functions 237

**9 Sound** **241**

Programming for sound 241
Programming the ports for sound 246

**10 The Serial and Parallel Ports** **247**

The serial port hardware 247
Programming the serial port 249
Parallel port hardware 253
Programming the parallel ports 254
Time-out errors 257
The Print Screen function 258

**11 Disks and Disk Drives** **261**

Floppy disk drives 261
Disks 263
Drive numbers 264
Disk architecture 265
Sector numbering 266
Formatting floppy disks 267
Formatting hard disks 273
Interleaving 274
Reading and writing disk sectors 275
Disk status 280
Resetting the drive 283
Disk compression 283

**12 The Disk Directory and FAT** **287**

The DOS FORMAT command 287
The directory structure 288
The file attributes 294
Volume labels 297
Sub-directories 298
The current drive 299
The current directory 301
Manipulating sub-directories 302
The file allocation table (FAT) 304
Fragmentation 305

| | |
|---|---|
| FAT structure | 306 |
| Recovering FAT information | 309 |
| Deleting files | 311 |
| Disk access | 311 |
| **13 Files** | **313** |
| Data transfer areas | 313 |
| Disk buffers | 314 |
| File specifications | 315 |
| Ambiguous file specifications | 316 |
| DOS error codes | 319 |
| File handles and FCBs | 324 |
| Operations with file handles | 324 |
| Creating and opening files | 326 |
| File types | 333 |
| The file pointer | 333 |
| Reading and writing data | 335 |
| Closing files | 336 |
| Duplicating file handles | 338 |
| End-of-file markers | 339 |
| ASCII files | 339 |
| Comma-delimited files | 339 |
| Files in networks | 340 |
| Renaming files | 343 |
| Deleting files | 343 |
| Date and time stamps | 344 |
| File Control Blocks (FCBs) | 345 |
| Finding files | 346 |
| Parsing the command line | 347 |
| File size | 348 |
| Creating and opening files | 348 |
| Reading and writing sequential files | 349 |
| Reading and writing random access files | 350 |
| Closing FCB files | 352 |
| Renaming and deleting files with FCBs | 353 |
| Redirection, pipes and filters | 354 |
| **14 Device Drivers** | **355** |
| Standard device drivers | 355 |
| Installable device drivers | 357 |
| Device types | 357 |
| Structure of device drivers | 359 |
| The request header | 362 |
| Device driver procedures | 364 |
| The BIOS Parameter Block (BPB) | 364 |
| IOCTL (Input/Output Control) | 365 |
| Device commands | 366 |
| ANSI.SYS | 366 |
| **Interrupt Summary** | **369** |
| **Index** | **395** |

# Preface

The majority of business computers are classed as PC-compatible: that is, they are either IBM PCs or machines that are compatible with them. All these computers follow the same basic rules of operation.

To get the best out of these machines, programmers and advanced users need to understand how the computers work. This book takes you inside the computer, showing you how each component functions and how it may be used to best effect. Each section is illustrated by a small segment of machine code. Reference tables on PC features, such as interrupts and video modes, are included.

The book is based on the IBM PC range, including 8086, 80286, 80386 and 80486 models. The information in the book is relevant to all true IBM-compatibles; anywhere that incompatibilities may cause problems is highlighted. Versions of DOS up to and including DOS 6 are covered.

As well as providing instruction in the programming of the computer, the book can also be used as a reference guide to the inner workings of the machine.

This book should appeal to all programmers and computer enthusiasts. Since most commercial programs are written or adapted for the PC-compatibles, it is relevant to programmers at all levels.

**Disk offer**

Lack of space in this Pocket Book has not permitted me to include as many programs as I would have liked. Those that are here are fairly rudimentary and certainly not guaranteed to be perfect. They are intended as a guide for the user and not as complete programs, to be copied blindly into the computer.

However, there is nothing more frustrating than keying in a long listing, only to discover that it is full of typing errors or does not work as well as may have hoped. For this reason there is a disk offer associated with this book. The disk comes with all the routines included here. There are also many routines that had to be excluded from the book due to lack of space. Details of how to obtain a copy are given at the back of the book.

It should be noted that some routines are used in other programs in the book; in these cases the figure number of the original routine is given for reference.

**Disclaimer**

Every effort has been taken to ensure that the information given in this book is accurate and complete. However, in any work of this size there will inevitably be omissions and errors, for which I apologise. Obviously I cannot take responsibility for any problems that may arise from use of the information contained in this book.

**Acknowledgments**

This book is a revised edition of the *Newnes PC User's Pocket Book* by Jim Reid. I would like to thank all those who were involved in the original book and Emily Morris for all her additional work. I would also like to thank Microsoft Corporation for their technical assistance during the production of this book.

Preparing this Pocket Book has been an interesting and absorbing task. I hope that all who read this Pocket Book and delve into the intricacies of the PC find that their time is equally well rewarded.

# 1 Components of the System

The IBM PC and compatibles, AT-compatibles and PS/2s are all based on a series of Intel processors known collectively as the 80x86 chips. This common basis means that programs written for one PC – whether an IBM or a clone – can generally be expected to work just as well on any other member of the family. This book describes the common workings of this range of microprocessors, and highlights the differences that may be encountered.

The first chapter describes the components that are generally found on any standard PC. It also includes coverage of some of the optional extras.

## The 80x86 family

The original IBM PC and IBM PC-XT were based on an Intel 8088 processor. Although this is a 16-bit processor it has only an 8-bit data bus (as described later).

Later PC-compatibles mainly used the 8086 processor. The main difference between this and the 8088 is its 16-bit data bus. This chip also forms the core of the PS/2 models 25 and 30.

The 80286 is used by the IBM PC-AT and compatibles, as well as the PS/2 models 50 and 60. This chip operates at higher speeds, has an expanded instruction set and supports multi-tasking.

The 80386 forms the basis of many AT-compatibles, as well as the PS/2 model 80. This 32-bit processor provides additional instructions and operates at even greater speeds.

Finally, the 80486 incorporates all of the features previously provided by the 80x87 maths co-processors (with the exception of the SX and SL models). It forms the core of the PS/2 model 90.

## 80x87 maths co-processors

Performing any arithmetic calculation, even something so simple as multiplying two small numbers together, takes a comparatively long time in computer terms, especially when floating point arithmetic is required. If a more complex computation needs to be made, such as a sine or square root, the processing time can become very significant. If the main CPU has to carry out these calculations, then it is tied up for a very long time, slowing down processing in the rest of the program.

To overcome this problem, you can install a chip specifically for the task of performing mathematical calculations. This is the 80x87 maths co-processor chip. The specific chip that is installed must match the CPU it is to work with: 8087, 80287 or 80387. There is no 80487, since the floating point functions are incorporated in the 80486 itself. The 80x87 chip, being dedicated to floating point arithmetic, can perform calculations very quickly, with the added advantage that the main CPU is freed to continue with other work.

The main disadvantage is that the chip can only be used if the application programs have been designed for it. A detailed description of the 80x87 chip is beyond the scope of this book.

## The system clock

The computer operates by processing a sequence of independent electrical pulses. These pulses are emitted at regular periods by an 8284A clock chip (or equivalent). This regular pulse is the heartbeat of the computer system and is central to its entire operation. All clock, timing and sound operations are based upon the system clock.

Some PC-compatibles and all other members of the family from the AT upwards also have a *Real Time Clock (RTC)*, which is battery-backed and maintains the current date and time even when the computer is switched off.

The system clock and RTC are described in further detail in Chapter 5.

## Programmable Interval Timer (PIT)

Since timing is such an important feature of the computer system, the IBM PC contains a special device, the *8253 Programmable Interval Timer (PIT)*, to co-ordinate certain timing tasks. On the AT, the 8254 chip is used. The PIT has three timers, which are used as follows:

- Timer 0, a general-purpose timer, may be used in application programs.
- Timer 1 is accessed by channel 0 of the DMA (see below).
- Timer 2 is used when generating sound (see Chapter 9).

Each of these timers maintains a pulse count, which can be read or changed via ports 40h to 42h (described later). Each of these ports holds a word (two bytes) of data but the values can only be accessed a byte at a time.

In addition, the PIT uses port 43h to control access to the other three ports. In general, if you want to read or write a value to ports 40h to 42h, you must first put a value in port 43h. This selects the operation mode that is to follow and determines the port to be accessed. Having prepared the way, a single byte can be read or written. The use of the ports is shown in Figure 1.1.

**PIT Ports**

| Port | Counter | Use |
|---|---|---|
| 40h | 0 | General purpose timer |
| 41h | 1 | Memory refresh (channel 0 of DMA) |
| 42h | 2 | Sound generation |
| 43h | - | PIT control |

*Figure 1.1*

The PS/2s have their own customised chips to achieve the same purpose. The model 50 and above have a fourth channel that monitors the non-maskable interrupt.

## Direct Memory Access (DMA)

The next chapter demonstrates that a 16-bit address is sufficient to uniquely define only 64K of memory locations. The address cannot exceed this size because of the limitations of the 16-bit system bus. To overcome this problem, the computer's memory is divided into 64K segments and each individual address refers to a location within a particular segment. In this way, the range of addresses is extended from 64K to 1 megabyte. A more detailed description of addressing procedures is given in Chapter 2.

The *Direct Memory Access (DMA) Controller* controls the flow of data between specific devices and addresses in memory. It allows data to be moved around without involving the CPU – for example, during disk accesses – freeing the CPU for other tasks.

The DMA has four channels: that is, it can control addresses for four locations at a time.

The first of these, channel 0, is used to refresh the memory; the other three are specific to the expansion slots. Each of these three channels has an associated *page register port* that determines which of the sixteen possible 64K segments are to be used. Since these segments must begin at a 64K boundary the values sent to the ports have to be in the range 00h to 0Fh. Having determined the segment, data is transferred within that area.

The segments in current use are stored at ports 81h to 83h. The DMA controller also uses ports 00h to 0Fh.

The use of the DMA controller is illustrated in Figure 1.2.

**8287-4 DMA channels**

| Channel | Use | Port |
|---|---|---|
| 0 | 8253 Timer Counter 1 | - |
| 1 | External SDLC serial port | 82h |
| 2 | External floppy disk controller | 83h |
| 3 | External hard disk controller | 81h |

*Figure 1.2*

## Programmable Interrupt Controller (PIC)

Devices frequently need to grab the attention of the CPU when a particular event occurs or when they need to get some message across. For example, every time a key is pressed the keyboard circuits need to pass that information on to the CPU. This is done by sending an *interrupt*. An interrupt is a signal that an event has occurred which, as a general rule, the CPU must act upon immediately. Interrupts arrive from a number of devices, as well as being generated by the software, so these all need careful control. All this activity is overseen by the *Programmable Interrupt Controller (PIC)*.

From the 80286 upwards, two PICs are used, increasing the number of hardware interrupts that can be dealt with.

## Other components

In addition to the components described above, each computer will have a number of other special components built into it. These will include devices such as the *Floppy Disk Controller (FDC)* and the *Power Supply Unit* (PSU).

Those components that can be controlled from within a program are described in the appropriate chapters. The majority of other components are beyond the control of the application programmer.

## Memory

Memory falls into two categories:

- *Random Access Memory (RAM)*, which is memory whose contents can be changed at any time
- *Read-Only Memory (ROM)*, which is memory whose contents have been permanently fixed and cannot be changed

The RAM is used for storing application programs and their data, the operating system and a block of essential system data. A section of *video RAM* stores the data that makes up the screen display.

RAM is *volatile* which means that when the mains power is turned off, the values in memory are lost. To keep its data, the contents of RAM must be constantly refreshed.

The ROM stores all the permanent routines that are supplied with the computer, such as those that come into effect when the computer is switched on. Many of the routines that are used to access the hardware are also stored in ROM.

Each location in memory is given a unique *address*. The first megabyte of addresses are labelled (in hexadecimal) from 00000h to FFFFFh. (See Chapter 2 for more details of the hexadecimal notation.) As a general rule, this memory is divided into blocks for specific purposes. Figure 1.3 shows a general memory map.

## User RAM

The first 640K of memory, from 00000H to 9FFFFh, is allocated to the *user RAM*. The PC is supplied with anything from 64K of RAM upwards but this can be extended up to the maximum 640K by adding further RAM chips.

The first 640K is often referred to as *conventional memory*.

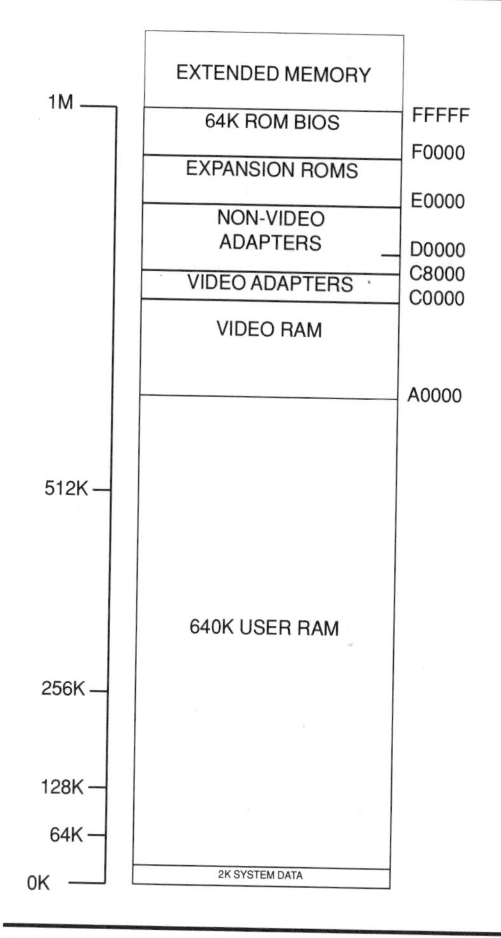


*Figure 1.3*

**Parity checking**

For every byte of RAM there is an additional memory bit which is used for *parity checking*. The value of this bit is determined by whether the sum of the bits in the corresponding byte is even or odd. Every time the CPU reads or writes a byte of RAM the parity bit is checked. If the bit is found to be incorrect at any time, the system halts and a memory error message is displayed. When the computer is switched on the system checks every memory location. If any error is found, the system will go no further and a memory parity error message is displayed. On many PCs the amount of memory that has been checked is counted through on the screen in 16K blocks. The time taken to complete the check on the early machines is considerable.

## Video RAM

The next 128K of RAM, from A0000h to BFFFFh, is allocated to the *video RAM*. It is here that the data intended for the screen display is stored. This data is read by the display adaptor and used to create the text or graphics screens.

The physical location of this memory varies; often it will be found on the display adaptor board itself. Wherever it is physically located, it is always treated as a normal part of memory by the CPU. As a result, it is quite permissible to put values directly into video RAM and, indeed, this is a process used by many programs to speed up the display of screen data. Further information on the use of video RAM is given in Chapter 8.

## Expansion ROMs

Immediately above the video RAM, the memory from C0000h to EFFFFh is reserved for *expansion ROMs*. This ROM is used by any additional card that is slotted into the computer system board. For example, the display adaptors frequently use the region C0000h to C7FFFh for their screen-handling routines and for storing the screen fonts. If the computer has a hard disk, the ROM routines for this device will be found in C8000h onwards.

Other ROM is used by additional boards and devices. The actual addresses selected are fairly arbitrary, the only rule being that the ROM must start at an 8K (2000h) boundary. The user must always check that any new device that is installed does not have a ROM that conflicts with existing ROMs.

## The BIOS

The top 64K of standard memory, from F0000h to FFFFFh, is reserved for the PC's *Basic Input/Output System (BIOS)*. This is the set of routines that perform almost all of the hardware operations. The BIOS takes full control of the computer as soon as it is switched on and until it hands over control to the operating system. Even then, it remains an important part of the system, the BIOS routines being used heavily by the corresponding operating system functions.

Although the BIOS is of major importance and extensively used in all programs, it may only require as little as 16K of memory. For technical reasons, the BIOS may be repeated several times in the top of memory.

The ROM BIOS for the PS/2, from model 50 upwards, starts at E0000h.

## Upper Memory Area (UMA)

The 384K above conventional memory is known as the *Upper Memory Area* (UMA) or *Upper Memory Blocks* (UMB). Some of this memory may be used for programs, depending on the memory allocation strategy (see Chapter 2).

DOS 5 frees more conventional memory for application programs by loading DOS itself into the UMA, along with TSRs, network drivers and device drivers.

For UMA to be used, CONFIG.SYS must contain the following lines:

```
DOS = UMB
DEVICE = HIMEM.SYS
```

The EMM386.EXE memory-management program (or equivalent) must also be loaded.

## High Memory Area (HMA)

The first 64K of extended memory (above 1M) is called the *High Memory Area* (HMA). This area can be used by DOS (on 286 machines and above) if the following lines are included in CONFIG.SYS:

```
DOS = HIGH
DEVICE = HIMEM.SYS
```

## The system RAM variables

The first 2K of RAM is reserved by the computer for storing information relating to the operation of the computer. A large portion of this holds the *system variables*. For the programmer, some of these locations yield important information about the way in which the computer works. Some values can be changed, with care, to modify the operation of the computer. The layout of this part of memory is shown in Figure 1.4, with the main system variable area detailed in Figure 1.5.

Many of these system variables are referred to throughout this book.

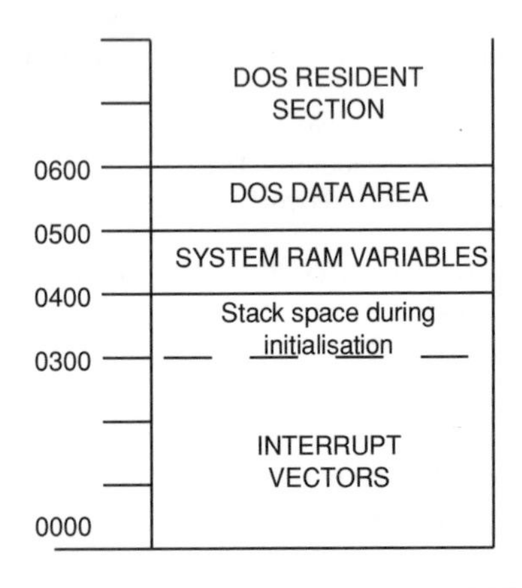


*Figure 1.4*

## RAM system variables

| Address | Number bytes (hex) | Use |
|---|---|---|
| 0300 | 100 | Stack space during system initialisation |
| 0400 | 2 | Port address of logical serial device 0 (initially the standard serial port) |
| 0402 | 2 | Port address of logical serial device 1 (initially the external asynchronous serial port; 0 if not installed) |
| 0404 | 4 | Reserved |
| 0408 | 2 | Port address of logical parallel device 0 (initially the standard parallel port) |
| 040A | 2 | Port address of logical parallel device 1 (initially the external parallel port or the external monochrome controller; 0 if neither installed) |
| 040C | 2 | Port address of logical parallel device 2 (initially the external monochrome controller if the external parallel port is fitted; 0 if only one is installed) |
| 040E | 2 | Reserved |
| 0410 | 2 | System configuration |
| 0412 | 1 | Reserved |
| 0413 | 2 | User RAM size (in kilobytes) |
| 0415 | 2 | Extra RAM size (in kilobytes): User RAM size - 64 |
| 0417 | 1 | Keyboard status |
| 0418 | 1 | Keys-pressed status |
| 0419 | 1 | Number being entered with Alt and numeric keypad |
| 041A | 2 | Pointer to next character in keyboard buffer, as offset from 0400h |
| 041C | 2 | Pointer to next free space in keyboard buffer, as offset from 0400h |
| 041E | 20 | Keyboard buffer |
| 043E | 1 | Floppy disk restore and interrupt flags |
| 043F | 1 | Floppy drive motor flags |
| 0440 | 1 | Drive motor timeout count |
| 0441 | 1 | Disk status |
| 0442 | 7 | Disk parameters |
| 0449 | 1 | Current video mode |
| 044A | 2 | Number of columns in current mode |
| 044C | 2 | Current video mode page size (in bytes, including surplus bytes at end of page) |
| 044E | 2 | Offset of current display page |

| Add-ress | Number bytes (hex) | Use |
|---|---|---|
| 0450 | 10 | Cursor position (row and column) for each display page |
| 0460 | 1 | Last raster line of cursor |
| 0461 | 1 | First raster line of cursor |
| 0462 | 1 | Current display page |
| 0463 | 1 | Port used for CRTC interface (03B4h for mono, 03D4h for colour) |
| 0465 | 1 | Contents of current video mode control port |
| 0466 | 1 | Contents of EGA colour select port |
| 0467 | 5 | Reserved |
| 046C | 4 | System clock count |
| 0470 | 1 | Midnight flag (01h if midnight passed) |
| 0471 | 1 | Break status |
| 0472 | 2 | Power-up memory check indicator |
| 0474 | 1 | Hard disk completion status |
| 0475 | 1 | Number of hard disks connected |
| 0476 | 2 | Reserved (by hard disk BIOS) |
| 0478 | 3 | Parallel printer timeout counts (for printers 0 to 2) |
| 047B | 1 | Reserved |
| 047C | 2 | Serial printer timeout counts (for printers 0 and 1) |
| 047E | 2 | Reserved |
| 0480 | 2 | Offset of absolute start of keyboard buffer, from 0400h |
| 0482 | 2 | Offset of absolute end of keyboard buffer, from 0400h |
| 0484 | 1 | Number of display rows - 1 |
| 0485 | 1 | Space used to store each character in character table |
| 0487 | 4 | Video adapter status |
| 048B | 0B | Disk status data |
| 0498 | 9 | RTC data |
| 04A8 | 4 | EGA parameter address |
| 04AC | 74 | Not used |
| 0500 | 1 | Print-screen status |
| 0501 | 1 | Reserved |
| 0504 | 1 | Single floppy drive indicator (0=A,1=B) |
| 0505 | 0B | Reserved |
| 0510 | 0E | Used by BASIC |

*Figure 1.5*

## The system board dip switches

The IBM PC range, and most IBM-compatibles, have one or more banks of *dip switches* on the system board. These are arrays of small switches, each of which can be set either on or off. The dip switches are used to determine features such as the language that is used for error messages when the computer is switched on, the initial video mode, the type of monitor attached and the amount of user RAM available. When the computer is first started, it checks the settings of these switches and sets initial values for some of the system variables accordingly.

The switches that are available and their uses vary from one PC to another. The settings of the switches are of little interest to the programmer, since most of the information they provide can be gleaned from the appropriate system variables.

## Checking the configuration list

Working in assembly language, it is important to know exactly what hardware devices are at your disposal; making assumptions about the hardware configuration can have disastrous effects on your programs. Therefore, in many cases, the first stage is to check out the configuration list.

Information on the components of the system is held in the byte at memory location 0410h. While you could extract this information by reading the contents of this byte, you can achieve the same effect with BIOS interrupt 11h.

---

*Interrupt:* 11h
*Service:* Get configuration list
*Entry values:* None
*Exit values:* AX=configuration list code

---

This interrupt returns in register AX a code that represents the current system configuration. The format is identical to that of 0410h; in effect, all this interrupt does is to read the contents of that

**System configuration word (0410h)**

| Bit | Use |
|---|---|
| 15 | } Number of parallel ports (1 - 3) |
| 14 | } |
| 13 | Not used |
| 12 | Set if games adapter installed |
| 11 | Not used |
| 10 | } Number of serial ports (1 - 2) |
| 9 | } |
| 8 | Not used |
| 7 | } No. of floppy drives installed - 1 |
| 6 | } |
| 5 | } Default display mode |
| 4 | } |
| 3 | } System RAM indicator |
| 2 | } |
| 1 | Set if 80x87maths co-processor installed |
| 0 | Set if floppy drives installed |

*Figure 1.6*

memory location into AX. The meanings of the various bits in this word are shown in Figure 1.6. Registers and interrupts are explained in Chapters 2 and 5 respectively.

Theoretically you can change the configuration (as far as the computer is concerned) by adjusting the value in this byte. However, it is not very good practise to do so.

Figure 1.7 contains a listing of a short program that extracts the relevant information from this byte.

```
CONFIG:         ;Displays configuration list

        ;The configuration code is read from
        ;the word at 0410h and converted into
        ;a simple screen display. An enhanced
        ;version of this program provides a
        ;more friendly screen and the chance
        ;to change some of the values.
        ;Can be called as routine from another
        ;program
        ;Calls DISSTR, DISLIN, DISBYT (Fig 8.10)
```

```
      ;Entry values: None
      ;Exit values:  AX,BX,CX,DX,ES changed

      jmp configst          ;Jump to start of
                            ;program

m1          db '8087 installed$'
m2          db 'No 8087$'
m3          db 'Default display mode = $'
m4          db 'Two floppy drives$'
m5          db 'One floppy drive$'
m6          db 'Number of serial ports = $'
m7          db 'Games adapter installed$'
m8          db 'No games adapter$'
m9          db 'Number of parallel ports = $'

configst:
      lea es,0000h          ;Point to start of
                            ;memory
      mov bx,0410h          ;BX points to
                            ;configuration word
      push bx               ;Save BX
      mov ax,bx
      call diswrd           ;Display
                            ;configuration word
      call newlin           ;Start new line
      and bl,02h            ;Isolate bit 1
      cmp bl,00h            ;Is it 0?
      jz dism2              ;If so, jump
      lea dx,m1             ;Otherwise, point to
                            ;message 1
      jmp part2
dism2:
      lea dx,m2             ;Point to message 2
part2:
      call dislin           ;Display message
      pop bx                ;Recover BX
      push bx               ;Save BX
      and bl,30h            ;Isolate bits 5 and 6
                            ;of BL
      lea dx,m3             ;Display message 3
      call disstr
      mov al,bl
      mov cl,04h
      shr al,cl             ;Convert to number
                            ;(0-3)
      call disbyt           ;Display default mode
      call newlin           ;Move to next line
      pop bx
      push bx               ;Save BX
      and bl,40h            ;Isolate bit 6 of BL
```

```
        cmp bl,00h              ;Is it 0?
        jz dism5                ;If so, jump
        lea dx,m4               ;Otherwise, point to
                                ;message 4
        jmp part3
dism5:
        lea dx,m5               ;Point to message 5
part3:
        call dislin             ;Display message
        pop bx
        push bx                 ;Save BX
        and bh,30h              ;Isolate bits 1 and 2
                                ;of BH
        lea dx,m6               ;Display message 6
        call disstr
        mov al,bh
        call disbyt             ;Display number of
                                ;serial ports
        call newlin             ;Move to next line
        pop bx
        push bx                 ;Save BX
        and bh,10h              ;Isolate bit 4 of BH
        cmp bl,00h              ;Is it 0?
        jz dism8                ;If so, jump
        lea dx,m7               ;Otherwise, point to
                                ;message 7
        jmp part4
dism8:
        lea dx,m8               ;Point to message 2
part4:
        call dislin             ;Display message
        pop bx                  ;Recover BX
        push bx                 ;Save BX
        and bh,0C0h             ;Isolate bits 6 and 7
                                ;of BH
        lea dx,m9               ;Display message 9
        call disstr
        mov al,bh
        mov cl,06h
        shr al,cl               ;Convert to number
                                ;(0-3)
        call disbyt             ;Display number of
                                ;parallel ports
        call newlin             ;Move to next line
        pop bx
        int 20h                 ;End program- change
                                ;to RET if routine
                                ;is to be run from
                                ;another program
```

*Figure 1.7*

## Detecting the RAM size

For large programs, or those that require a substantial amount of memory allocation, it is important to know exactly how much user RAM is available. This is held in memory location 0413h. As for the configuration list, this value can be obtained with an interrupt, in this case BIOS interrupt 12h.

| | |
|---|---|
| *Interrupt:* | 12h |
| *Service:* | Get user RAM |
| *Entry values:* | None |
| *Exit values:* | AX=user RAM |

The value in AX is identical to that in the word at 0413h and can be extracted by a routine such as that in Figure 1.8.

```
RAMSIZE:        ;Displays user RAM size

       ;Program uses interrupt 12h to display
       ;the number of 1K blocks

       ;Can be called as routine from another
       ;program

       ;Limitations - only display hex value.
       ;Call DEC2HEX to convert

       ;Calls DISSTR, DISBYT, DISLIN (Fig 8.10)

       ;Entry values: None
       ;Exit values:  AX=RAM size
       ;              DX changed

       jmp ramst

rammes         db 'User RAM size=$'
rammes2        db ' Kilobytes (in hex)$'

ramst:
       int 12h                   ;Get user RAM size
                                 ;in Kbytes
       lea dx,rammes
       call disstr               ;Display message
       call diswrd               ;Display size
```

```
        lea dx,rammes2
        call dislin                 ;Display message and
                                    ;start new line
        int 20h                     ;Replace with RET
                                    ;for calls from
                                    ;another program
```

*Figure 1.8*

As a matter of interest, the word at 0415h holds the amount of memory above the first 64K. This measure of 'additional' RAM is left over from the early days of the IBM PC, when 64K was the basic amount of user memory supplied.

**Extended memory**

For the 80286 upwards you can check the amount of extended memory with interrupt 15h, function 88h.

| | |
|---|---|
| *Interrupt:* | 15h |
| *Function:* | 88h |
| *Service:* | Get extended memory size (not PCs) |
| *Entry values:* | AH=88h |
| *Exit values:* | AX=extended memory (K) |

The value returned includes extended memory above 1M but excludes any expanded memory (EMS).

## Real and protected modes

The 8086 and 8088 microprocessors execute all programs in *real mode*. The programs can access only the first 1M of memory without the use of sophisticated programming features, operating with extended and expanded memory. Running two or more program concurrently requires some complex memory organisation.

The 80286 onwards can operate either in real mode – in which case, programs run the same as on the 8086 – or in *protected mode*. Each protected-mode application is allocated its own section of

RAM. The CPU ensures that no program can interfere with any other. There is no need for expanded memory in this mode.

## The main system board

The Intel *Central Processing Unit (CPU)* is comprised of two separate sections: the bus interface unit and the execution unit.

### Bus interface unit

The *bus interface unit* is used for overall control of the computer and comprises the following:

- The *segment registers*, which store the internal addresses of programs and associated data
- The *instruction pointer*, which identifies the next instruction to be processed
- The *instruction queue*, where instructions that are waiting to be processed are stored
- The *control system*, which takes overall control of the computer

The bus interface unit also controls the system bus, described below.

### Execution unit

The actual processing of instructions takes place in the *execution unit*, which is comprised of the following:

- The *general registers*, which are used for temporary storage and are the main variables in any program
- The *operands area*, which is where the instructions in any program are translated into simpler operations that the computer can understand
- The *Arithmetic and Logic Unit (ALU)*, which is the main part of the system, where all calculations are carried out
- The *flags register*, where a number of important single-bit flags are stored

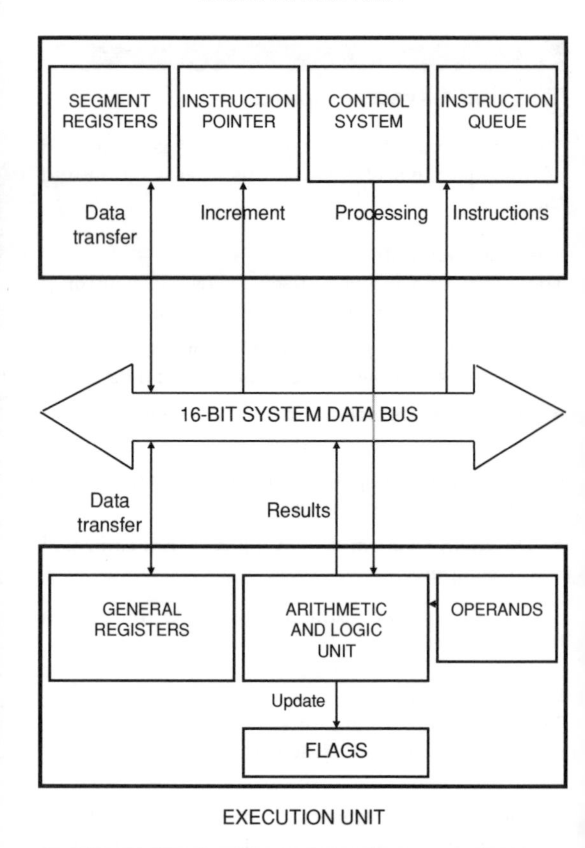


*Figure 1.9*

The registers, instruction pointer, general registers, operands and flags register are described in further detail below.

The 80486 also includes a *Floating Point Unit (FPU)*, which takes on the operations previously handled by the 80x87.

**Instruction flow**

When instructions arrive at the bus interface unit they are stored in the instruction queue. The first instruction in the queue is passed on by the control system to the execution unit, when the processor has completed the previous instruction. The operand from the instruction is transferred into the ALU, along with the contents of any registers that are to be used in the calculation. Any relevant data from memory is also called up.

Once the calculation is complete, the results are put on the system bus to be stored in memory or passed to the relevant device. The flags register is updated according to the calculation result and the instruction pointer is incremented.

## The system bus

The *system bus* is the means by which any instruction or item of data travels from one part of the computer to another. A bus simply consists of a set of parallel data lines; each line can take one bit of information but all the lines are used at the same time. As a general rule, a bus will have 8, 16, 32 or 64 lines. An 8-bit data bus can transport 8 bits of data – a single byte – at a time. The number of lines on a data bus is one means of categorising the computer.

Computers are designed with more than one bus, and any mixture of bus sizes may be used. Many IBM PC compatibles are true 16-bit computers, having both a 16-bit processor and a 16-bit bus. The original IBM PC, however, had only an 8-bit data bus even though it used a 16-bit processor. As a result, the processor has to wait for two separate bytes to arrive on the bus before they can be processed (resulting in slightly slower processing times).

Buses are used for a number of purposes:

- The data bus transports data from one part of the system to another.

- The address bus transmits addresses, indicating the location where information is to be sent or is ready to be collected.
- The control bus sends control information from one part of the system to another.
- The expansion bus transfers data to and from the expansion cards.

Any information sent along the bus is preceded by a code, indicating the destination of the information. Each hardware component that is linked into the bus checks this header data as it passes to see whether the information that follows is relevant. If it is, the device extracts the information from the bus as it passes.

### MCA

The PS/2, from model 50 onwards, uses a different type of bus based on Micro Channel Architecture (MCA). This provides faster operation but its main effect is on the hardware that is connected into the bus. MCA-based hardware is not compatible with standard PCs. From the programmer's point of view, there is no difference in operation and compatibility between programs is maintained.

If writing programs for the PS/2, there are some extra interrupts dedicated to MCA-based machines.

## Ports

The points on the data bus to which the various devices are connected are referred to as *ports*. When any device wishes to transfer information to some other part of the system, the data is placed in one of the ports ready to be picked up on the bus. Alternatively, information intended for a device is delivered to the relevant port for that device. All data that is transferred in the system is either placed in one of the ports or stored directly in the memory locations.

For example, each time a key is pressed, the keyboard controller puts the relevant key code into one of its ports. The CPU reads the value from the port and acts accordingly.

**PC System Ports**

| Numbers | I/O | Use |
|---|---|---|
| 00-0F | IO | 8237 DMA Controller |
| 10-1F | - | Reserved |
| 20-21 | IO | 8259 Interrupt Controller |
| 22-3F | - | Reserved |
| 40-42 | IO | 8253 PIT Counters (0,1,2) |
| 43 | I | 8253 PIT Mode |
| 44-5F | - | Reserved |
| 60-65 | IO | Keyboard Controller |
| 66 | O | System reset |
| 66-6F | - | Reserved |
| 70 | O | RTC Address |
| 71 | IO | RTC Data |
| 72-80 | - | Reserved |
| 81 | O | DMA Page Register Channel 2 |
| 82 | O | DMA Page Register Channel 3 |
| 83 | O | DMA Page Reg Channels 0,1 |
| 84-9F | - | Reserved |
| A0 | O | NMI Mask Control |
| A1-FF | - | Reserved |

*Figure 1.10*

**PC Device Ports**

| Numbers | I/O | Use |
|---|---|---|
| 0378 | IO | Parallel Printer data |
| 0379 | I | Parallel Printer status |
| 037A | IO | Parallel Printer control |
| 037B-037F | IO | Reserved |
| 03B0-037F | IO | Monochrome mode CRTC |
| 03C0-03CF | IO | Video Controller |
| 03D0-03DF | IO | Colour Mode CRTC |
| 03F0-03F1 | - | Reserved |
| 03F2 | O | Drive selection |
| 03F3 | - | Reserved |
| 03F4 | I | FDC status |
| 03F5 | IO | FDC data |
| 03F6-03F7 | - | Reserved |
| 03F8-03FF | IO | Serial Data Control |

*Figure 1.11*

Some ports are capable only of sending data out, some are used for input and others are available for transfer of data in either direction. Every port is given a unique reference number and this number is used in all instructions relating to that port.

The main system ports are listed in Figure 1.10. These ports generally refer to the internal devices of the PC.

Another selection of ports, with higher addresses in the range 0200h to 03FFh, relate to the various standard external devices: the parallel printer, the monitor and the floppy disk controller (see Figure 1.11).

**Expansion board slots**

As described above, the expansion bus is used to transfer data to and from the circuits on any expansion cards connected into the expansion slots. The actual ports that are used depend upon the specific cards that have been installed but each group of port numbers is generally used for a particular purpose. The standard uses of the expansion port numbers is given in Figure 1.12.

**Expansion bus ports**

| Numbers | Use |
|---|---|
| 0200-020F | External Game Control Interface |
| 0210-0217 | External Bus Extension Unit |
| 0220-024F | Reserved |
| 0278-027F | External Printer Port |
| 02F0-02F7 | Reserved |
| 02F8-02FF | External Asynchronous RS232C Port |
| 0300-031F | External Prototyping Card |
| 0320-032F | External Hard Disk Controller |
| 0380-038F | External SDLC RS232C Port |
| 03A0-03AF | Reserved |
| 03B0-03BB | External Monochrome Display Controller |
| 03BC-03BF | Printer Port |
| 03C0-03CF | External Graphics Display Controller |
| 03D0-03DF | Extrnl Colour/Graphics Display Controller |

*Figure 1.12*

**Use of the internal ports**

Most of the time you can steer clear of the ports. As a general rule, the input/output for particular ports is handled by the corresponding interrupt routines, which should be used in any program.

In fact, it is generally a good policy *never* to read from or write to a port unless it is absolutely essential. The ports do not always behave in the manner you might expect; indeed, even reading the value held by a port can sometimes have an unexpected effect.

There are occasions, of course, when it is either necessary or desirable to access a port directly. In particular, to produce sound you *must* work directly with the relevant ports.

**Terminology**

Do not confuse the *internal* ports, which are merely addresses to which information is sent or from which data is received, with the physical *external* ports, to which devices such as a printer or mouse may be connected. Remember also that the port address numbers are completely different to the equivalent, RAM addresses.

You may also see internal ports referred to as *registers*. You should make the distinction between these and the CPU registers (described in Chapter 2).

# 2 Programming Principles

This book does not set out to be an assembly language tutorial; its main task is to describe the internal workings of the IBM PC and PS/2 families. However, in order to fully explore the potential that working directly with the hardware or the operating system can provide, some knowledge of assembly language and basic programming methods is necessary. Therefore, a brief outline of the basic principles of assembly language programming is given here.

The main consideration is given to programming the 8086, since programs that use the special facilities of the 80286 upwards are limited to these machines and will not run on the standard PC.

## Binary

The first requirement is a working knowledge of the units of measurement that are applied within computer systems. Any communication with the computer, no matter what the level, requires a degree of translation from the instructions and information we provide into a format that the machine can understand. Whether entering English-like instructions in a fourth generation language or the almost unintelligible assembly language code, a transformation of these instructions must take place before the computer can even begin to act upon them. This is because of the way the computer's memory is organised, being based entirely upon the *binary* system.

Binary, like decimal, is just an organised way of representing numeric values. Binary and decimal work in exactly the same way, the only difference being that binary has just two possible values for each digit, compared with the decimal system's ten.

### Bits

The basic unit that is used throughout the computer system is the *bit*, short for *binary digit*. This unit can take only two possible values: 0 and 1. The limitless combinations of 0s and 1s together form the native language of the computer.

Each memory location is made up of a string of magnetic locations, whose polarity is directly translated into 0 or 1; data stored on disk uses a similar approach. Information transferred within the internal circuits of the computer, or through its ports to the outside world, is represented by a series of pulses. Depending on the devices concerned, each pulse can be either a high or low voltage, again being directly translated into 0 or 1. Alternatively, the 0 or 1 may represent the absence or presence of a current.

In this way, the computer thinks, talks, writes and remembers in a language made up of strings of binary digits. The strings of 0s and 1s form the binary system of counting.

This same language is used both for program code and data. Numbers are held directly in binary format. Instructions to the CPU are also encoded as binary. In addition, any item of text can be converted into a binary string that the computer can understand, by assigning numeric codes to letters, punctuation marks and symbols. The CPU knows how to interpret each string – as a further instruction, a number or a piece of text – by the instruction that precedes it. Figure 2.1 shows how a base 10 value is translated into binary.

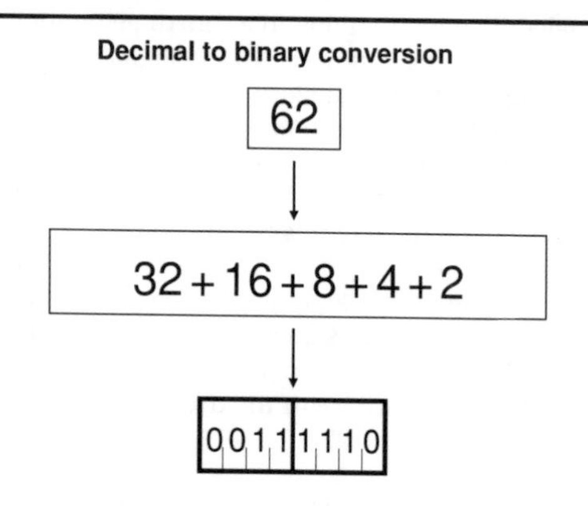


*Figure 2.1*

### Bytes

Given that the computer cannot understand plain English and that we could not possibly hope to converse with the machine in binary, some happy medium has to be found. The first stage towards finding a common language is to group a number of bits together. Thus the main unit of data in the 80x86 family of computers consists of a string of eight bits, termed a *byte*. Since each bit in the byte can take either of two possible values, the eight bits between them may take 256 different combinations (i.e. $2^8$).

As far as the computer is concerned, a byte held in memory is just a piece of data. However, our programs may interpret the byte in many different ways. A byte may be part of the code of a program, a representation of a text character or a numeric value.

When bytes are used to represent numbers, they may be referred to as *signed bytes*, where the value can be either positive or negative, in the range -128 to +127; alternatively, they may be *unsigned bytes*, taking positive values only, in the range 0 to 255.

As another alternative, a byte may be subdivided so that groups of bits represent different information. There is an example of this in the configuration list bytes of Chapter 1.

In such cases, where the position of an individual bit is important, the bits are numbered from 0 to 7. Bit 0 is the rightmost bit and is referred to as the *least significant bit (LSB)*; changing this bit makes a difference of 1 to the total value represented by the byte. Similarly, bit 7, the leftmost bit, is the *most significant bit (MSB)*. In an unsigned byte, this bit makes a difference of 128 to the value; in a signed byte, the MSB is used to determine whether a byte is positive (MSB = 0) or negative (MSB = 1). In this case, the MSB may also be referred to as the *sign bit*. Figure 2.2 shows how the bits in the byte are numbered.

### Words

The byte is a convenient unit and forms the basis of all other units of measurement within the computer system. Some data is transferred along an 8-bit

**Bit numbering**

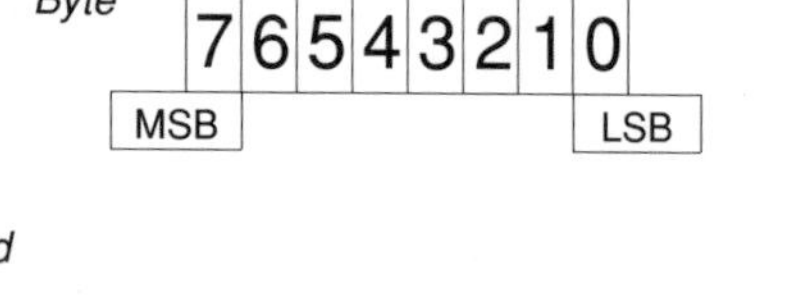


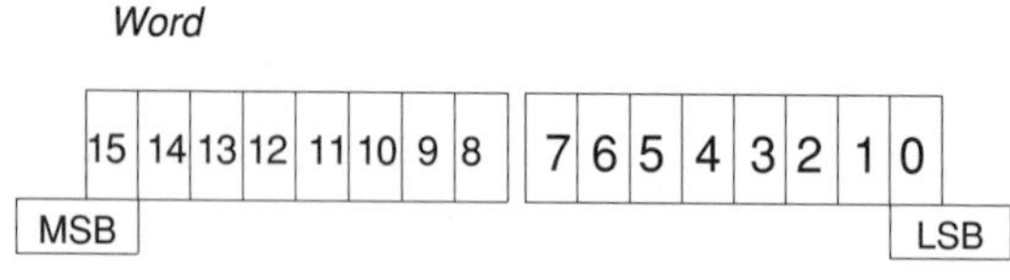


*Figure 2.2*

data bus, which has eight parallel lines that can transmit a whole byte of data at a time.

However, the IBM PC and compatibles are, to a greater or lesser extent, 16-bit computers. The 8086 and 80286 CPU all operate with sixteen bits of data at a time. The AT and many IBM compatibles also have 16-bit data buses.

The 8-bit byte, representing values up to a maximum of 255, is also somewhat limiting in calculations. Therefore, much of time, two bytes are used at a time, forming a unit called a *word*.

A word is simply two 8-bit bytes next to each other in memory. A 16-bit data bus can carry a word at a time and a 16-bit processor can work with that number of bits simultaneously.

As for bytes, words may be either signed or unsigned. A signed word can represent values from -32768 to +32767 (which will be familiar to anyone who has ever done any sort of programming) while an unsigned word can reach a maximum of 65535.

Where necessary, individual bits are numbered from 0 to 15: the rightmost bit, bit 0, being the LSB with the MSB, or sign bit, being on the extreme left at bit 15.

Unfortunately, the term 'word' is used in a rather sloppy fashion in the computer world, often referring to any collection of bytes. For example, when reference is made to mainframe computers, the term 'word' will often mean a 4-byte or larger unit. This book always uses 16-bit 'words'.

The 80386 and 80486 have 32-bit buses that transfer *double-words*.

**Larger units**

In programming terms, bytes and words are generally the most convenient items to handle. When it comes to overall data storage and memory size, however, the numbers become large and other units are required. Because everything in the binary system is related to powers of 2, and there is no easy conversion to our everyday decimal system, precise translations can become a little tricky.

When considering large sections of memory or disk space, it is usual to talk in terms of *kilobytes*, *megabytes* and *gigabytes*. One kilobyte (1K) is 1024 bytes. Not everyone is so precise, however, and you may see 1K being used to represent 1000 bytes. (It was common in the early days of mass-produced PCs for computers with 64K of memory – actually 65536 bytes – to be advertised as '65K computers'.)

You need to be even more careful with megabytes. Technically speaking, 1 megabyte (1M) is 1024K or 1,048,576 bytes. However, 'rounding errors' may again creep in here.

With the limits of memory and storage space expanding, the term gigabyte (1G) is now often used, representing 1024M.

## Hexadecimal

The computer's binary system (base 2) is not practical for regular use and our own decimal system (base 10) does not link closely enough to the computer's way of thinking. What is needed is a numbering system that can be mapped directly onto binary and yet uses commonsense units that we can better understand. The system most usually adopted is that of *hexadecimal*, which is base 16.

Hexadecimal, generally abbreviated to *hex*, needs sixteen digits. The last six of these are represented

| Decimal | Binary | Hexadecimal |
|---|---|---|
| 0 | 0000 | 0 |
| 1 | 0001 | 1 |
| 2 | 0010 | 2 |
| 3 | 0011 | 3 |
| 4 | 0100 | 4 |
| 5 | 0101 | 5 |
| 6 | 0110 | 6 |
| 7 | 0111 | 7 |
| 8 | 1000 | 8 |
| 9 | 1001 | 9 |
| 10 | 1010 | A |
| 11 | 1011 | B |
| 12 | 1100 | C |
| 13 | 1101 | D |
| 14 | 1110 | E |
| 15 | 1111 | F |

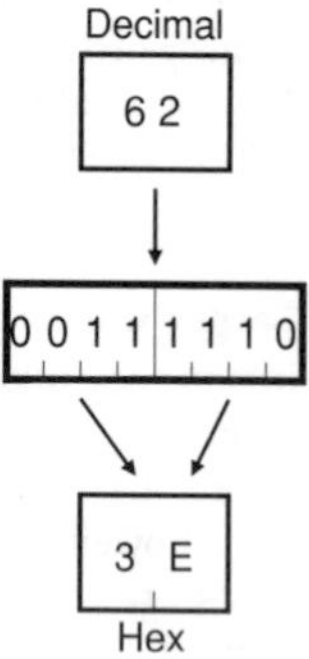

*Figure 2.3*

by the letters A to F. The decimal values 0 to 15 can therefore be represented by the hex numbers:

```
0 1 2 3 4 5 6 7 8 9 A B C D E F
```

A single hex digit represents exactly four binary digits. Thus a byte is represented by a two-digit hex number and a word by four hex digits. Figure 2.3 shows how the decimal values 0 to 15 correspond to their binary and hexadecimal equivalents.

Computer jargon, being very modern, has more than its fair share of bad puns. Four bits, or half a byte, is often referred to as a *nibble*. In a byte, the top four bits make up the high nibble while the bottom four are the low nibble.

**Conventions**

Many different conventions have evolved for representing hexadecimal numbers when written, and it is obviously important to be able to distinguish a hex number from a standard decimal figure. The convention most widely used, and adopted throughout this book, is to append the letter 'h' to any hex number. For example, decimal 16 is represented by 10h while 26 is written as 1Ah.

When hex figures are written down they are frequently padded with leading zeros to make them up to an even number of digits; thus bytes generally have two digits and words four digits, no matter how small the number may be. When referring to memory locations, ports, interrupts and other values for use in programs, hexadecimal is generally used in preference to decimal. Decimal figures are reserved for 'real world' values.

**Important values**

It helps to become familiar with a few standard conversions:

- 1 byte can take 100h (256) different values. These are in the range 00h to FFh, the values 80h to FFh being negative in a signed byte.
- A word can take 10000h (64K) different values. The range here is 0000h to FFFFh, negative values being 8000h to FFFFh in a signed word.
- A kilobyte is 400h, a megabyte is 100000h.

A table of such conversions is given in Figure 2.4.

**Hexadecimal values**

| Hex | | | Decimal |
|---|---|---|---|
| 10h | 1/64K | Paragraph | 16 |
| 100h | 1/4K | Byte maximum | 256 |
| 400h | 1K | Kilobyte | 1,024 |
| 1000h | 4K | Page | 4,096 |
| 4000h | 16K | | 16,384 |
| 10000h | 64K | Word max | 65,536 |
| 40000h | 256K | | 262,144 |
| 100000h | 1M | Megabyte | 1,048,576 |
| 40000000h | 1G | Gigabyte | 1,073,741,824 |

*Figure 2.4*

Figure 2.5 shows a decimal-to-hex conversion table while the reverse process is carried out with Figure 2.6.

**Decimal to Hexadecimal**

| | 00 | 10 | 20 | 30 | 40 | 50 | 60 | 70 | 80 | 90 |
|---|---|---|---|---|---|---|---|---|---|---|
| 0 | 00 | 0A | 14 | 1E | 28 | 32 | 3C | 46 | 50 | 5A |
| 1 | 01 | 0B | 15 | 1F | 29 | 33 | 3D | 47 | 51 | 5B |
| 2 | 02 | 0C | 16 | 20 | 2A | 34 | 3E | 48 | 52 | 5C |
| 3 | 03 | 0D | 17 | 21 | 2B | 35 | 3F | 49 | 53 | 5D |
| 4 | 04 | 0E | 18 | 22 | 2C | 36 | 40 | 4A | 54 | 5E |
| 5 | 05 | 0F | 19 | 23 | 2D | 37 | 41 | 4B | 55 | 5F |
| 6 | 06 | 10 | 1A | 24 | 2E | 38 | 42 | 4C | 56 | 60 |
| 7 | 07 | 11 | 1B | 25 | 2F | 39 | 43 | 4D | 57 | 61 |
| 8 | 08 | 12 | 1C | 26 | 30 | 3A | 44 | 4E | 58 | 62 |
| 9 | 09 | 13 | 1D | 27 | 31 | 3B | 45 | 4F | 59 | 63 |

| | 100 | 110 | 120 | 130 | 140 | 150 | 160 | 170 | 180 | 190 |
|---|---|---|---|---|---|---|---|---|---|---|
| 0 | 64 | 6E | 78 | 82 | 8C | 96 | A0 | AA | B4 | BE |
| 1 | 65 | 6F | 79 | 83 | 8D | 97 | A1 | AB | B5 | BF |
| 2 | 66 | 70 | 7A | 84 | 8E | 98 | A2 | AC | B6 | C0 |
| 3 | 67 | 71 | 7B | 85 | 8F | 99 | A3 | AD | B7 | C1 |
| 4 | 68 | 72 | 7C | 86 | 90 | 9A | A4 | AE | B8 | C2 |
| 5 | 69 | 73 | 7D | 87 | 91 | 9B | A5 | AF | B9 | C3 |
| 6 | 6A | 74 | 7E | 88 | 92 | 9C | A6 | B0 | BA | C4 |
| 7 | 6B | 75 | 7F | 89 | 93 | 9D | A7 | B1 | BB | C5 |
| 8 | 6C | 76 | 80 | 8A | 94 | 9E | A8 | B2 | BC | C6 |
| 9 | 6D | 77 | 81 | 8B | 95 | 9F | A9 | B3 | BD | C7 |

| | 200 | 210 | 220 | 230 | 240 | 250 |
|---|---|---|---|---|---|---|
| 0 | C8 | D2 | DC | E6 | F0 | FA |
| 1 | C9 | D3 | DD | E7 | F1 | FB |
| 2 | CA | D4 | DE | E8 | F2 | FC |
| 3 | CB | D5 | DF | E9 | F3 | FD |
| 4 | CC | D6 | E0 | EA | F4 | FE |
| 5 | CD | D7 | E1 | EB | F5 | FF |
| 6 | CE | D8 | E2 | EC | F6 | |
| 7 | CF | D9 | E3 | ED | F7 | |
| 8 | D0 | DA | E4 | EE | F8 | |
| 9 | D1 | DB | E5 | EF | F9 | |

*Figure 2.5* *(continues...)*

| Decimal | Hex | Decimal | Hex | Decimal | Hex |
|---|---|---|---|---|---|
| 100 | 0168 | 1000 | 04EC | 10000 | 2814 |
| 200 | 01CC | 2000 | 08D4 | 20000 | 4F24 |
| 300 | 0230 | 3000 | 0CBC | 30000 | 7634 |
| 400 | 0294 | 4000 | 10A4 | 40000 | 9D44 |
| 500 | 02F8 | 5000 | 148C | 50000 | C454 |
| 600 | 035C | 6000 | 1874 | 60000 | EB64 |
| 700 | 03C0 | 7000 | 1C5C | | |
| 800 | 0424 | 8000 | 2044 | | |
| 900 | 0488 | 9000 | 242C | | |

*Figure 2.5 (continued)*

**Hexadecimal to Decimal**

| | 00 | 10 | 20 | 30 | 40 | 50 | 60 | 70 |
|---|---|---|---|---|---|---|---|---|
| 0 | 0 | 16 | 32 | 48 | 64 | 80 | 96 | 112 |
| 1 | 1 | 17 | 33 | 49 | 65 | 81 | 97 | 113 |
| 2 | 2 | 18 | 34 | 50 | 66 | 82 | 98 | 114 |
| 3 | 3 | 19 | 35 | 51 | 67 | 83 | 99 | 115 |
| 4 | 4 | 20 | 36 | 52 | 68 | 84 | 100 | 116 |
| 5 | 5 | 21 | 37 | 53 | 69 | 85 | 101 | 117 |
| 6 | 6 | 22 | 38 | 54 | 70 | 86 | 102 | 118 |
| 7 | 7 | 23 | 39 | 55 | 71 | 87 | 103 | 119 |
| 8 | 8 | 24 | 40 | 56 | 72 | 88 | 104 | 120 |
| 9 | 9 | 25 | 41 | 57 | 73 | 89 | 105 | 121 |
| A | 10 | 26 | 42 | 58 | 74 | 90 | 106 | 122 |
| B | 11 | 27 | 43 | 59 | 75 | 91 | 107 | 123 |
| C | 12 | 28 | 44 | 60 | 76 | 92 | 108 | 124 |
| D | 13 | 29 | 45 | 61 | 77 | 93 | 109 | 125 |
| E | 14 | 30 | 46 | 62 | 78 | 94 | 110 | 126 |
| F | 15 | 31 | 47 | 63 | 79 | 95 | 111 | 127 |

| | 80 | 90 | A0 | B0 | C0 | D0 | E0 | F0 |
|---|---|---|---|---|---|---|---|---|
| 0 | 128 | 144 | 160 | 176 | 192 | 208 | 224 | 240 |
| 1 | 129 | 145 | 161 | 177 | 193 | 209 | 225 | 241 |
| 2 | 130 | 146 | 162 | 178 | 194 | 210 | 226 | 242 |
| 3 | 131 | 147 | 163 | 179 | 195 | 211 | 227 | 243 |
| 4 | 132 | 148 | 164 | 180 | 196 | 212 | 228 | 244 |
| 5 | 133 | 149 | 165 | 181 | 197 | 213 | 229 | 245 |
| 6 | 134 | 150 | 166 | 182 | 198 | 214 | 230 | 246 |
| 7 | 135 | 151 | 167 | 183 | 199 | 215 | 231 | 247 |
| 8 | 136 | 152 | 168 | 184 | 200 | 216 | 232 | 248 |

| | 80 | 90 | A0 | B0 | C0 | D0 | E0 | F0 |
|---|---|---|---|---|---|---|---|---|
| 9 | 137 | 153 | 169 | 185 | 201 | 217 | 233 | 249 |
| A | 138 | 154 | 170 | 186 | 202 | 218 | 234 | 250 |
| B | 139 | 155 | 171 | 187 | 203 | 219 | 235 | 251 |
| C | 140 | 156 | 172 | 188 | 204 | 220 | 236 | 252 |
| D | 141 | 157 | 173 | 189 | 205 | 221 | 237 | 253 |
| E | 142 | 158 | 174 | 190 | 206 | 222 | 238 | 254 |
| F | 143 | 159 | 175 | 191 | 207 | 223 | 239 | 255 |

| Hex | Decimal | Hex | Decimal |
|---|---|---|---|
| 100 | 256 | 1000 | 4096 |
| 200 | 512 | 2000 | 8192 |
| 300 | 768 | 3000 | 12288 |
| 400 | 1024 | 4000 | 16384 |
| 500 | 1280 | 5000 | 20480 |
| 600 | 1536 | 6000 | 24576 |
| 700 | 1792 | 7000 | 28672 |
| 800 | 2048 | 8000 | 32768 |
| 900 | 2304 | 9000 | 36864 |
| A00 | 2560 | A000 | 40960 |
| B00 | 2816 | B000 | 45056 |
| C00 | 3072 | C000 | 49152 |
| D00 | 3328 | D000 | 53248 |
| E00 | 3584 | E000 | 57344 |
| F00 | 3840 | F000 | 61440 |
| | | 10000 | 65536 |

*Figure 2.6*

Making conversions with a table such as this can become quite fast once you are familiar with the system, but doing so in a program is surprisingly tricky. Figures 2.7 includes routines for performing the conversion either way. The DEC2HEX routine can be included in any program requiring such calculations. The routines for converting hex to decimal are included in the companion disk for this book – see the back page for details.

```
D2H:      ;Program to convert decimal to hex

      ;Value to be converted is included
      ;as command line parameter
      ;(e.g. D2H 12345)

      ;Limitations: No checking for validity
      ;of parameter. Maximum 65536.

      ;Calls PARSE (2.19), NEXTPARM (2.19),
      ;DISWRD (8.10), DEC2HEX

      jmp d2hstart

declen      db ?              ;Number of digits in
                              ;decimal parameter

d2hstart:
      call parse              ;Parse the command
                              ;line
      mov al,[paramlen]       ;Get no. digits and
                              ;save in DECLEN
      mov [declen],al
      call nextparm           ;Read decimal into
                              ;PARAMETER
      cld
      xor cx,cx
      mov cl,05h
      mov al,00h
      lea di,decin
      rep stosb               ;Fill DECIN with
                              ;nulls
      lea si,parameter
      lea di,decin
      mov cl,[declen]         ;Transfer contents
                              ;of PARAMETER
      rep movsb               ;to DECIN
      call dec2hex            ;Decimal-to-hex
                              ;conversion
      call diswrd             ;Display result
      int 20h

;-----------------------------------------------

DEC2HEX:      ;Convert decimal value to hex

      ;Entry values: DECIN holds decimal
      ;              value
      ;Exit values:  AX=hex value
      ;              AX,BX,CX,DX,SI changed
```

```
      jmp decstart

decin        db '     ',00
      ;Decimal value to be converted, as
      ;ASCII string, terminated by null
      ;character.  Maximum value 65535.
      ;Routine does not check that number
      ;is valid.

decstart:
      xor ax,ax                 ;Set AX=0 (AX will
                                ;hold hex value)
      xor bx,bx                 ;Clear BX
      mov bl,0Ah                ;Move 10 into BX
      xor si,si                 ;Clear SI (pointer
                                ;to next decimal
                                ;digit)

startcon:
      xor cx,cx                 ;Clear CX
      mov cl,decin[si]          ;Get next decimal
                                ;digit
      cmp cl,00h                ;Check against 0
      jz endcon                 ;If 0, conversion is
                                ;complete
      mul bx                    ;Otherwise, multiply
                                ;value in AX by 10
      sub cl,30h                ;Otherwise, subtract
                                ;30h to convert ASCII
                                ;number to actual val
      add ax,cx                 ;Add new digit
      inc si                    ;Increase SI, point
                                ;to next digit
      jmp startcon              ;Jump to start of
                                ;loop
endcon:
      ret
```

*Figure 2.7*

**Paragraphs and pages**

There is no shortage of jargon words when it comes to numbering systems, and a group of 10h (16) bytes of memory – 8 words – is often called a *paragraph*. Even more common is the term *page*, referring to 1000h (4096 or 4K) bytes of memory. A simple calculation shows that there are 100h paragraphs in a page.

### Low-high storage

To complicate matters still further, a two-byte word is not stored in memory as you might expect, with the high byte first and then the low byte; rather, it is stored in reverse order, the low-order byte being stored in the low-order memory. For example, the word 026Fh would appear in memory as:

```
6F 02
```

There are times when it is important to know exactly which byte is stored first.

## Binary operations

While a complete study of the binary system is not relevant to normal programming procedures, some of the side effects of the binary system are worthy of discussion.

### Binary subtraction

As described above, signed bytes are negative when they are in the range 80h to FFh; similarly, signed words are negative in the range 8000h to FFFFh. Converting these values into binary, you will see that the negative values are those where the most significant bit is 1.

So what happens when a number increases beyond its limit? In the case of a signed byte, the result of adding 1 to +127 is the number -128. Subtracting 1 from -128 takes you back to +127. The result is a cycle of numbers, as illustrated in Figure 2.8. The same principle applies to two-byte words, where +32767 is immediately followed by -32768.

The diagram in Figure 2.8 displays a certain symmetry. It has been arranged so that the numbers on either side are slightly out of step. That is, 0 is opposite -1, 1 is opposite -2, and so on. Inspecting the binary values of the numbers, you will see that the numbers on the right are the *complement* of those on the left and vice versa. That is, if you switch the 0s and 1s that make up a number on one side you

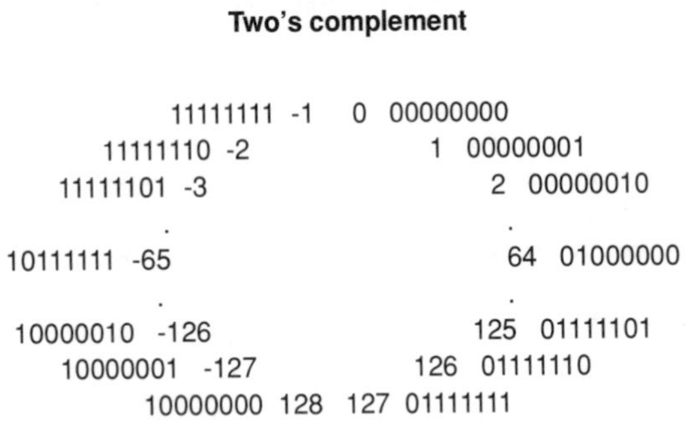

**Two's complement**

```
        11111111 -1   0 00000000
     11111110 -2             1 00000001
   11111101 -3                  2 00000010
          .                      .
10111111 -65                     64 01000000
          .                      .
 10000010 -126                 125 01111101
   10000001  -127           126 01111110
       10000000 128  127 01111111
```

*Figure 2.8*

will get the number opposite. Switching the 0s to 1s in a number is referred to as *taking the complement* of the number.

Thus if you take the complement of any number and add 1, the result is the negative of the original number. For example:

```
complement(1) + 1 = -2 + 1 = -1
```

The procedure works in both directions:

```
complement(-1) + 1 = 0 + 1 = 1
```

This operation is true of all numbers in the cycle and is known as *two's complement*. The process forms the basis of all computer subtraction, which can be transformed into a series of additions. For example:

```
  6 - 4
= 6 + (-4)
= 6 + (complement(4) + 1)
= 6 + (-5 + 1)
= 1 + 1
= 2
```

**The carry bit**

The frequent result of binary addition is that a *carry bit* is set. The carry bit – or *flag* – indicates that the numbers added together required more digits than were available. For example, adding two unsigned bytes holding the values 129 and 130 produces the result:

```
  10000001
+ 10000010
= 00000011
```

The maximum value a byte can hold is 256. Therefore, the result is only 3 but the carry bit is set, indicating that the true answer is 256 + 3 = 259.

Using two's complement arithmetic, the carry bit will be set in places we do not expect. For example, the calculation of 6-4, when converted to binary, becomes:

```
  00000110
+ 11111011
+        1
= 00000010
```

Strictly speaking, the addition of the two binary numbers produces the result:

```
100000010
```

However, the additional bit on the left, the carry bit, is ignored.

On other occasions, the fact that we have passed over from one side of the circle to the other *is* important. For example, adding 1 to 127 in a signed byte gives the result -128, which is clearly wrong. In this case, the carry bit is not set:

```
01111111 + 00000001 = 10000000
```

In binary terms, this is perfectly acceptable. However, with signed bytes the result is clearly something that should be noted. The same happens when subtracting from large negative numbers.

So that we are aware that this happens, the computer flags the situation by setting an *overflow flag*. Like the carry flag, this indicates that a certain situation has arisen. This time, however, rather than indicating that the calculation took us over the top of the circle (which is quite in order), the overflow flag is set when the calculation takes us round the bottom of the circle, indicating that the result needs to be treated with care.

Most of the time, it does not matter whether the carry or overflow flags are set but it is as well to be aware of their meanings when a calculation is complete.

## ASCII representations

So much for the storage of numbers. Clearly we must be able to store a variety of text as well, including upper and lower case letters, punctuation marks, symbols and so on. Since the computer is only able to understand binary, the solution is to represent all the characters that may be needed by a special binary code (in much the same way that Morse code can represent letters and symbols by a sequence of dots and dashes).

The coding system generally applied on the PC range is that of ASCII (the American Standard Code for Information Interchange). This system is used throughout the computer world and is a means of representing 128 different letters and symbols by a standard set of numeric codes.

### ASCII control codes

The first 32 ASCII characters (00h to 1Fh) are special *control codes*. These codes are used to represent common computer operations rather than specific characters. For example, ASCII code 13 (0Dh) represents a carriage return (CR), while 12 (0Ch) produces a form feed (FF) and 27 (1Bh) is the escape character (Esc). The ASCII control codes are listed in Figure 2.9, along with the names and standard abbreviations that are normally attached to them.

### Standard ASCII characters

The codes 20h to 2Fh represent a series of symbols. The numeric digits (when used as text rather than for their numeric content) start at 30h. The upper case letters start at 41h and lower case at 61h. Finally, the remaining gaps are filled with a set of arithmetic symbols, punctuation marks and other characters in common usage.

The standard ASCII character set is given in Figure 2.10.

**ASCII control codes**

| Dec | Hex | Abbrev | Meaning |
|---|---|---|---|
| 0 | 00 | NUL | Null character |
| 1 | 01 | SOH | Start of header |
| 2 | 02 | STX | Start text |
| 3 | 03 | ETX | End text |
| 4 | 04 | EOT | End of transmission |
| 5 | 05 | ENQ | Enquiry |
| 6 | 06 | ACK | Acknowledge |
| 7 | 07 | BEL | Bell |
| 8 | 08 | BS | Backspace |
| 9 | 09 | HT | Horizontal tab |
| 10 | 0A | LF | Line feed |
| 11 | 0B | VT | Vertical tab |
| 12 | 0C | FF | Form feed |
| 13 | 0D | CR | Carriage return |
| 14 | 0E | SO | Shift out |
| 15 | 0F | SI | Shift in |
| 16 | 10 | DLE | Data line escape |
| 17 | 11 | DC1 | Device control 1 |
| 18 | 12 | DC2 | Device control 2 |
| 19 | 13 | DC3 | Device control 3 |
| 20 | 14 | DC4 | Device control 4 |
| 21 | 15 | NAK | Negative acknowledge |
| 22 | 16 | SYN | Synchronisation idle |
| 23 | 17 | ETB | End transmission block |
| 24 | 18 | CAN | Cancel |
| 25 | 19 | EM | End of medium |
| 26 | 1A | SUB | Substitute |
| 27 | 1B | ESC | Escape |
| 28 | 1C | FS | File separator |
| 29 | 1D | GS | Group separator |
| 30 | 1E | RS | Record separator |
| 31 | 1F | US | Unit separator |

*Figure 2.9*

**ASCII character set**

| Dec | Hex | Char | Dec | Hex | Char | Dec | Hex | Char | Dec | Hex | Char |
|---|---|---|---|---|---|---|---|---|---|---|---|
| 0 | 00 | NUL | 32 | 20 | Space | 64 | 40 | @ | 96 | 60 | ` |
| 1 | 01 | SOH | 33 | 21 | ! | 65 | 41 | A | 97 | 61 | a |
| 2 | 02 | STX | 34 | 22 | " | 66 | 42 | B | 98 | 62 | b |
| 3 | 03 | ETX | 35 | 23 | # | 67 | 43 | C | 99 | 63 | c |
| 4 | 04 | EOT | 36 | 24 | $ | 68 | 44 | D | 100 | 64 | d |
| 5 | 05 | ENQ | 37 | 25 | % | 69 | 45 | E | 101 | 65 | e |
| 6 | 06 | ACK | 38 | 26 | & | 70 | 46 | F | 102 | 66 | f |
| 7 | 07 | BEL | 39 | 27 | ' | 71 | 47 | G | 103 | 67 | g |
| 8 | 08 | BS | 40 | 28 | ( | 72 | 48 | H | 104 | 68 | h |
| 9 | 09 | HT | 41 | 29 | ) | 73 | 49 | I | 105 | 69 | i |
| 10 | 0A | LF | 42 | 2A | * | 74 | 4A | J | 106 | 6A | j |
| 11 | 0B | VT | 43 | 2B | + | 75 | 4B | K | 107 | 6B | k |
| 12 | 0C | FF | 44 | 2C | , | 76 | 4C | L | 108 | 6C | l |
| 13 | 0D | CR | 45 | 2D | - | 77 | 4D | M | 109 | 6D | m |
| 14 | 0E | SO | 46 | 2E | . | 78 | 4E | N | 110 | 6E | n |
| 15 | 0F | SI | 47 | 2F | / | 79 | 4F | O | 111 | 6F | o |
| 16 | 10 | DLE | 48 | 30 | 0 | 80 | 50 | P | 112 | 70 | p |
| 17 | 11 | DC1 | 49 | 31 | 1 | 81 | 51 | Q | 113 | 71 | q |
| 18 | 12 | DC2 | 50 | 32 | 2 | 82 | 52 | R | 114 | 72 | r |
| 19 | 13 | DC3 | 51 | 33 | 3 | 83 | 53 | S | 115 | 73 | s |
| 20 | 14 | DC4 | 52 | 34 | 4 | 84 | 54 | T | 116 | 74 | t |
| 21 | 15 | NAK | 53 | 35 | 5 | 85 | 55 | U | 117 | 75 | u |
| 22 | 16 | SYN | 54 | 36 | 6 | 86 | 56 | V | 118 | 76 | v |
| 23 | 17 | ETB | 55 | 37 | 7 | 87 | 57 | W | 119 | 77 | w |
| 24 | 18 | CAN | 56 | 38 | 8 | 88 | 58 | X | 120 | 78 | x |
| 25 | 19 | EM | 57 | 39 | 9 | 89 | 59 | Y | 121 | 79 | y |
| 26 | 1A | SUB | 58 | 3A | : | 90 | 5A | Z | 122 | 7A | z |
| 27 | 1B | ESC | 59 | 3B | ; | 91 | 5B | [ | 123 | 7B | { |
| 28 | 1C | FS | 60 | 3C | < | 92 | 5C | \ | 124 | 7C | ¦ |
| 29 | 1D | GS | 61 | 3D | = | 93 | 5D | ] | 125 | 7D | } |
| 30 | 1E | RS | 62 | 3E | > | 94 | 5E | ^ | 126 | 7E | ~ |
| 31 | 1F | US | 63 | 3F | ? | 95 | 5F | _ | 127 | 7F | ⌂ |

*Figure 2.10*

## ASCII extended character set

| Dec | Hex | Char | Dec | Hex | Char | Dec | Hex | Char | Dec | Hex | Char |
|---|---|---|---|---|---|---|---|---|---|---|---|
| 128 | 80 | Ç | 160 | A0 | á | 192 | C0 | └ | 224 | E0 | α |
| 129 | 81 | ü | 161 | A1 | í | 193 | C1 | ┴ | 225 | E1 | β |
| 130 | 82 | é | 162 | A2 | ó | 194 | C2 | ┬ | 226 | E2 | Γ |
| 131 | 83 | â | 163 | A3 | ú | 195 | C3 | ├ | 227 | E3 | π |
| 132 | 84 | ä | 164 | A4 | ñ | 196 | C4 | ─ | 228 | E4 | Σ |
| 133 | 85 | à | 165 | A5 | Ñ | 197 | C5 | ┼ | 229 | E5 | σ |
| 134 | 86 | å | 166 | A6 | ª | 198 | C6 | ╞ | 230 | E6 | µ |
| 135 | 87 | ç | 167 | A7 | º | 199 | C7 | ╟ | 231 | E7 | τ |
| 136 | 88 | ê | 168 | A8 | ¿ | 200 | C8 | ╚ | 232 | E8 | Φ |
| 137 | 89 | ë | 169 | A9 | ⌐ | 201 | C9 | ╔ | 233 | E9 | Θ |
| 138 | 8A | è | 170 | AA | ¬ | 202 | CA | ╩ | 234 | EA | Ω |
| 139 | 8B | ï | 171 | AB | ½ | 203 | CB | ╦ | 235 | EB | δ |
| 140 | 8C | î | 172 | AC | ¼ | 204 | CC | ╠ | 236 | EC | ∞ |
| 141 | 8D | ì | 173 | AD | ¡ | 205 | CD | ═ | 237 | ED | φ |
| 142 | 8E | Ä | 174 | AE | « | 206 | CE | ╬ | 238 | EE | ε |
| 143 | 8F | Å | 175 | AF | » | 207 | CF | ╧ | 239 | EF | ∩ |
| 144 | 90 | É | 176 | B0 | ░ | 208 | D0 | ╨ | 240 | F0 | ≡ |
| 145 | 91 | æ | 177 | B1 | ▒ | 209 | D1 | ╤ | 241 | F1 | ± |
| 146 | 92 | Æ | 178 | B2 | ▓ | 210 | D2 | ╥ | 242 | F2 | ≥ |
| 147 | 93 | ô | 179 | B3 | │ | 211 | D3 | ╙ | 243 | F3 | ≤ |
| 148 | 94 | ö | 180 | B4 | ┤ | 212 | D4 | ╘ | 244 | F4 | ⌠ |
| 149 | 95 | ò | 181 | B5 | ╡ | 213 | D5 | ╒ | 245 | F5 | ⌡ |
| 150 | 96 | û | 182 | B6 | ╢ | 214 | D6 | ╓ | 246 | F6 | ÷ |
| 151 | 97 | ù | 183 | B7 | ╖ | 215 | D7 | ╫ | 247 | F7 | ≈ |
| 152 | 98 | ÿ | 184 | B8 | ╕ | 216 | D8 | ╪ | 248 | F8 | ° |
| 153 | 99 | Ö | 185 | B9 | ╣ | 217 | D9 | ┘ | 249 | F9 | ∙ |
| 154 | 9A | Ü | 186 | BA | ║ | 218 | DA | ┌ | 250 | FA | · |
| 155 | 9B | ¢ | 187 | BB | ╗ | 219 | DB | █ | 251 | FB | √ |
| 156 | 9C | £ | 188 | BC | ╝ | 220 | DC | ▄ | 252 | FC | $^n$ |
| 157 | 9D | ¥ | 189 | BD | ╜ | 221 | DD | ▌ | 253 | FD | $^2$ |
| 158 | 9E | ₧ | 190 | BE | ╛ | 222 | DE | ▐ | 254 | FE | ■ |
| 159 | 9F | ƒ | 191 | BF | ┐ | 223 | DF | ▀ | 255 | FF | |

*Figure 2.11*

**Extended ASCII**

While the standard ASCII codes cover most of the standard letters, numbers and symbols that are needed, there are a great many other characters that are useful: the box-drawing characters, currency symbols, foreign characters and so on.

Fortunately, the standard ASCII set requires just 7 bits of data for the 128 codes. Since it is usual to work in terms of 8-bit bytes, this leaves one bit spare. In other words, there are an extra 128 codes that can be used without needing to go beyond a single byte.

As a general rule, these 128 extra codes are used for the *extended ASCII* character set, which ranges from 80h to FFh.

The only problem is, this extended set is not quite as standard as the normal ASCII character set. The usual implementation of the extended ASCII characters in the UK is given in Figure 2.11 but it is important to bear in mind that the extended ASCII characters might not always be coded exactly as you expect.

It is also worth mentioning that these codes are not always available as an option. For example, some communications links use the eighth bit of each byte for error checking, meaning that only the standard ASCII codes can be transferred. Some programs use the extra bit for storing extra information; for example, some versions of WordStar uses the MSB to indicate that a character comes at the end of a word.

**ASCIIZ**

Some of the interrupts described in this book expect data to be stored in memory as an ASCIIZ (ASCII with zero) string. This is simply a string of standard ASCII characters, terminated by the null character (00h).

## Organisation of memory

As described in Chapter 1, the PC has internal memory locations for storing data. The computer needs to be able to identify each of these memory locations uniquely, so that information can be transferred to and from them without confusion. To do this, each memory location is given a unique *address*.

This address works in exactly the same way as the address of a house. Any data is transferred to a particular location as a 'packet' of information, with the data itself preceded by the address of the destination location, in much the same way that information sent by letter is enclosed in an envelope carrying the recipient's address.

To store a piece of information in a memory location, the CPU sends the address down the data bus, followed by the item of data itself. The hardware ensures that the data is delivered to the correct location.

On the 16-bit 8086, this apparently limits the maximum address to 65536 (64K). While this was enough for the earlier computers, clearly it is insufficient for today's large-capacity machines. However, the 8086 has a 20-bit address bus, capable of transferring values up to 1M.

To identify a slot in memory, the 8086 gives each memory location an address that is made up of two parts, each a single word in length. These are the *segment* and *offset*. The segment is the address of a general 64K area in memory while the offset is the position of a memory location relative to the start of the segment.

The segment can start at any paragraph boundary (that is, at a multiple of 16 bytes from the start of memory). Therefore, the last digit is always 0 and consequently ignored. For example, the segment B800 actually begins at location B8000h. The offset can take values from 0000h to FFFFh which, when added to the segment address B800, gives a range from B8000h to C7FFFh.

The full address of any location is given by combining the segment and offset; for example,

B800:00A0 represents the 80th byte (00A0h) in the segment starting at B8000h. To calculate an address precisely, multiply the segment by 16 and add the offset. In the example above:

```
  B800:00A0
= (B800 x 10h) + 00A0h
= B8000h + 00A0h
= B80A0h
```

This method of addressing means that each location can be referred to by many different addresses. There is no hard and fast rule as to which segment you should choose on any occasion; it is a matter of convenience. The overlapping of addresses is illustrated in Figure 2.12.

The use of segments means that the 8086 can address up 1M of memory.

The 80286 has a 24-line address bus, giving it an addressing capability of 16M, while the 80386's 32-line address bus extends the addressing range to 4G. However, to ensure that programs are compatible across the entire PC range, you should keep within the IM limit.

**8086 addresses**

| Actual address | First segment | Second segment | Third segment |
|---|---|---|---|
| 00000 | 0000:0000 | | |
| 00001 | 0000:0001 | | |
| ... | ... | | |
| 0000F | 0000:000F | | |
| 00010 | 0000:0010 | 0001:0000 | |
| 00011 | 0000:0011 | 0001:0001 | |
| ... | ... | ... | |
| 0001F | 0000:001F | 0001:000F | |
| 00020 | 0000:0020 | 0001:0010 | 0002:0000 |
| 00021 | 0000:0021 | 0001:0011 | 0002:0001 |
| ... | ... | ... | ... |

*Figure 2.12*

**Expanded and extended memory**

On the 8086, the IM limit can be increased by the use of LIM EMS. (Lotus-Intel-Microsoft Expanded Memory Specification). EMS maps additional memory onto the standard 1M memory space, allowing access to 32M of memory. Special programming methods are needed to access EMS.

The 80286 upwards allow the use of *extended* memory. This is standard memory above the 1M limit, which can be accessed directly via the enlarged address bus.

Programs that use expanded memory are compatible across the entire PC range but those that access extended memory require a minimum 80286 processor.

## The registers

Being able to uniquely identify any location in memory is not enough for programming purposes. You cannot perform calculations directly with data in memory. Likewise, the 80x86 does not allow you to transfer data directly from one part of memory to another. There are also times when you wish to temporarily store information away without the bother of transferring it to an identifiable location in memory. These problems are overcome by the use of the registers and stack.

All calculations are carried out using special areas of workspace called *registers*, contained in the CPU itself. These form the basic variables for machine code programming.

The registers, since they are not part of the computer RAM or pre-programmed ROM, do not have addresses in the usual sense. Instead, each one is given a name.

When any data is to be used in calculations it is first transferred to a register. When an item of data is moved from one part of memory to another it must move via one of the registers. Registers are also used to point to the start of the program and data area, to keep track of the current position in a

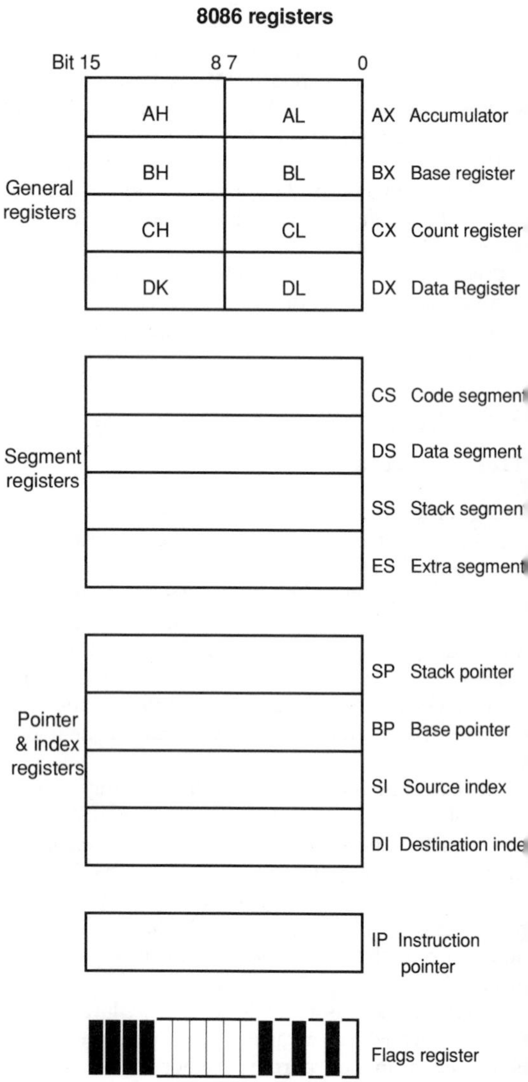

**8086 registers**

Bit 15 8 7 0

General registers

| AH | AL | AX Accumulator |
|---|---|---|
| BH | BL | BX Base register |
| CH | CL | CX Count register |
| DK | DL | DX Data Register |

Segment registers

CS Code segment
DS Data segment
SS Stack segmen
ES Extra segment

Pointer & index registers

SP Stack pointer
BP Base pointer
SI Source index
DI Destination inde

IP Instruction pointer

Flags register

*Figure 2.13*

program and to identify the stack area (described below).

The number of registers available varies depending on the processor type. The 8086 registers are illustrated in Figure 2.13.

**The general registers**

The 8086 contains four *general registers*: AX, BX, CX and DX. Although there are some circumstances where specific registers must be used, these registers are usually available to the programmer as general-purpose variables; for example:

```
MOV AX,[data1]
ADD AX,0005h
MOV [data1],AX
```

The effect of these three lines is to add 5 to the value of the memory location we have referred to as DATA1. This is achieved by moving the current value of DATA1 into AX (the accumulator), adding 5 to it and then storing the result back in DATA1. In the BASIC programming language, such a feat would be achieved with the instruction:

```
DATA1 = DATA1 + 5
```

When compiled, this high-level instruction would be converted into the three machine code steps described above. In practice, any of the general registers could have been used as the basis for this calculation.

**Single-byte registers**

Although the general registers can each contain a word of data, it is sometimes more convenient to work with individual bytes. Therefore, each of the registers can be split into two separate single-byte registers. The second character of the register name is H or L, instead of X, indicating the high and low bytes respectively. For example, the high byte of AX is AH and its low byte is AL. The principle is the same for all the general registers.

**The segment registers**

The start of various sections of memory needs to be known at all times by the computer. This is done by storing the segment addresses in the four *segment registers*. In these cases, the registers are used to identify 64K blocks of memory, which may be completely independent of each other, may coincide or may overlap. The purpose of these four registers is as follows:

- CS (the Code Segment) is the memory segment where the program code is stored.
- DS (the Data Segment) is the main data storage area.
- SS (the Stack Segment) is the part of memory for storing the program stack.
- ES (the Extra Segment) is used to point to an additional data storage area, particularly when moving data from one location to another.

For small programs, these four segments are often the same. When the program, its data and stack area can all fit comfortably into a 64K block of memory, it is convenient for all four segments to start at the same position, with different offsets for each individual section.

These registers are automatically set up when any program is run and should only be changed when absolutely necessary. In particular, you should not change CS or SS unless you are absolutely certain of what you are doing; always make sure to restore them after carrying out any operation.

**The pointer registers**

Two registers are used to point to particular bytes in memory. SP (the Stack Pointer) points to the current top of stack; this is described in more detail below. BP (the Base Pointer) identifies an offset in memory for certain operations. This offset is usually given relative to the Base Register, BX.

SI (the Source Index) is another type of pointer, generally used to identify the start point of a block of data that is to be moved. DI (the Destination Index) is similarly used to point to the start of an area of memory where data is to be stored. Generally, the Source Index is given as an offset to the Data Segment while the Destination Index is an offset of the Extra Segment. Therefore, when moving a block of data, the source is given as DS:SI while the destination is ES:DI.

IP (the Instruction Pointer) is an offset to the Code Segment and indicates the next instruction in memory to be executed. Each time an instruction is processed, IP is updated. The location of the current instruction is identified by CS:IP.

**The flags register**

The final register on the 8086 is also a word in length but does not store a single 16-bit value; rather, each individual bit is used to indicate a particular situation. This is the *flags register*. Each bit can take the value 0 or 1 and is referred to as a *flag*. The flags are constantly changing and tell us what is happening in the system at any time. For example, if any calculation results in an overflow the overflow flag is set (i.e. given a value of 1); if the calculation does not result in an overflow, that flag is cleared (i.e. given a value of 0).

The flags are used for a variety of purposes within programs. There are also special instructions that test the values of flags and act accordingly, that set or clear individual flags, and that push the flags register onto the stack or pop it off again.

The organisation of the flags register, along with the names, common abbreviations and use of the individual bits, is given in Figure 2.14. The abbreviations used by the DEBUG utility when the flags are set or clear are also noted.

The general use of the flags is as follows:

- The *overflow flag* indicates that an operation has resulted in a number that is either too large or too small. As a rule, the flag is set if the sign of the result of a calculation is logically incorrect (for example, adding 1 to 127 to get -128 will produce an overflow); otherwise, the flag is cleared.
- The *direction flag* is used by the 8086 string instructions which operate on entire sections of memory. The value of the flag indicates the direction in which the instruction is to work. For example, the SI register usually points to the start of the source data. If the direction flag is

**Flags register**

| Bit | Abbr | Name | DEBUG Clear | DEBUG Set | Meaning if set |
|---|---|---|---|---|---|
| 0 | CF | Carry flag | NC | CY | Result too large or too small for register |
| 1 | | Unused | | | |
| 2 | PF | Parity flag | PO | PE | Result has even no. of bits set to 1 |
| 3 | | Unused | | | |
| 4 | AF | Auxiliary flag | NA | AC | BCD operation requires adjustment |
| 5 | | Unused | | | |
| 6 | ZF | Zero flag | NZ | ZR | Result of operation was zero |
| 7 | SF | Sign flag | PL | NG | Result of operation was negative |
| 8 | TF | Trap flag | - | - | Single-step mode |
| 9 | IF | Interrupt flag | DI | EI | Interrupts enabled |
| 10 | DF | Direction flag | UP | DN | Direction for string ops is negative |
| 11 | OF | Overflow flag | NV | OV | Operation resulted in arithmetic overflow |
| 12 | | Unused | | | |
| 13 | | Unused | | | |
| 14 | | Unused | | | |
| 15 | | Unused | | | |

*Figure 2.14*

clear, this register is increased by 1 after each operation; otherwise it is decreased.

- The *interrupt flag* determines whether or not the system responds to interrupts. When the flag is set, hardware interrupts are processed. Occasionally it is necessary to disable interrupts by clearing this flag; in such circumstances the flag should be kept clear only as long as is absolutely necessary.
- The *trap flag* is set when you want the processor to execute only one instruction at a time before returning control to a calling program. For example, it is used by DEBUG to trace through a

program. The point of setting the trap flag is that you can step through a program one instruction at a time, at each step being free to inspect the contents of memory and the registers before continuing.

- The *sign flag* is set when an operation results in a negative value, and cleared when the result is positive.
- The *zero flag* is set when an operation results in a zero value, otherwise it is cleared. (Take care with this flag. When the flag has a value of 1, the result was 0; when the flag is 0, the result was non-zero.)
- The *carry flag* is used to hold the extra bit when an addition results in a value that needs to be carried over to the next part of the calculation.

### 80286, 80386 and 80486 registers

The 80286 has several additional registers that are required for programming in protected mode. These registers provide access to extended memory, among other things. DOS cannot operate in this mode, so these extra registers are not covered here.

The 80386 and 80486, being 32-bit processors, provide extended 32-bit registers (EAX, EBX, etc.) plus two extra segment registers (FS and GS). They also have a 32-bit flags register. All 8086 programs will operate successfully on the 80386 and 80486.

## The stack

Because the number of registers is limited you often need to use the same register for many different operations. In some cases, you need to hang on to the existing values so that they can be used again later. While it would be possible to transfer the contents of the registers to specific locations in memory, this is often inconvenient. In particular, you do not always know how many values need to be stored; for example, when calling a subroutine the address of the current instruction must be temporarily held so that the program can continue with the next instruction when it returns; there may be many of these addresses, when a number of subroutines are 'nested'.

The way round this is to set aside a part of memory as a general storage area. Any data can be stored in this area without worrying about precisely where it is. Such an area is referred to as a *stack*.

Imagine that you are writing a series of notes. As each note is completed, the piece of paper is added to a pile. As you add each note to the pile, you record that fact. You do not need to know precisely where in the pile any particular note is. What is important is that you should know how far it is from the top. For example, if you write a particular note and then add four more on top, you can recover the original note by removing a total of five sheets from the pile.

The computer stack works in exactly the same way. You can store any information you like by simply adding it to the stack; you don't need to know exactly where it is in memory. As long as you take items off the stack in the reverse order (and in the same subroutine) you can recover any item at any reasonable time. The contents of any register can be stored in the stack with the PUSH instruction; the corresponding POP instruction pulls the item back off again. These instructions are used extensively in all assembler programs.

You should also bear in mind that the processor uses the same stack space. When a subroutine is called, for example, the location of the next instruction to be processed in the calling routine is pushed onto the stack. When the subroutine ends, this address is popped off the stack again so that the processor knows where to find the next instruction. This means that some care is needed when pushing and popping around subroutines. You can push one or more registers onto the stack before calling a subroutine and pop them off again immediately afterwards, secure in the knowledge that the correct values will have been recovered (assuming the subroutine is well behaved). However, if you push a value onto the stack, call a subroutine and, from within the subroutine, try to pop the value back off, you will not get the results you expect.

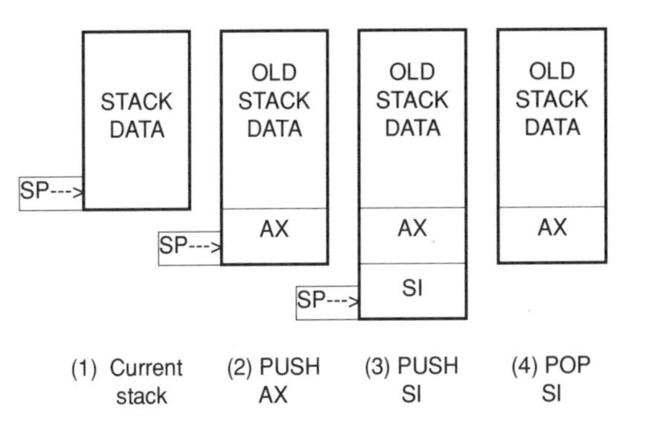


*Figure 2.15*

The use of the stack is illustrated in Figure 2.15.

**The Stack Segment**

The location of the area of memory that is allocated for storing the stack can be found in the Stack Segment (SS). Often the Stack Statement coincides with the Data Segment but, since the size of the stack cannot be defined in advance, confusion is avoided by always filling the stack from the highest memory location down. The last item to have been stored on the stack is identified by the stack pointer (SP). The SP always points to the *top of stack*. Don't be confused by this; since the stack works from high memory down, as each new item is added the top of stack moves down into a lower part of memory.

The great advantage is that it becomes possible to store a substantial program, its data and stack entirely in a 64K segment. Since the size of the program is fixed, the program code is stored at the bottom of the segment. The data area follows immediately on from this and can grow upwards, while the stack starts at the other end of the segment and works down. This is the case with COM programs, for example. All will be well as long as there is plenty of leeway to allow the stack to expand. If the area becomes too tight then you will run out of stack space and the program will collapse with an 'out of stack space' message.

The top of stack is identified by SS:SP. SS points to the start of the segment; SP starts at FFFFh and works down. Although you can adjust the stack pointer yourself it is not generally a good idea to do so. Each time a subroutine is called or an item is pushed onto or popped off the stack, the stack pointer is automatically updated by the system. Take great care if you do change the stack segment or stack pointer; careless alterations will completely wreck the operation of a program.

## Addressing modes

In assembly language programs, it is often necessary to point to specific places in memory; in particular, you need to identify a location for storing a particular value or a point in the program as the destination for a jump. To make life easier, you can give names to the memory locations, and labels to subroutines and specific points in the program. The rules to be followed by these names are defined by the assembler being used but the principles are always the same. When the program is compiled, the names are replaced by the actual offset.

Most operations require the manipulation of one or more pieces of data. The 80x86 provides a number of different ways of referring to data. These are the *addressing modes*.

### Immediate addressing

The simplest form, *immediate addressing*, refers to a specific, fixed value. For example, to move the value 7 into AX takes the instruction:

```
MOV AX,0007h
```

After this instruction, AX holds the value 7. To load a different value requires a different instruction.

Similarly, an offset can be moved into AX as follows:

```
MOV AX,DATA1
```

If DATA1 points to a location at offset 0200h in the data segment, AX now contains the value 0200h.

### Direct addressing

Much of the time you need to work with the contents of a memory location, without knowing what the actual value is. In this case an area of memory is used as a variable: this is *direct addressing*. For example, the contents of offset 0200h can be moved into AX with either of these instructions:

```
MOV AX,[0200h]
MOV AX,[DATA1]
```

When compiled, these two instructions are identical. If DATA1 contains 0007h, AX now holds the value 7. The square brackets can be read as 'contents of'.

### Register addressing

The third mode, *register addressing*, transfers the contents of one register into another. For example:

```
MOV AX,BX
```

The value in BX is now replicated in AX. Note that in this case square brackets [ ] are not used. Any pair of registers can be used in this form of addressing.

### Indirect addressing

If the location of the value to be loaded varies (that is, you are using a different variable each time), then operations need to be carried out using *indirect addressing*. For example:

```
MOV AX,[BX]
```

Here the register AX takes the value held in the location that is pointed to by BX (relative to DS). For example, if BX has been loaded with the offset 0200h, AX will now hold the value 7, this being the contents of the location pointed to by BX.

For this mode, the registers are limited. As well as BX you may use SI or DI (both relative to DS) and BP (relative to SS).

**Based addressing**

If you want to store an array of data in memory, then you can identify an individual byte or word by extending the principles of indirect addressing. With *based addressing* a register points to the start of an array and you can then specify an offset from that point. Continuing with the example above, if 0200h is the start of an array of data, the ninth byte of the array (offset 08h from start) can be loaded into AX with the command:

```
MOV AX,[BX + 08h]
```

For based addressing you may use either BX (relative to DS) or BP (relative to SS).

**Indexed addressing**

To identify a variable offset from the start of an array, use *indexed addressing*. Here the first byte of the array must be specified explicitly rather than as a value in BX or BP. For example, if DATA1 is the start of an array and the element number has been stored in SI, the value in that location can be loaded with either of the instructions:

```
MOV AX,[DATA1 + SI]
MOV AX,DATA1[SI]
```

These two instructions are identical. SI is an index for the array. With indexed addressing either SI or DI are applicable.

**Based index addressing**

Finally, *based index addressing* combines the previous two modes by allowing you to specify a variable base point, in either BX or BP, and an offset in either SI or DI. As a further modification, an immediate value can be added to extend the displacement further.

The same items as before can be loaded into memory with the instructions:

```
MOV AX,[BX + SI]
MOV CX,[BX + SI + 02h]
```

These two instructions load two consecutive words into AX and CX respectively.

These addressing modes are demonstrated by the program in Figure 2.16.

```
ADDRESS:        ;A program to test addressing
                ;modes

      ;Calls DISLIN, DISBYT, NEWLIN (Fig 8.10)

      jmp addrst

message1      db 'Immediate addressing  $'
message2      db 'Direct addressing     $'
message3      db 'Register addressing   $'
message4      db 'Indirect addressing   $'
message5      db 'Based addressing      $'
message6      db 'Indexed addressing    $'
message7      db 'Based index addressing$'
data1:        dw 0b312h,45a3h,77ffh,0087h,0088h
              ;The address of data1 is 01A4h

addrst:
      lea dx,message1
      call dislin
      mov ax,01A4h              ;Immediate - load
                                ;value
      call diswrd
      call newlin
      mov ax,data1              ;Immediate - load
                                ;address
      call diswrd
      call newlin

      lea dx,message2
      call dislin
      mov ax,[01A4h]            ;Direct
      call diswrd
      call newlin
      mov ax,[data1]            ;Direct- alternative
                                ;using label
      call diswrd
      call newlin

      lea dx,message3
      call dislin
      mov bx,1122h              ;Set up BX
                                ;(immediate)
      mov ax,bx                 ;Register
      call diswrd
      call newlin
```

```
lea dx,message4
call dislin
mov bx,data1            ;Set up BX
                        ;(immediate)
mov ax,[bx]             ;Indirect
call diswrd
call newlin

lea dx,message5
call dislin
mov bx,data1            ;Set up BX
                        ;(immediate)
mov ax,[bx+06h]         ;Based
call diswrd
call newlin

lea dx,message6
call dislin
mov si,0006h            ;Set up SI
                        ;(immediate)
mov ax,[01a4h+si]       ;Indexed
call diswrd
call newlin
mov ax,data1[si]        ;Indexed -
                        ;alternative syntax
call diswrd
call newlin

lea dx,message7
call dislin
mov bx,data1            ;Set up BX
                        ;(immediate)
mov si,0006h            ;Set up SI
                        ;(immediate)
mov ax,[bx+si]          ;Based index
call diswrd
call newlin
mov ax,[bx+si+02h]      ;Based index - next
                        ;word
call diswrd
call newlin
int 20h
```

*Figure 2.16*

**Protected modes**

The 80286, running in protected mode, uses *segment descriptor tables* to address areas beyond the first megabyte. The tables contain 24-bit addresses. There are special instructions for using this extended memory.

The 80386, while maintaining compatibility with its predecessors, also uses 32-bit segment and offset addresses to extend its range still further. This chip also has a Virtual 8086 addressing mode. In this mode, the 8086 address space is mapped onto any 1M area of extended memory, allowing more than one 8086 program to be run concurrently.

## 80x86 instructions

All programs are comprised of a series of instructions. Each instruction tells the computer to carry out a particular task. In high-level languages a single command is converted into several machine code instructions when the program is compiled, as illustrated in the previous section. With programs written in assembly language there is no further subdivision. The assembly language instructions are translated on a one-to-one basis to their machine code equivalents. In general, each machine code instruction is allocated its own individual portion of the CPU's arithmetic and logic unit (ALU). The assembly language instructions therefore form the basic building blocks for all programs.

The 8086/8088 processors provide over 100 machine code instructions; the 80286 adds a further 20 while the 80386 gives you another 35. The addition of an 80x87 maths coprocessor adds another 80 or so instructions. Finally, the 80486, which incorporates all the functions of the maths co-processor within the main CPU, takes the total number of instructions to over 250.

### Syntax

A machine code instruction consists of a sequence of hex digits. The first two or three digits represent the instructions to be performed, the remainder (if any) are the values, locations or registers that are to be processed. In assembly language these hex digits are directly represented by mnemonics and operands.

The *mnemonic* is the instruction itself: for example, `MOV`, the command to move a value from one location to another. The *operands* are the values to be processed. In a MOV instruction, for instance, the operands are the location that is to be changed and the value it is to receive. In the instruction `MOV AX,07h` the operands are AX and 07h.

Assembly language programs will also contain a variety of *labels*. These are convenient names for memory locations that are converted to offset values when assembled. Each label refers to a particular byte of memory.

For example, the instruction `JMP END` tells the program the jump to a byte labelled END.

Similarly, labels can be used for memory locations when moving data. For example, `MOV AX,END` moves the *address* of the memory location END into AX; the instruction `MOV AX,[END]` moves the contents of the memory location into the register. Whether the CPU interprets the second operand as an actual value or the contents of a memory location depends upon the particular MOV instruction that is coded.

It should be noted at this point that the translation of a mnemonic to its machine code equivalent is not quite as simple as you might expect. There is not just one instruction for each mnemonic but several: a different one for each addressing mode. For example, the MOV instruction when moving an immediate value into a register is different to that for moving the contents of a register into a memory location. However, that is generally a problem for the assembler to deal with. The only time you need to be able to translate backwards is when you are inspecting the contents of memory.

**Variations**

Some instructions have more than one mnemonic: for example, Jump If Greater (JG) and Jump if Not Less or Equal (JNLE). Some assemblers also have their own individual mnemonics not included in the standard set. (The mnemonics are a feature of the assembler software, so different assemblers will have different sets of mnemonics.) When assembled, these are converted to more than one machine code instruction.

Similarly, *psuedo-ops* are found in almost all assembly languages. These are special instructions that tell the assembler what to do when the code is actually compiled. They are not actually translated into machine code but are a feature of the assembler and are ignored here.

The rigid structure that is required by many assemblers – which insist upon a large number of psuedo-ops being used and being applied precisely – can make assembly language programming unduly arduous. The examples in this book are based on A86, a no-nonsense assembler that generally ignores psuedo-ops wherever possible. Using this assembler, the programs given here can be typed in directly without any of the other trimmings that are required by some assemblers. If you do compile these examples with another assembler, then you must remember to add whatever psuedo-ops are required by that program. A86 is a shareware program; further details of how it may be obtained are given at the back of the book.

**Effect on the flags**

Many instructions change one or more of the flags. Some always set or clear particular flags; some flags return values that are useful; and some flags return indeterminate or unpredictable values.

## Assembler operation

The process of converting an original assembler file into an executable program consists of several stages.

The original file is referred to as the *source file*. This is usually an ASCII text file. The examples in this book are all source files. The assembler converts this into an *object file*. This is a file in which the mnemonics and operands have been converted into the corresponding machine code and any labels have been converted into offsets. The assembler usually takes two passes through the file to achieve this; on the first pass a list of the labels and their locations is constructed, the second pass slots the correct offsets into the gaps.

If some routines are used regularly, in a number of different assembler files, these may be stored in a *library file*. The next stage, *linking*, takes the object file and replaces any external references to routines in the library files with the correct code.

The result is an *executable file*. This is a program with an EXE extension that can be run at the DOS prompt. The final stage, for small programs, is to convert the executable file into a *binary file*, for a COM extension. This is usually achieved with a program such as EXE2BIN.

## Binary and executable files

There are some important differences between the two forms of program that can be executed from the DOS prompt. Binary (COM) files are suitable for small programs. The basic requirement for a binary file is that the code, data and stack areas must all fit into a single 64K segment. A binary file is loaded into memory at the lowest possible point and, because it is small, executes very quickly.

For executable (EXE) files, on the other hand, there is no limit to the size. The program code, data area and stack can be in different segments and the program itself can be loaded into any part of memory. However, a table of information is always loaded into memory at the first available place. This table points to the main section of program code. The executable file has the advantage that it can be much larger than a COM file and is not confined to a particular part of memory; the trade-off is that DOS has to do a lot more work when the program is loaded, so it is much slower to get started.

If you are creating an application that will be operating for some considerable time, the extra time taken to load the program is of little importance and an EXE file may be most suitable. If you have created a small utility that performs its work very quickly, then you will not want the user to wait too long while the program is loaded, so a COM file should be considered.

## DEBUG

All DOS systems are supplied with a copy of DEBUG. This is a very simple assembler program. Like many of the DOS utilities (such as EDLIN, the text editor that appears not to have changed for twenty years) DEBUG is extremely basic. However, it can be a very good starting point for creating, running and debugging assembler code. A complete discussion of DEBUG is beyond the scope of this book but the DEBUG instructions are briefly described in Figure 2.17.

**DEBUG commands**

| Command | Name | Syntax | Effect |
|---|---|---|---|
| A | Assemble | A<br>A address | Assembles code directly |
| C | Compare | C range, address | Compares memory in range with memory starting at address |
| D | Dump | D<br>D range | Displays next 128 bytes or range |
| E | Enter | E address<br>E address, data | Enters data at specified address |
| F | Fill | F range, data | Fills range with data |
| G | Go | G | Executes program from start or from address |
| H | Hexadecimal | H value, value | Adds two hex numbers and subtracts second from first |
| I | Input | I port | Inputs value from port |
| L | Load | L address<br>L address, sectors | Loads a file or disk sectors |
| M | Move | M range, address | Moves a range of memory to a new address |
| N | Name | N filename | Names a file to load or save |
| O | Output | O data,port | Outputs data to a port |
| P | Proceed | | |
| Q | Quit | Q | Quits DEBUG |

| Command | Name | Syntax | Effect |
|---|---|---|---|
| R | Register | R<br>R register | Displays contents of registers |
| S | Search | S range, data | Searches range for data |
| T | Trace | T<br>T=address<br>T steps | Traces program, optionally from a specified address and/or a number of steps |
| U | Unassemble | U range | Unassembles a range of code |
| W | Write | W<br>W address<br>W address, sectors | Writes a section of code to a file or directly to disk |

*Figure 2.17*

## The program segment prefix

When you run a program, the first thing DOS does is to create a block of data in the first available space in memory. This data is vital to the operation of the program and is called the *Program Segment Prefix (PSP)*.

The PSP is 100h (256) bytes long. Therefore, the actual instructions in a COM file always begin at offset 0100h from the start of the code segment. In the case of an EXE file, the PSP is still created and stored in the first 100h bytes of available memory but the instruction code itself could be anywhere else in memory.

The contents of the PSP are shown in Figure 2.18.

### Locating the PSP

Before you can make use of the data in the PSP, you need to identify its location. Although it is possible to calculate the position with a COM file, since it must be the 100h bytes immediately before the start of the code, this is not always easy. For an EXE file, the main program could be anywhere and the PSP is not necessarily attached to it.

DOS 2 provides a function to locate the PSP: function 51h of interrupt 21h. (Function 62h is identical.)

**The Program Segment Prefix**

| Offset (hex) | Bytes (hex) | Use |
|---|---|---|
| 00 | 2 | INT 20h instruction |
| 02 | 2 | Top of memory |
| 04 | 1 | Reserved |
| 05 | 1 | Op code (redundant: for CP/M compatibility) |
| 06 | 4 | Number of bytes in segment (CP/M) |
| 0A | 4 | Terminate address |
| 0E | 4 | Ctrl-Break address |
| 12 | 4 | Critical error address |
| 16 | 16 | Reserved |
| 2C | 2 | Environment segment |
| 2E | 22 | Reserved |
| 50 | 2 | DOS call |
| 52 | 0A | Reserved |
| 5C | 10 | File Control Block 1 |
| 6C | 14 | File Control Block 2 |
| 80 | 1 | Length of command line |
| 81 | 7F | Command line parameters |

N.B. All segment:offset addresses are stored in reverse order with the low byte of the offset first.

*Figure 2.18*

| | |
|---|---|
| *Interrupt:* | 21h |
| *Function:* | 51h (or 62h) |
| *DOS version:* | 2 |
| *Service:* | Get PSP segment address |
| *Entry values:* | AH=51h (or AH=62h) |
| *Exit values:* | BX=segment address of PSP |

A further function allows you to change the PSP address.

|  |  |
|---|---|
| *Interrupt:* | 21h |
| *Function:* | 50h |
| *DOS version:* | 2 |
| *Service:* | Set PSP address |
| *Entry values:* | AH=50h |
|  | BX=segment address of PSP |
| *Exit values:* | None |

**The command line parameters**

The PSP contains several important pieces of data, not least the command line parameters. These are additional items of text entered on the command line, following the program name; typically, the parameters consist of filenames or *switches* – additional instructions telling the program how the command is to be processed. The command line parameters are stored in the final 7Fh (127) bytes of the PSP.

The total length of the parameters is given at offset 80h. This length excludes the program name but includes any space before the parameters.

The routines in Figure 2.19 demonstrate how to extract the parameters. They assume that there is a space between each pair of parameters, although it is fairly easy to change the program to accept other characters as well (for example, '/', as DOS does). The routine can be included in any program that gives the user the option of supplying filenames or special instructions when the program is run.

```
PARSTEST:       ;Program to test parsing routines

      ;Prints parameters parsed from
      ;command line

      ;Calls PARSE, NEXTPARSE, DISLIN

      call parse
getp:
      call nextparm
      jc endparse
      lea dx,parameter
      call dislin
      jmp getp
endparse:
      int 20h
```

```
;---------------------------------------------

PARSE:      ;Parse the command line

      ;Finds the first item of text after
      ;the command and the length of the
      ;command line parameters
      ;NEXTPARM will return subsequent
      ;parameters

      ;Entry values: None
      ;Exit values:  PARAMST=offset address
      ;               of parameters
      ;              PARAMLEN=parameters
      ;               total length
      ;              BX,CX,DX changed

      jmp parsestart

paramst       db ?            ;Start of next
                              ;parameter (offset
                              ;from 82h)
paramlen      db ?            ;Length of remaining
                              ;parameters

parsestart:
      lea bx,80h              ;Point to start of
                              ;command line data
      mov cl,byte ptr [bx]    ;Move parameter
                              ;length into CX
      cmp cl,00h
      jz noparam              ;Jump if no
                              ;parameters
      dec cl                  ;Ignore leading space
noparam:
      mov [paramlen],cl       ;Store parameter
                              ;length
      mov byte ptr [paramst],00h  ;Store start
                              ;of parameter
                              ;(as offset from 82h)
      ret

;---------------------------------------------

NEXTPARM:      ;Get next parameter

      ;Routine does not allow for multiple
      ;spaces or for / characters
      ;Limited to 64-character parameters
      ;Parameter cannot include $
```

```
      ;Entry values: None
      ;Exit values:  PARAMETER= next parameter
      ;              CF=1 if no parameter
      ;              AX,BX,CX,SI,DI changed

      jmp npstart

parameter     db 64 dup ('&') ;Parameter to be
                              ;returned
ends          db '$'          ;$ to end for string
                              ;display function

npstart:
      xor cx,cx               ;Set CL to hold
                              ;length of remainder
      mov cl,[paramlen]       ;of parameters
      cmp cl,00h
      jnz getparam            ;Jump if there are
                              ;more parameters
      stc
      jmp nextend
getparam:
      mov al,' '              ;AL contains search
                              ;character (space)
      cld
      xor bx,bx               ;Point to start of
                              ;parameter
      mov bl,[paramst]
      add bl,82h
      lea di,bx
      repnz scasb             ;Search for space or
                              ;end of parameters
      jnz endline1            ;Jump if at end of
                              ;line
      dec di                  ;Otherwise, move DI
                              ;back to space at
                              ;end of parameter
endline1:
      sub di,82h              ;Calculate offset of
                              ;end of parameter
      xor ax,ax
      mov al,[paramst]
      sub di,ax               ;Calculate parameter
                              ;length
      mov cx,di
      push cx                 ;Save parameter
                              ;length
      lea di,parameter        ;Point to PARAMETER
      push cx
      mov cx,40h
      mov al,' '
```

```
      rep stosb                  ;Clear PARAMETER
      pop cx
      xor bx,bx                  ;Point to start of
                                 ;parameter for source
      mov bl,[paramst]
      add bl,82h
      lea si,bx
      lea di,parameter           ;Point to PARAMETER
                                 ;for destination
      rep movsb                  ;Copy parameter out
                                 ;of PSP
      mov al,[paramst]           ;Calculate start of
                                 ;next parameter
      pop cx                     ;Recover parameter
                                 ;length
      add al,cl
      inc al                     ;Ignore following
                                 ;space
      mov [paramst],al
      mov al,[paramlen]          ;Calculate length of
                                 ;remainder
      sub al,cl
      cmp al,00h
      jz endline2                ;Jump if at end of
                                 ;line
      dec al                     ;Ignore space
endline2:
      mov [paramlen],al
nextend:
      ret
```

*Figure 2.19*

**Duplicating the PSP**

Prior to DOS version 2, if you wanted to run another program from an existing program, you had to start by making a duplicate of the PSP in memory. This was achieved with interrupt 21h, function 26h.

| | |
|---|---|
| *Interrupt:* | 21h |
| *Function:* | 26h |
| *DOS version:* | 1 |
| *Service:* | Create PSP |
| *Entry values:* | AH=26h |
| | DX=segment address |
| *Exit values:* | None |

The only input required to this interrupt is the address at which the new PSP is to be created. An exact replica of the PSP is created at the new address.

Later versions of DOS make life considerably easier by using function 4Bh (described later).

## Ending a program

Once switched on, the computer never stops working. The internal programs have no end as such; they simply keep looping around waiting for something to happen.

Theoretically, it is possible to load a program without the aid of DOS and run it directly: if you do so, you will have no way of stopping the program, apart from rebooting, since such a program would have nowhere to go. It would also have to be totally self-contained.

However, assuming that you are running your programs under DOS – and you need a very good reason not to do so – then an instruction is needed that will halt the processing of an application program and return control to the operating system. There are two equivalent interrupts to end a program.

---

| | |
|---|---|
| *Interrupt:* | 20h |
| *DOS version:* | 1 |
| *Service:* | Terminate program |
| *Entry values:* | CS=PSP address |
| *Exit values:* | None |

---

| | |
|---|---|
| *Interrupt:* | 21h |
| *Function:* | 00h |
| *DOS version:* | 1 |
| *Service:* | Terminate program |
| *Entry values:* | AH=00h |
| | CS=PSP address |
| *Exit values:* | None |

---

Before invoking either of these interrupts, you must ensure that the code segment (CS) points to the start of the PSP (this check is necessary only if CS has been changed by the program). Once one of these interrupts has been executed, control returns to the operating system. These instructions are absolutely final: the program can never come back.

Note that neither of these interrupts closes any open files. It is the programmer's responsibility to ensure that everything has been tidied up before the program ends. For information on closing files, see Chapter 13.

## Address interrupts

Three of the DOS interrupts are not really interrupts in the conventional sense: rather, they are addresses of code where execution is to continue in certain circumstances.

- Interrupt 22h stores the address where execution will resume when the current program finishes.
- Interrupt 23h points to a routine that handles the Ctrl-Break key combination.
- Interrupt 24h handles critical errors, such as a drive not being ready.

When the program is initially run, these three addresses are copied to the three double-words at offset 0Ah to offset 15h of the PSP. If DOS is to operate normally when the program finishes, it is vital that the three address interrupts should be restored to their original values. Therefore, when a program completes its execution, DOS automatically copies the three addresses from the defaults stored in the PSP back to their original location.

This has great advantages, in that a program can replace any of these interrupts – for example to create your own Ctrl-Break routine or a customised critical-error handler – yet be secure in the knowledge that DOS will restore the defaults when the program has finished. You could change the defaults as well, of course, with the result that whatever routines you have installed would still be used by DOS afterwards, but this is not good practice. Any program should leave the computer as it finds it.

The exception to this rule is that you may change interrupt 22h when running another program (see below).

## Calling other programs

It is sometimes useful to be able to call one program from within another, or to load in an extra piece of code as an overlay. This is achieved with function 4Bh of interrupt 21h.

| | |
|---|---|
| *Interrupt:* | 21h |
| *Function:* | 4Bh |
| *DOS version:* | 2 |
| *Service:* | Load/execute program |
| *Entry values:* | AH=4Bh |
| | AL= 00h (Load and run) |
| | 01h (Load but do not run) |
| | 03h (Load overlay) |
| | 05h (Set execution state – DOS 5) |
| | DS:DX=address of ASCIIZ file specification |
| | ES:BX=address of control block |
| *Exit values:* | AX=return code |

Certain information must be made available before the interrupt is invoked so that the PSP for the new program can be created. This information is stored in a *control block*, the address of which is pointed to by ES:BX. The layout of the control block is shown in Figure 2.20. The contents of this control block can be created directly by copying the PSP.

The specification of the file to be executed or loaded must be stored as an ASCIIZ string, pointed to by DS:DX. Notice that if you want the original program to resume from its current position, once the sub-program has been completed, it is necessary to change interrupt 22h.

**Overlays control block (Function 4Bh; AL=03h)**

| Offset | Bytes | Use |
|---|---|---|
| 00 | 2 | Overlay address segment |
| 02 | 2 | Relocation factor |

**Execution control block (Function 4Bh; AL=00h)**

| Offset (hex) | Bytes | Use |
|---|---|---|
| 00 | 2 | Environment address segment |
| 02 | 4 | Command line address |
| 06 | 4 | First FCB address |
| 0A | 4 | Second FCB address |

NB: All segment:offset addresses are given in reverse order, with the offset low byte first.

*Figure 2.20*

**Allocating memory**

In some cases it is essential to allocate memory for a program. Memory is allocated in units of paragraphs (10h) with interrupt 21h, function 48h.

| | |
|---|---|
| *Interrupt:* | 21h |
| *Function:* | 48h |
| *DOS version:* | 2 |
| *Service:* | Allocate memory |
| *Entry values:* | AH=48h |
| | BX=memory (in paragraphs) |
| *Exit values:* | AX= seg address of allocated mem |
| | error code (if CF=1) |
| | BX=largest memory size |
| | (if allocation failed) |

The program returns with the segment address of the memory that has been allocated or, if the allocation failed, an error code and the largest amount of memory that could be allocated.

Similarly, you can modify the amount of memory allocated to the program with function 4Ah.

| | |
|---|---|
| *Interrupt:* | 21h |
| *Function:* | 4Ah |
| *DOS version:* | 2 |
| *Service:* | Modify allocated memory |
| *Entry values:* | AH=4Ah |
| | BX=memory (paragraphs) |
| | ES=segment of block |
| *Exit values:* | AX=error code (if CF=1) |
| | BX=largest memory size (if allocation failed) |

Finally, you can free memory that was previously allocated with function 49h.

| | |
|---|---|
| *Interrupt:* | 21h |
| *Function:* | 49h |
| *DOS version:* | 2 |
| *Service:* | Free memory |
| *Entry values:* | AH=49h |
| | ES=segment of block to return |
| *Exit values:* | AX=error code (if CF=1) |

All three of these functions work in a similar way.

You should free memory as soon as possible after it is no longer required, so that programs are not unnecessarily restricted in the future.

**Upper Memory Area**

If a program is to use the Upper Memory Area (UMA), then you need to decide on a strategy for allocating memory. This is achieved with the function 58h. The current strategy is returned with subfunction 00h and changed with function 01h. Before changing the allocation strategy, the current strategy must be saved and then restored before the program terminates.

| | |
|---|---|
| *Interrupt:* | 21h |
| *Function:* | 58,00h |
| *DOS version:* | 3 |
| *Service:* | Get allocation strategy |
| *Entry values:* | AH=58h |
| | AL=00h |
| *Exit values:* | AX=allocation strategy |

| | |
|---|---|
| *Interrupt:* | 21h |
| *Function:* | 58,01 |
| *DOS version:* | 3 |
| *Service:* | Set allocation strategy |
| *Entry values:* | AH=58h |
| | AL=01h |
| | BX=allocation strategy |
| *Exit values:* | CF= 0 (success) |
| | 1 (failure) |

The meaning of the allocation strategies is shown in Figure 2.21.

**Memory Allocation strategies**

| Strategy | Meaning |
|---|---|
| 0000h | Conventional memory, lowest address (default) |
| 0001h | Conventional memory, block closest to requested size |
| 0002h | Conventional memory, highest address |
| 0040h | UMA (only), lowest address |
| 0041h | UMA (only), block closest to requested size |
| 0042h | UMA (only), highest address |
| 0080h | UMA, lowest address; if none use conventional memory |
| 0081h | UMA, block closest to requested size; if none use conventional memory |
| 0082h | UMA, highest address; if none use conventional memory |

*Figure 2.21*

If the UMBs are to be used, then (under DOS 5) a link must be created. The link is tested with subfunction 02h of function 58h and set with subfunction 03h. The existing link must be saved, and restored when the program terminates.

---

| | |
|---|---|
| *Interrupt:* | 21h |
| *Function:* | 58,02h |
| *DOS version:* | 5 |
| *Service:* | Get upper memory link |
| *Entry values:* | AH=58h |
| | AL=02h |
| *Exit values:* | AL= 0 (not linked) |
| | 1 (linked) |

---

| | |
|---|---|
| *Interrupt:* | 21h |
| *Function:* | 58,03h |
| *DOS version:* | 5 |
| *Service:* | Set upper memory link |
| *Entry values:* | AH=58h |
| | AL=03h |
| | BH=00h |
| | BL= 0 (link) |
| | 1 (unlink) |
| *Exit values:* | CF= 0 (success) |
| | 1 (failure) |

---

**Terminating sub-programs**

Main programs are terminated with interrupt 20h or function 00h of interrupt 21h. To terminate a sub-program – and return to the main program rather than the DOS command line – use function 4Ch.

---

| | |
|---|---|
| *Interrupt:* | 21h |
| *Function:* | 4Ch |
| *DOS version:* | 2 |
| *Service:* | Terminate sub-program |
| *Entry values:* | AH=4Ch |
| *Exit values:* | AL=error code |

---

When the sub-program ends, a code is returned. This code can be extracted by the main program with function 4Dh.

---

| | |
|---|---|
| *Interrupt:* | 21h |
| *Function:* | 4Dh |
| *DOS version:* | 2 |
| *Service:* | Get return code of sub-program |
| *Entry values:* | AH=4Dh |
| *Exit values:* | AL=return code |

These codes are listed in Figure 2.21. When a sub-program ends by returning to the DOS command line, the code can be tested by ERRORLEVEL in a batch file.

**Sub-program return codes (Functions 4Ch and 4Dh)**

| Code | Meaning |
|---|---|
| 00 | Normal termination |
| 01 | Ended by Ctrl-Break |
| 02 | Critical error |
| 03 | Ended by interrupt 31h call (TSR) |

*Figure 2.22*

## Critical errors

Many errors can be dealt with quite easily from within the program but other major errors, called *critical errors*, have no easy solution and processing ceases. For example, if a program needs to write data away to a file but the disk is not ready, the program cannot continue until the fault has been dealt with. The fault occurs while an interrupt routine is being processed, at which stage the main program has no control.

Critical errors always relate to hardware of one sort or another: disk errors, memory faults, etc.

When such an error occurs, DOS invokes interrupt 24h, the critical error handler. The default address for the critical error handler is stored in the PSP and it is this address that DOS uses, rather than the original interrupt address. Therefore, even if you change the address of interrupt 24h, DOS will still use the original routine. This routine is the one that produces the familiar 'Ignore, Retry, Abort' message.

If no allowance is made for critical errors, the error message will appear in the middle of the program. As soon as the user responds with one of the required key presses, the program continues from where it left off. This has the advantage that you can write a small program without having to worry too much about critical errors; they are automatically taken care of. The disadvantage is that this can make a mess of the screen.

You can replace this interrupt with your own routine. Obviously such a routine can be useful only for recoverable errors – in particular, disk errors – as the other, more serious errors will just cause the system to crash, sometimes fatally.

**Critical error codes (AH)**

| Code (hex) | Error |
|---|---|
| 00 | System files read error |
| 01 | System files write error |
| 02 | FAT read error |
| 03 | FAT write error |
| 04 | Directory read error |
| 05 | Directory write error |
| 06 | Data read error |
| 07 | Data write error |
| 80-FF | Non-specific, non-disk error |

*Figure 2.23*

**Detailed error codes (DI low byte)**

| Code (hex) | Error |
|---|---|
| 00 | Disk is write-protected |
| 01 | Invalid drive |
| 02 | Disk drive not ready |
| 03 | Invalid command |
| 04 | CRC error |
| 05 | Request header invalid |
| 06 | Disk seek error |
| 07 | Bad media |
| 08 | Sector not found |
| 09 | Out of paper (printer) |
| 0A | Disk write error |
| 0B | Disk read error |
| 0C | General error |

*Figure 2.24*

There are many codes available to an error routine to describe what is going on. Register AH holds the general type of error, as shown in Figure 2.23. The low byte of DI holds further information (Figure 2.24) and the stack contains the values of all the registers as they stood when the error occurred.

Any error-handling program has to sift out the most important of this wealth of information to decide what to do. The routine must try to make the best of the situation without further use of the hardware. (If a disk error has occurred, it is no good trying to read an error-handling routine from disk!) However, you *can* get instructions from the user as to how to handle the error. Having done so you may exit the routine and allow DOS to take over. You must tell DOS how to handle the error by supplying a code in AL as follows:

**0** Ignore

**1** Retry

**2** Abort

## Multi-tasking

As a general rule, the 80x86 can only work on one task at a time. However, because of the speed of the CPU, it is possible for the computer to give the appearance of handling more than one thing at a time. This is done with a process called *multi-tasking* (or *multiplexing*).

The main program, referred to as the *foreground* program, takes most of the processing time (and should be the one that requires most user input). Meanwhile the other *background* programs are allocated smaller amounts of time and must be the type of program that can operate without requiring constant attention from the user. As far as the user is concerned, all the programs are running simultaneously.

The computer achieves this piece of magic by allocating small chunks of computer time, called *time slices*, to each program in turn. Each time slice consists of a number of clock ticks. Usually, the foreground program has the largest proportion of clock ticks. For example, the DOS print spooler, PRINT, is allocated two ticks in each slice as opposed to the eight for the current foreground program. Since the time slices are so brief, each program is accessed many times a second and, in theory at least, the user should not notice any difference in the operation of the foreground program.

Multi-tasking is appropriate when the foreground program does not require a great deal of processing time. For example, word processing makes an ideal foreground program, since the CPU is not doing anything for the majority of the time. In the time taken to press a key, the background program may have been called several times. On the other hand, the background program must require little or no input from the user; for example, a print spooler is a suitable application since, once under way, it can get on with its work whenever there is time available.

However, there are occasions when multi-tasking can slow down the operation of the foreground quite considerably, notably when any disk access is required. Since all processing must stop while the disk is being accessed, this can cause problems. It is all right if it is the foreground program that is accessing the disk, since the user expects to have to wait, but if the background program requires a great deal of disk access this can slow up progress considerably (especially on the 8086/8088).

The user must also take care if the background program accesses the printer to make sure that the printer is always ready. Otherwise, everything comes to a halt while the background program waits for the printer to timeout before it allows control to return to the foreground.

**Multiplex numbers**

DOS requires that each background program be given a unique *multiplex number*. This an identification number that is essential to locate the program once installed in memory.

DOS reserves the multiplex numbers 00h to BFh (and a few higher ones) for itself. Those that have been used are listed in Figure 2.25. You are free to use multiplex numbers 80h to FFh but it is safest to start at C0h.

**Multiplex numbers**

| Number | Use |
|---|---|
| 01h | PRINT.EXE |
| 06h | ASSIGN.COM |
| 10h | SHARE.EXE |
| 11h | Network redirection |
| 14h | NLSFUNC.EXE |
| 1Ah | ANSI.SYS |
| 43h | HIMEM.SYS |
| 48h | DOSKEY.COM |
| 4Bh | Task switching |
| ADh | KEYB.COM |
| AEh | APPEND.EXE |
| B0h | GRAFTABL.COM |
| B7h | APPEND.EXE |

*Figure 2.25*

**Installation**

A multi-tasking program is installed by loading a *handler* into memory. This is a piece of code that determines the actions to be taken whenever the program is called. Each handler begins with a section of header information that gives the multiplex number and also points to the next handler in the chain. The procedure is identical to that of device drivers (see Chapter 14).

**Access**

You can request action from a background program with interrupt 2Fh.

| | |
|---|---|
| *Interrupt:* | 2Fh |
| *DOS version:* | 3 |
| *Service:* | Access background program |
| *Entry values:* | AH=multiplex number |
| | AL=function code |
| *Exit values:* | Various (depending on program) |

This interrupt became available with DOS 3. It checks each handler in the chain in turn for the required multiplex number. When found, the function number that is passed across in the interrupt is used to tell the handler what action to take. The handler executes the relevant routine in the background program. It is up to the background program to devise the actions that are necessary and to deal with invalid function numbers.

Any function can be used for any purpose, with the exception of 00h, which is reserved. This function is used to get information about the background program; there are three possible responses, as illustrated in Figure 2.26.

Although multi-tasking is an appealing idea, the problems of speed have generally meant that it has not really been applied to any great extent.

**Multiplex return codes**

| Code | Meaning |
|---|---|
| 00 | Handler not yet installed but it is all right to do so |
| 01 | Handler not installed; you may not install the handler |
| 02 | Handler installed |

*Figure 2.26*

## Terminate and Stay Resident programs (TSRs)

Creating a multi-tasking program is complex and rarely worth the effort. Most of the time you want to temporarily suspend one program in order to do something else, rather than have the first program carrying on its work. This can be done with a Terminate and Stay Resident (TSR) program. The program is loaded into memory in much the same way as a background program, and there it stays until it is invoked by the user. When invoked, the main program ceases and control passes to the TSR; when the TSR has finished its work, control is passed back to the main program again. There are many TSRs commercially available, examples including Borland's Sidekick and a variety of programs to produce screen dumps.

Usually, TSRs are accessed via special key presses (although this is not essential). Again, the program is in two parts. One part is used to load the TSR into memory and invoke it for the first time; the other part is executed on future occasions.

The general procedure for operating a TSR is as follows:

**1** The TSR is initially executed from the DOS command line.

**2** The program is in two parts: a resident section and an initialisation section. The initialisation section marks out the part of memory that is to be safeguarded while the main application is running. This part of memory includes the resident section but does not usually include the initialisation portion, since this can be overwritten once its work is complete.

**3** The program modifies the selected interrupt so that it can be invoked later. Usually this is the keyboard interrupt but other interrupts are a possibility. (More information on interrupts is given in Chapter 4.)

**4** The TSR terminates with interrupt 21h, function 31h, rather than the normal interrupt 20h. You must specify the amount of memory that is to be reserved for the TSR, so that it is not overwritten by any application program. The memory must be specified in terms of paragraphs. This memory must include the TSR's PSP (10h paragraphs) but may exclude the initialisation portion if the program is designed in such a way that this comes at the end of the code. DOS now keeps this area free from any further updates.

**5** The user can now run an application program. To reactivate the resident portion of the TSR, the user presses the special combination of keys (or uses any other method that has been chosen).

**6** The main section of the TSR is executed. Obviously some way is needed of getting out of the

TSR, such as the **Esc** key. The TSR must end by restoring everything to its original state. This ensures the same TSR can be invoked many times in one session.

**7** The TSR remains resident in memory until the system is rebooted, unless the user runs a program that will free memory or such a routine is included in your TSR.

---

*Interrupt:* 21h
*Function:* 31h
*Service:* Terminate and stay resident
*Entry values:* AH=31h
AL=termination code
DX=no. paragraphs to keep
*Exit values:* AX=error code

---

When replacing any interrupt, always end the new interrupt by calling the original one: this ensures that more than one TSR can use the same interrupt, as long as they do not use the same trigger.

# 3 DOS

This chapter describes the DOS operating system that is used by almost all members of the IBM PC family. An operating system is a set of programs that allows you to store data on disk, load and run programs, and generally make life easier when trying to control the computer. The files that make up the DOS operating system are described here, along with the procedures that are followed when the computer is first switched on.

Theoretically, it is possible to ignore DOS and work directly with the hardware. Then, however, you are not able to manipulate files on disk and data-handling operations become extremely difficult. Although this is acceptable for some applications (particularly those that require little data-handling), it is usual to accept the limitations that DOS provides so as to take full advantage of the numerous features that it offers.

Other operating systems are available, of course, but most these are not widely used on the PC. The main rival to DOS in the past, CP/M, is rarely used these days while its younger cousin, OS/2 has yet to make any major impact outside the PS/2 range of computers. Since this book is intended mainly for PC users and programmers, no description of the inner workings of other operating systems is given. Since the PS/2 range are based on the same family of microprocessors as the PCs, the hardware operates in the same way.

## Versions of DOS

DOS made its first appearanace in 1981, along with the first IBM PC. Developed by Microsoft, the version for the IBMs is known as PC-DOS. When IBM-compatibles began to arrive, they were bundled with an almost identical operating system, MS-DOS. The difficulty is that, although many clones claim to be 100% IBM-compatible, inevitably there are differences in the hardware. As a result, there must be differences in the operating system. Microsoft licences these *original equipment manufacturers* (OEMs) to adapt MS-DOS to fit their systems. The OEMs will usually rename the operating system (such as Compaq DOS or Z-DOS) but functionally it remains the same as the original MS-DOS; to the user and the programmer there *should* be no difference in operation, though peculiarities will crop up from time to time.

It is interesting to note that Microsoft has never sold MS-DOS as a standalone product; it is always supplied as a customised, integral part of a machine. However, with DOS 5 and DOS 6 Microsoft has started selling upgrade packs; these will allow a user to upgrade any existing DOS version (from DOS 2.11 onwards). These are not bootable systems so cannot be installed directly onto a machine with no operating system.

DOS 1 contained the core of modern MS-DOS; although a number of its functions have now been superseded, the vast majority are still supported. A DOS 1 program should still run under DOS 6. The main restriction in DOS 1 was that only single-sided 5¼" floppies were allowed, with only 64 files per disk.

The limitations on directory size that were a feature of DOS 1 were overcome by the introduction of DOS 2 in 1983. This version allowed the use of subdirectories and introduced a number of other programming facilities.

DOS 3 arrived the following year, allowing for large capacity floppy and hard disks. Version 3.1 provided support for networks while 3.2, introduced in 1986, permitted 3½" disks. With the arrival of the PS/2 range in 1987, Microsoft released version 3.3 (along with OS/2).

1988 saw the emergence of DOS 4, a re-organised version of the operating system with a standard user 'front-end'. This version was not a success, and a whole series of version 4.01 bug fixes were released in rapid succession. Most people returned to DOS 3.3 or never upgraded.

Despite the shortcoming of DOS 4, it was not until 1991 that the next version, DOS 5 arrived. This version freed more 'conventional' memory (the first 64K) by relocating DOS itself in the High Memory Area on 286 machines and above; for 386 or higher, many TSRs, device drivers and network drivers are loaded into the Upper Memory Blocks, freeing still more space. DOS 5 also came with an improved front-end shell, a Task Swapper to switch between programs, and additional utilities, including Undelete and Unformat.

DOS 6, introduced in 1993, concentrated on adding further utilities, rather than an overhaul of the operating system itself. The new features include a new Backup tool, file defragmentation and anti-virus software, as well as improvements to the memory management software, Undelete program and SmartDrive. The system also includes automatic disk compression with a program called DoubleSpace (which uses a new interrupt).

This history is summarised in Figure 3.1.

**DOS versions**

| Vers. | Year | Modifications |
|---|---|---|
| 1.0 | 1981 | Original version for IBM PC |
| 1.1 | 1981 | Minor bugs fixed |
| 1.25 | 1982 | Double-sided disks allowed |
| 2.0 | 1983 | Introduction of sub-directories |
| | | First appearance of file handles |
| 2.01 | 1983 | International symbols introduced |
| 2.10 | 1983 | Minor bugs fixed |
| 2.11 | 1983 | Minor bugs fixed |
| 2.25 | 1983 | Extended ASCII character set |
| 3.0 | 1984 | High capacity floppy and hard disks |
| 3.1 | 1984 | Networking capabilities |
| 3.2 | 1986 | 3½" disks allowed |
| 3.3 | 1987 | Support for PS/2 |
| 4.0 | 1988 | Enhanced user interface |
| | | Hard disks > 32M |
| 4.01 | 1988 | Minor bugs fixed |
| 5.00 | 1991 | Enhanced functions and memory-handling |
| 6.00 | 1993 | Disk compression and other utilities |

*Figure 3.1*

**Version number**

The DOS version number is shown on the screen when the computer is booted. The user can also check the version at any time with the VER command. However, application programs cannot 'see' the screen in this way so they use a DOS interrupt to check the version number.

---

| | |
|---|---|
| *Interrupt:* | 21h |
| *Function:* | 30h |
| *DOS version:* | 2 |
| *Service:* | Check DOS version number |
| *Entry values:* | AH=30h |
| *Exit values:* | AH=minor version number<br>AL=major version number<br>BX,CX changed |

---

This interrupt returns the main version number in the AL register, with the decimal part in AH. The minor number always consists of two digits and is returned as a binary value. For example, if AL = 03h and AH = 14h, this represents DOS version 3.20.

DOS 5 provides a new function, which return additional information.

---

| | |
|---|---|
| *Interrupt:* | 21h |
| *Function:* | 33,06h |
| *DOS version:* | 5 |
| *Service:* | Get DOS version details |
| *Entry values:* | AH=33h<br>AL=06h |
| *Exit values:* | BH=minor version number<br>BL=major version number<br>DH= 00h (DOS is in conventional memory)<br>08h (DOS is in ROM)<br>10h (DOS is in HMA)<br>DL=revision number (bits 0-2) |

---

**Compatibility**

Many computer manufacturers produce their own versions of DOS. Although these different versions of DOS may appear the same to the casual user, moving DOS from one machine to another is not recommended (and not usually necessary, of course). The main point about DOS is that it deals with all the tricky hardware operations. Therefore, for a different set of hardware, different DOS routines are needed. Even though two PCs may be said to be compatible, there will usually be some differences in their internal make-up which will require slightly different DOS routines.

However, all equivalent versions of DOS should present the same front end to the user and programmer. Therefore, if you put the same input into two different incarnations of DOS each will send its own individual set of instructions to the hardware in order to achieve the same effect. So, even though the operations carried out in the middle may be different, if you put the same information in you should get the same results out.

This contrasts with what will happen if you try to give the same instructions to the hardware directly. Most of the time everything will be fine but there will be some occasions when the same instructions will produce different results.

This is particularly true of those operations that involve the battery-backed RAM, the mouse and other non-standard devices, whose effects vary from one hardware configuration to another.

Some direct hardware access is acceptable – notably some forms of screen handling and sound production, which are described later – but, wherever possible, you should use DOS rather than direct access to the hardware.

Working through DOS has some disadvantages, of course:

- In some cases, the operations are carried out much more slowly.
- If you write a program to work with a particular version of DOS you are then stuck with that operating system.

**Minimum version numbers**

Perhaps the most important decision to be made is the minimum DOS version number that will be required for a program.

Each version of DOS introduces a new set of capabilities, generally via the DOS interrupts. If you use a particular feature, then the version in which this was introduced is the minimum version that is required for the operation to be carried out successfully. Therefore the highest version number of all the features used in the program becomes the minimum requirement for the operating system under which the program will run. For example, if you use interrupt 21h, function 41h to delete a file, the minimum requirement is DOS 2.0. However, interrupt 21h, function 13h existed in DOS 1.0 and performed a similar function. If you use function 13h that part of the program will work on any version of DOS.

All DOS versions are *upwardly compatible*. That is, a routine that works under one version of DOS should also work under all later versions.

Some of the points to consider when choosing a minimum version are:

- The later the DOS version you work with, the more limited will be the program's portability.
- To run on all versions of DOS, use only DOS 1 commands. Such a program may be highly portable but it will also be extremely limited and hard work to program.
- Almost all PCs now have at least DOS 2.0 and this version of the operating system provides most of the facilities you are likely to need. This may be a good option unless your requirements are particularly advanced (for example, networking).
- DOS 3.2 is necessary if you want to provide programs that can be networked. A decision to restrict the program to DOS 3.2 and higher versions is not unreasonable; virtually all computers currently being marketed have DOS 3.2 or later.
- Features such as code pages can only be used if you insist on a minimum of DOS 3.3. This could severely restrict the use of a program and should be avoided.

- A minimum of DOS 4.0 is unlikely to be acceptable for programs that are going to be made widely available, though it may be suitable

```
DOSVER:       ;Check DOS version number

      ;Entry values: DX=Minimum DOS version
      ;               number
      ;Exit values:  AX=DOS version no.
      ;              BX=(0 Version OK
      ;                 (1 Version not OK
      ;AX,BX,CX,DX changed

      jmp verst

vermess       db 'Program requires minimum DOS'
              db 'version 3.2$'

verst:

      mov dl,03h                ;Set minimum major
                                ;version no.
      mov dh,14h                ;Set minimum minor
                                ;version no.
                                ;03h,14h =3.20

                                ;(Error message
                                ;VERMESS may need to
                                ;change)
      mov ah,30h
      int 21h
      cmp dl,al
      jl ok                     ;Return if major
                                ;version OK
      jg notok                  ;Display error
                                ;message if not OK
      cmp dh,ah                 ;Otherwise, check
                                ;minor versions
      jle ok                    ;Jump if minor
                                ;version OK

notok:
      lea dx,vermess
      call disstr               ;Display text

ok:
      ret
```

*Figure 3.2*

for individual programs aimed at specific computer set-ups.

The program in Figure 3.2 checks the version number and displays an error message if necessary.

**Changing DOS versions**

Sometimes you may want to switch from one version of an operating system to another, particularly on a hard disk. Although it is possible to switch versions by simply replacing the DOS system files (as well as COMMAND.COM and the utility programs) by the new versions, this is not recommended. For versions of DOS prior to 3.3 the system files must be on the first available sectors of the disk and must be in consecutive blocks. Since the system files tend to grow from one version to another, this means that you have to ensure that there is sufficient blank space at the beginning of the disk to take the complete files. In addition, some application programs access the DOS files directly and assume that they are of a particular size, so changing the version for one with files of a different size may cause problems. If you are going to change DOS versions, it is usually far safer to copy everything off the hard disk, reformat the disk with a new version and then re-install all your programs and data. This takes longer but success is more likely.

Care also needs to be taken with equivalent versions of DOS from different manufacturers (as opposed to different versions of DOS from the same manufacturer). The version numbers may be the same but, because each DOS is written for its own computer, there may be particular hardware problems.

Some of these problems are now being alleviated with the arrival of DOS 5 and DOS 6, which allow a user to update any prior version of DOS to an official Microsoft version.

## The DOS boot record

The first sector on every disk – both hard and floppy – contains a *boot record*. This will exist on the disk regardless of whether or not it is a *system disk* and

**The boot record (DOS 1, 2, 3)**

| Offset (hex) | No. Bytes | Use |
|---|---|---|
| 00 | 3 | Jump instruction (long jump or short jump plus NOP) |
| 03 | 8 | Manufacturer name and DOS version and number |
| 0B | 2 | Number of bytes per sector |
| 0D | 1 | Number of sectors per cluster |
| 0E | 2 | Number of reserved sectors |
| 10 | 1 | Number of FATs |
| 11 | 2 | Number of root directory entries |
| 13 | 2 | Number of sectors on volume |
| 15 | 1 | Media type code (see Figure 12.9) |
| 16 | 2 | Number of sectors per FAT |
| 18 | 2 | Number of sectors per track |
| 1A | 2 | Number of heads |
| 1C | 2 | Number of hidden sectors |
| 1E | - | Boot routine |

Note: Bytes 0Bh - 1Dh are the BIOS parameter block (BPB) – see Figure 14.6

**The boot record (DOS 4, 5, 6)**

| Offset (hex) | No. Bytes | Use |
|---|---|---|
| 00 | 1Ch | As for DOS 1, 2, 3 |
| 1C | 4 | Number of hidden sectors |
| 20 | 4 | Number of sectors (if value at 13h = 0) |
| 24 | 1 | Drive number |
| 25 | 1 | Not used |
| 26 | 1 | ID byte = 29h |
| 27 | 4 | Serial number of volume |
| 2B | 0Bh | Volume label |
| 36 | 8 | Type of FAT as ASCII string: 'FAT12' or 'FAT16', followed by two spaces |
| 3E | - | Boot routine |

Note: Bytes 0Bh-23h are the BIOS parameter block (BPB) – see Figure 14.6

*Figure 3.3*

regardless of the operating system. When you start up the computer, the ROM BIOS routines complete their initial tasks and then try to execute this piece of code on the floppy disk – if one has been loaded – or the hard disk.

If the disk is a system disk, the code in the boot record loads the operating system into memory and starts it running. On a non-system disk, the boot record merely contains a table of disk data.

In the case of DOS the boot record takes the form of a jump (JMP) instruction to skip to the main *boot code*. The part of the record that is skipped contains a table of disk information. The boot code itself loads the first DOS file into memory and executes it. The layout of the DOS boot record is shown in Figure 3.3.

DOS 4 onwards stores additional information in the boot record.

The boot *sector* ends in two bytes with the value AA55h.

## The DOS BIOS

The first real file on a system disk forms the DOS Basic Input/Output System (BIOS). This file contains all the routines that are needed to communicate with the standard hardware devices (keyboard, screen and disk drives).

All requests for a hardware operation, unless sent directly to the ROM BIOS, are channelled through the code in the DOS BIOS.

The DOS BIOS contains a series of *device drivers*, one for each of the standard hardware devices. A device driver simply provides sets of instructions to cope with every operation that the hardware might be required to perform. In fact, most devices only perform a very few operations; their more sophisticated operations are built from these few simple building blocks.

Any non-standard devices – the mouse, for example – require their own individual routines to be separately loaded in the form of device drivers (see Chapter 14).

The DOS BIOS includes modifications to the ROM BIOS interrupt routines.

The DOS BIOS exists on disk in a file called either IBMBIO.COM (PC-DOS) or IO.SYS (MS-DOS). In versions prior to DOS 3.3, the file must be stored immediately after the boot record.

The actual contents of this file depend upon the hardware of the PC for which it is intended. Therefore, the precise code varies from one implementation to another. The instructions it can cope with are the same for all equivalent DOS versions. As described above, this is a very good reason why you should work through DOS. If you talk to the hardware directly, you may need to change the code for different computers; via DOS, the same program should work across the entire PC family.

## The kernel

The second DOS system file is often referred to as the *kernel*. This part is independent of the hardware. It receives all the requests for hardware operations from the application programs and channels them to the BIOS in the correct format. In its spare time, it performs additional activities, such as loading and executing the command interpreter. This file contains all the DOS interrupts.

Physically, the kernel exists as a file called either IBMDOS.COM (PC-DOS) or MSDOS.SYS (MS-DOS). It is stored on disk immediately after the BIOS. Note that both the BIOS and kernel are hidden files and that, for versions of DOS prior to 3.3, they must exist in consecutive sectors on disk. DOS 3.3 has relaxed the rules a little, allowing these files to move around if necessary.

## The command interpreter

The command interpreter, COMMAND.COM, is the 'visible' portion of DOS. It provides the interface between the user and the operating system. Its task is to receive commands and process them, display error and information messages, and generally cater for the user's needs.

This file is not hidden and, although it usually resides in the root directory of the system disk, it does not need to be there. The physical position of COMMAND.COM on disk is irrelevant; you can change the directory it is in with the PATH statement or the COMSPEC directive. The name of the file can even be changed, as long as you use SHELL to identify it. You can change the default name by editing the kernel, where it is hard-coded; however, you need a very good reason to do this. If you are really keen, you can even replace COMMAND.COM with your own command interpreter.

COMMAND.COM has three separate portions.

**The resident section**

The resident part of COMMAND.COM is loaded into low memory immediately after the BIOS and kernel. There it stays until you reboot. If an application overwrites this portion, the system will crash when the program finishes.

This section handles the input/output errors and is responsible for displaying the familiar 'Not ready' error message. It also handles the address interrupts: 22h, 23h and 24h.

When the resident section is executed for the first time, its first task is to load the transient portion.

**The transient section**

The transient portion of COMMAND.COM is loaded into the top of memory. This part of the program displays the prompt and processes user commands. It contains all the code for the internal commands (DIR, COPY, etc.)

It is called the *transient* section because it can be overwritten if necessary. It sits at the top of memory, so any large program will overwrite it; in this case, when the application finishes, the resident section checks to see if the transient portion is there; if not, it tries to reload it from the system disk. If it can't find it (when the system disk is a floppy and is no longer there), the 'Insert disk with COMMAND.COM' message is displayed.

If you 'shell out' of a program, a second copy of the transient section is temporarily loaded into memory. This allows you to execute standard DOS commands from within an application.

**The initialisation section**
The third part of COMMAND.COM, the *initialisation portion*, is loaded immediately above the resident section. This part of the program is only needed when the computer is first booted. Its task is to check for the existence of the AUTOEXEC.BAT file and, if it's there, to process it. If that file does not exist, the initialisation section prompts for the date and time.

Having completed these tasks, the initialisation portion becomes redundant. DOS updates its pointers so that the space that it occupied is freed and the first application that is run overwrites it.

## The environment

The way in which the computer operates is determined by the *environment*. This is a series of instructions, stored in the CONFIG.SYS file, which tell DOS how to set up the system. The contents of CONFIG.SYS are read into memory before AUTOEXEC.BAT is executed. Each item consists of an expression in the form:

*variable* = *value*

Environment expressions are used for a variety of purposes, such as telling the system which devices to install, setting the default path and giving the location of COMMAND.COM.

In some cases the order of items in the environment is important. For example, DOS will not search for the device drivers anywhere on disk apart from in the root directory, unless the PATH expression has been dealt with first.

There does not have to be a CONFIG.SYS file on the system disk but, if there is not, DOS assumes certain defaults. The main environment variables

**The environment variables**

| Directive | Default | Use |
|---|---|---|
| COUNTRY | 1 | Country information |
| COMSPEC | COMMAND.COM | Command processor |
| DEVICE | (Standard device) | Installs device drivers |
| BREAK | OFF | Frequency of checks for Break key |
| BUFFERS | 2 | Number of sectors for each disk buffer |
| DRIVPARM | (None) | Drive characteristics |
| FCBS | 4,0 | Maximum number of file control blocks |
| FILES | 8 | Maximum number of file handles |
| LASTDRIVE | E | Last drive accessible to DOS |
| SHELL | COMMAND.COM | Command processor |

*Figure 3.4*

are shown in Figure 3.4, along with the defaults that are adopted, where applicable.

**Modifying the environment**
The DOS SET command allows the user to set new variables, modify existing expressions or delete them altogether. The environment is stored in memory as a series of ASCII strings, almost identical to the original on disk. Each expression is separated from the next by a single null character (00h), the last variable concluding with two null characters. Following on from this – for DOS 3 onwards – there is a two-byte word that stores a count of the number of words needed to store the environment and then the file specification of the program to which the environment relates.

## Country-dependent information

Computers are supplied with different keyboards for different countries. Although the basic layout of the keys stays the same, their operation varies from one country to another. For example, Shift-3 on the UK keyboard produces the £ sign but for a US keyboard the result is a #.

DOS always assumes that you are working with a US keyboard unless told otherwise. That is, Shift-3 will give a # symbol regardless. DOS also assumes the American format (Month-Day-Year) for the date.

With DOS 1, no variation was allowed.

DOS 2 introduced programs such as KEYBUK.COM, which configures the keyboard for UK use and deals with certain other country-dependent information. KEYBUK can be run at any time. One of the aims of KEYBUK, and the other country programs, is to get or set the country information. It does this by calling DOS interrupt 21h, function 38h.

---

*Interrupt:* 21h
*Function:* 38h (DOS 2 version)
*DOS version:* 2
*Service:* Get or set country-dependent information
*Entry values:* AH=38h
AL=country code (0-2)
DS:DX=address of 32 byte buffer
*Exit values:* AX=error code (if CF=1)
BX=country code
DS:DX=address of information

---

This interrupt returns the country information in a 32-byte buffer, the layout of which is shown in

**DOS 2 country information buffer**

| Offset (hex) | Bytes (hex) | Use |
|---|---|---|
| 00 | 02 | Date and time format (see Fig. 3.6) |
| 02 | 02 | Currency symbol |
| 04 | 02 | Thousands separator |
| 06 | 02 | Decimal separator |
| 08 | 18 | Not used |

*Figure 3.5*

**DOS 2 country-dependent information**

| Country code | Area | Date format | Time format |
|---|---|---|---|
| 0 | America | mm-dd-yy | hh:mm:ss |
| 1 | Europe | dd-mm-yy | hh:mm:ss |
| 2 | Japan | yy-mm-dd | hh:mm:ss |

*Figure 3.6*

Figure 3.5. Under DOS 2, there are only three country codes (as shown in Figure 3.6) which are also set by KEYBUK and similar programs.

**DOS 3 country information**

DOS 3 extended – and therefore confused – the system. There are more KEYBxx programs but these affect the keyboard only.

In addition, DOS 3 introduced a new COUNTRY environment variable which sets the country-dependent information: the date and time, currency symbol, numeric separators and so on. Each country is identified by a three-digit code (see Figure 3.7). At the same time, function 38h was modified, changing the way the registers pass data.

*Interrupt:* 21h
*Function:* 38h (DOS 3 version)
*DOS version:* 3
*Service:* Get or set country-dependent information
*Entry values:* AH=38h
AL= 00h (current country)
01h - FEh (country code)
FFh (code>=255)
BX=country code (if AL=FFh)
DS:DX=address of 32 byte buffer
*Exit values:* AX=error code (if CF=1)
BX=country code
DS:DX=address of information

Register AL holds the country numbers but there are two special cases; AL=0 refers to the current

**DOS 3 keyboard programs**

| Country | Code | KEYBxx |
|---|---|---|
| Australia | 061 | |
| Belgium | 032 | |
| Brazil | 055 | |
| Canada/English | 001 | |
| Canada/French | 002 | |
| Czechoslovakia | 042 | |
| Denmark | 045 | KEYBDA |
| Finland | 358 | |
| France | 033 | KEYBFR |
| Germany | 049 | KEYBGR |
| Holland | 031 | |
| Hungary | 036 | |
| International (English) | 061 | |
| Israel | 972 | |
| Italy | 039 | KEYBIT |
| Latin America | 003 | |
| Middle East | 785 | |
| Norway | 047 | KEYBNO |
| Poland | 048 | |
| Portugal | 351 | |
| Spain | 034 | KEYBSP |
| Sweden | 046 | KEYBSW |
| Switzerland/French | 041 | KEYBCHF |
| Switzerland/German | 041 | KEYBCHG |
| United Kingdom | 044 | KEYBUK |
| USA | 001 | |
| Yugoslavia | 038 | |

*Figure 3.7*

country and, for country codes greater than 255, AL must be set to FFh, with the country code put in BX. Many more countries are supported, each with its own country data (Figure 3.8).

Incidentally, the country code is the same as the international dialling code.

Usually, the user will match the KEYBxx program with the corresponding country but this is no longer essential.

The data buffer is also used very differently (Figure 3.9). Therefore, programs need to allow for these

**DOS 3 country-dependent information**

| Country Code | Country | Date Format | Hour Format | Currency symbol |
|---|---|---|---|---|
| 001 | United States | mm-dd-yy | 1 - 12 | $ |
| 031 | Netherlands | dd-mm-yy | 0 - 23 | |
| 032 | Belgium | dd-mm-yy | 0 - 23 | F |
| 033 | France | dd-mm-yy | 0 - 23 | F |
| 034 | Spain | dd-mm-yy | 0 - 23 | Pt |
| 039 | Italy | dd-mm-yy | 0 - 23 | Lit. |
| 041 | Switzerland | dd-mm-yy | 0 - 23 | Fr |
| 044 | United Kingdom | dd-mm-yy | 0 - 23 | £ |
| 045 | Denmark | dd-mm-yy | 0 - 23 | DKR |
| 046 | Sweden | yy-mm-dd | 0 - 23 | SEK |
| 047 | Norway | dd-mm-yy | 0 - 23 | KR |
| 049 | Germany | dd-mm-yy | 0 - 23 | DM |
| 061 | Australia | dd-mm-yy | 0 - 23 | $ |
| 358 | Finland | dd-mm-yy | 0 - 23 | MK |
| 972 | Israel | dd-mm-yy | 0 - 23 | |

*Figure 3.8*

**DOS 3 country information buffer**

| Offset (hex) | Bytes (hex) | Use |
|---|---|---|
| 00 | 02 | Date format 0=M,D,Y<br>1=D,M,Y<br>2=Y,M,D |
| 02 | 05 | Currency symbol |
| 07 | 02 | Thousands separator |
| 09 | 02 | Decimal separator |
| 0B | 02 | Date separator |
| 0D | 02 | Time separator |
| 0F | 01 | Currency format<br>Bit 0: 0=Before, 1=After<br>Bits 1 and 2: No. of spaces between symbol and value |
| 10 | 01 | Decimal places for currency |
| 11 | 01 | Time format 0=12-hour<br>1=24-hour |
| 12 | 04 | Address of routine for defining upper and lower case usage |
| 16 | 02 | Data list separator |
| 18 | 08 | Not used |

*Figure 3.9*

variations by checking the version number first (see Figure 3.2). Note that the values in Figure 3.9 from 02h (currency symbol) to 0Eh (time separator) are all stored as ASCIIZ strings, as is the list separator (16h-17h).

**DOS 3.3 country information**

With the arrival of DOS 3.3, the KEYBxx programs were replaced by a single KEYB program which requires a range of parameters. This is accompanied by an even more complex COUNTRY variable.

DOS 3.3 also provides further country information through function 65h, which gives pointers to the addresses of various translation tables.

---

| | |
|---|---|
| *Interrupt:* | 21h |
| *Function:* | 65h |
| *DOS version:* | 3.3 |
| *Service:* | Extended country information |
| *Entry values:* | AH=65h |
| | AL= 01h (Get country information) |
| | 02h (Get character trans table) |
| | 04h (Get filename trans table) |
| | 05h (Get filename char table – DOS 5) |
| | 06h (Get collating sequence table) |
| | 07h (Get double-byte char table) (DOS4) |
| | 20h (Convert character – DOS 5) |
| | 21h (Convert string – DOS 5) |
| | 22h (Convert ASCIIZ – DOS 5) |
| | BX=code page (-1 for active code page) |
| | CX=buffer size (29h if AL=01h, otherwise 05h) |
| | DX=country code (-1 for default) |
| | ES:DI points to buffer |
| *Exit values:* | AX=error code (if CF=1) |
| | ES:DI points to data buffer |

---

For AL=01h, the information returned in the buffer is shown in Figure 3.10.

For the other subfunctions, the first byte in the buffer is the subfunction number, the next four bytes are the address. The filename character table

**DOS 3.3 country information buffer**

| Offset (hex) | Bytes (hex) | Use |
|---|---|---|
| 00 | 01 | ID byte (=01h) |
| 01 | 02 | Data buffer size - 3 |
| 03 | 02 | Country code |
| 05 | 02 | Code page |
| 07 | 02 | Date format |
| 09 | 05 | Currency symbol |
| 0E | 02 | Thousands separator |
| 10 | 02 | Decimal separator |
| 12 | 02 | Date separator |
| 14 | 02 | Time separator |
| 16 | 01 | Currency format |
| 17 | 01 | Decimal places for currency |
| 18 | 01 | Time format |
| 19 | 04 | Address of routine for defining upper and lower case usage |
| 1D | 02 | Data list separator |
| 1F | 0A | Not used |

Note: The values from 09h (currency symbol) to 15h (time separator) are all stored as ASCIIZ strings, as is the list separator (1Dh-1Eh).

*Figure 3.10*

lists the characters that may be used in filenames; the collating sequence table determines the order of characters when sorted. The three DOS 5 conversion functions translate strings to upper case.

**Code pages**

The translation table that converts numerical codes to the full ASCII character set is referred to as a *code page*. Prior to DOS 3.3, each version of DOS was supplied with a specific code page. The available pages were numbered 437, 860, 863 and 865, and were selected according to the country to which the computer was destined.

DOS 3.3 introduced a new code page, 850, which is intended to be a universal standard that should be used by all new applications. To allow for varia-

**DOS 3.3 KEYB codes and code pages**

| Country | Code | KEYB | Code pages |
|---|---|---|---|
| Australia | 061 | US | 437,850 |
| Belgium | 032 | BE | 437,850 |
| Canada/English | 001 | US | 437,850 |
| Canada/French | 002 | CF | 850,863 |
| Denmark | 045 | DK | 850,865 |
| Finland | 358 | SU | 437,850 |
| France | 033 | FR | 437,850 |
| Germany | 049 | GR | 437,850 |
| Holland | 031 | NL | 437,850 |
| Israel | 972 | | 437,850 |
| Italy | 039 | IT | 437,850 |
| Latin America | 003 | LA | 437,850 |
| Middle East | 785 | | 437,850 |
| Norway | 047 | NO | 850,865 |
| Portugal | 351 | PO | 850,860 |
| Spain | 034 | SP | 437,850 |
| Sweden | 046 | SV | 437,850 |
| Switzerland/French | 041 | SF | 437,850 |
| Switzerland/German | 041 | SG | 437,850 |
| United Kingdom | 044 | UK | 437,850 |
| USA | 001 | US | 437,850 |

*Figure 3.11*

tions in code pages, a procedure called *code page switching* has been made available.

When the system is booted the COUNTRY variable defines the code page. The code page for a device (which must have a driver that supports code page switching) can be changed with the DOS MODE, NLSFUNC and CHCP commands. MODE and CHCP are also available as OS/2 commands.

You can switch code pages within an application with DOS function 66h.

*Interrupt:* 21h
*Function:* 66h
*DOS version:* 3.3
*Service:* Code page switching
*Entry values:* AH=66h

| | |
|---|---|
| | AL= 01h (Get current code page) |
| | 02h (Set code page) |
| | BX=code page (if AL=02h) |
| *Exit values:* | AX=error code (if CF=1) |
| | BX=code page (if AL=01h) |
| | DX=default code page (if AL=01h) |

The code pages currently in use are:

| | |
|---|---|
| 437 | US |
| 850 | Multilingual |
| 852 | Slavic |
| 860 | Portuguese |
| 863 | Canadian-French |
| 865 | Nordic |

The KEYB codes and corresponding code pages are shown in Figure 3.11.

**DOS 4 country information**

The only addition DOS 4 makes is to provide the address of a table that can be used to translate two-byte codes into characters for languages where the ASCII character set is insufficient. This address is available from subfunction 07h of function 65h (above).

**Dip switches**

If all this isn't enough, it is worth noting that most PCs have a set of dip switches that can be set to determine the language that is used for error and information messages while the system is being booted.

## Booting up the computer

The process of starting up the computer is known as *booting*. This process is carried out by the first program in the ROM BIOS, called the *boot* or *bootstrap* program. This program begins at F000:FFF0.

When the computer is first switched on, it performs a *cold boot*. This includes the following tasks:

- Self-testing. This includes checks on the memory and hardware.
- Initialisation. Information about the system is stored in RAM.
- Loading the operating system.

Each of these tasks is outlined below.

**Self-testing**

The tests that are carried out vary from one PC to another, of course, but broadly speaking the principles are as follows:

1. The interrupts are disabled. The self-test program is stored in ROM so it cannot be changed; since no interrupts are allowed, it cannot be halted early.
2. The integrity of the ROM is verified by performing a checksum calculation.
3. The DMA controller and PIT are checked.
4. The speed of the RTC (if any) is checked.
5. The serial and parallel ports are initialised.
6. The mouse registers are cleared.
7. All RAM is tested. On the IBM PC, each 16K block is counted through on the screen as the test is performed.
8. The PIC is tested.
9. The disk drives are checked by moving the drive heads to a specific track. You will see the disk lights come on at this stage but the program is not trying to read anything.
10. The keyboard is tested.

Any errors, where possible, are notified by an error message on the screen. Usually, this is fairly meaningless to anyone other than a PC engineer. If the error lies with the monitor or associated boards, it is not possible to put up a message, of course; in such cases the error is notified by series of beeps. The language used for the error messages is read from links or dip switches on the main board.

**Initialisation**

When everything is deemed to be all right, the program goes on to the next stage:

1 If there is any battery-backed RAM, this is checked. If any error is encountered in the data (indicating that the power supply has been interrupted or the batteries are getting low), all values are reset to their defaults. An error message may be displayed.

2 The PIT is set to generate an interrupt on counter 0, a specific number of times per second (for example, 18.2 on the PC; see Chapter 4 for more details). Counter 1 is set to generate a signal every 15.13 microseconds. Counter 2 is disabled.

3 Channel 0 of the DMA controller is set to control the memory refresh function; the other channels are disabled.

4 Any dip switches are read, the RAM size is checked, and so on.

5 The system variables, at locations 0300h to 0500h in RAM, are set according to the hardware that is attached.

6 The first 32 interrupt vectors, from 00h to 1Fh, are placed in the first 80h bytes of RAM. The other interrupt vectors are loaded later by DOS, application programs, etc.

7 The disk interface is tested with interrupt 13h.

8 The keyboard is tested.

9 The video adaptor and video ROM are tested.

10 The interrupt controller is initialised. Interrupts 00h, 01h and 06h are enabled.

11 The non-maskable interrupt (NMI) is enabled.

12 Any external ROMs are identified and initialised.

13 The display adaptor ROM is initialised; the video RAM is tested, the video controller is initialised, the character fonts are loaded from ROM and the display mode is selected. The display mode chosen depends upon the adaptor and (on some

PCs) the setting of dip switches. Interrupt 10h is installed.

**14** The boot sector is loaded from disk. The first attempt is made to read the boot sector from floppy disk; if there is no disk, the program tries the hard disk (if fitted). If there is no suitable boot sector on either disk – or no floppy disk and no hard disk – an instruction to load a system disk is displayed; having loaded a disk and pressed a key, the step is repeated until successful. The system checks the last two bytes of the boot sector to see if a boot program is included: if it is, these bytes will have the values 55h and AAh. Once the boot sector has been loaded, the procedures are dependent upon the operating system.

On early IBM PCs, if no system disk is found, the ROM BASIC is loaded.

**The warm boot**

A *warm boot* or *system reset* takes place in a number of situations. Typically, it occurs when the user presses **Ctrl-Alt-Del** but a warm boot may also be forced by a program, by invoking interrupt 19h.

In fact, the procedures are almost identical. All that the routine that handles **Ctrl-Alt-Del** does is invoke interrupt 19h and reset parts of the system.

| | |
|---|---|
| *Interrupt:* | 19h |
| *Service:* | Restart system |
| *Entry values:* | None |
| *Exit values:* | None |

The interrupt 19h routine in ROM checks for a floppy disk; if one is found, the routine attempts to load the operating system. If not, the system is loaded from the hard disk's active partition.

The warm boot is most often used when a program crashes, to clear any resident programs from memory or, less frequently, to allow a different operating system to be loaded.

When deliberately generated by a program, the warm boot usually signifies that security has been violated; it may also occur accidentally, due to an erroneous call to interrupt 19h.

In any event, the effect is the same. Almost all the cold boot procedures are repeated, the most major difference being that the RAM is not tested – and therefore not cleared. (Note that, on the original IBM PC, interrupt 18h actives ROM BASIC.)

## Loading the operating system

Control now passes to the operating system. For DOS, the procedure is as follows:

**1** The boot program checks for the existence of the DOS BIOS and kernel. If these are incompatible, a 'Wrong operating system' message is displayed.

**2** The DOS BIOS and kernel are loaded into the low end of memory.

**3** The initialisation routine in the DOS BIOS is activated, almost immediately passing control to a routine in the kernel.

**4** This routine sets aside part of memory for the disk buffers and another for the file control blocks (FCBs). It identifies the hardware that is attached and sets up the status byte at 0410h, which is accessed via interrupt 11h.

**6** Control reverts to the BIOS, which loads the environment (if any). This routine also loads any device drivers referred to by the environment.

**7** The BIOS loads the resident portion of the command processor and executes it.

**8** The resident portion of COMMAND.COM loads the initialisation section to the memory immediately above and passes control to it.

**9** The initialisation portion checks the root directory of the boot disk for AUTOEXEC.BAT. If this file does not exist, it prompts for the date and time. If the file does exist, the AUTOEXEC.BAT instructions are executed.

The operating system is now fully loaded.

# 4 Interrupts

Under normal circumstances, the CPU follows its own course, sticking to a fairly limited, pre-defined cycle of activities. To get it to do anything of any worth, you need to grab its attention for a moment. This is done with the *interrupts*. These are signals to the CPU that it should cease whatever it is doing and carry out some specific task.

For example, when a key is pressed, the keyboard hardware generates an interrupt: the CPU deals with it and then goes about its business once more. In a similar way, programs can demand that certain routines be carried out by invoking interrupts.

## Interrupt vectors

There are many different types of interrupt. Each interrupt is identified by a number, rather than a name, and each one has its own piece of code, called an interrupt *handler*. This is a special type of subroutine. When the interrupt is called, the current activity is suspended, the code in the interrupt handler is executed, and then the main program resumes at the original point. The advantage of the interrupt routines is that they can exist anywhere. The hardware interrupt handlers are held in the ROM BIOS; the DOS interrupts form part of the DOS BIOS file; and you can create your own interrupt handlers in user RAM.

Interrupts do not have names; instead, each has a number. An interrupt handler is pointed to by its corresponding *interrupt vector*. This is the address of the start of the interrupt handler routine. The vector consists of two words, containing the segment and offset address of the interrupt handler.

Interrupts can occur at any time, when any piece of code is being processed. Therefore, the interrupt vectors are stored in the safest possible place, the very start of RAM. The vectors are stored sequentially, each one taking exactly four bytes. The first vector, for interrupt 00h, begins at 0000:0000. Up to 256 (FFh) vectors are allowed and it is assumed that all of these may exist. Therefore, 1K of RAM is

**80x86 interrupts**

| Interrupt | Type | Use |
|---|---|---|
| 00 | Hardware | Divide by zero |
| 01 | Hardware | Single step |
| 02 | Hardware | Non-Maskable Interrupt (NMI) |
| 03 | Hardware | Break points |
| 04 | Hardware | Overflow |
| 05 | Hardware | Print-Screen |
| 06 | Hardware | User mouse interrupt |
| 07 | Hardware | Reserved |
| 08 | Hardware | Clock tick |
| 09 | Hardware | Keyboard |
| 0A-0F | | Reserved |
| 10 | BIOS | Screen |
| 11 | BIOS | Equipment list |
| 12 | BIOS | Memory size |
| 13 | BIOS | Disk |
| 14 | BIOS | Serial port |
| 15 | BIOS | Cassette etc. |
| 16 | BIOS | Keyboard |
| 17 | BIOS | Parallel port |
| 18 | BIOS | ROM BASIC boot |
| 19 | BIOS | System reset |
| 1A | BIOS | Date and time |
| 1B | BIOS | Keyboard break |
| 1C | BIOS | Clock tick |
| 1D | Address | Video table |
| 1E | Address | Disk table |
| 1F | Address | Graphics character table |
| 20 | DOS | Terminate program |
| 21 | DOS | DOS functions |
| 22 | DOS address | Program termination |
| 23 | DOS address | Ctrl-Break address |
| 24 | DOS address | Critical error handler |
| 25 | DOS | Disk read |
| 26 | DOS | Disk write |
| 27 | DOS | Terminate and Stay Resident |
| 28-32 | | Reserved for DOS |
| 33 | DOS | Mouse |
| 34-3F | | Reserved for DOS |
| 40-5F | | Reserved for BIOS |
| 60-6F | | Available for programmers |
| 70-7F | | Reserved for 20286 BIOS |
| 80-FF | | Reserved for BASIC |

*Figure 4.1*

set aside for the vectors and you can calculate the position of any interrupt vector by multiplying the interrupt number by 4.

This has the advantage that programs written to use the interrupts are totally independent of the interrupt code, its position and size. If the interrupt code is changed in any way it makes no difference to the application program. Therefore, when a new version of DOS comes along – assuming that upwards compatibility has been maintained – you can be quite satisfied that existing programs will still operate in the same way as before.

There is a slight disadvantage, in that a program that relies on the DOS interrupts is tied in to DOS. However, this is a small price to pay for the power that is supplied by the DOS functions. To replace an interrupt routine with a new one, simply put a different address in the vector table.

The interrupts are divided into a number of groups. Each group is defined by a certain part of the system and some of the interrupt numbers have pre-defined uses (see Figure 4.1).

## Handling interrupts

The handling of interrupts is dealt with by the programmable interrupt controller (PIC). There are two *interrupt lines*, used by the hardware to signal that an interrupt has occurred. At each machine cycle, the CPU checks the interrupt lines for signals. If an interrupt is indicated, the CPU gets the interrupt number from the interrupt line, uses the appropriate interrupt vector to identify the address and diverts processing to that point. Even while processing an interrupt, the CPU continues to check the interrupt lines regularly, so another interrupt signalled results in further redirection. As a result, the CPU is able to deal with a chain of interrupts. At the end of each interrupt routine, processing continues at the point where the interrupt was called. Eventually, the process will get back to where it started and continue with the original program.

In some circumstances it is necessary to ensure that no further interruptions can occur. This is done by *disabling* the interrupts. Any such period should always be as short as possible and the interrupts should be re-enabled at the earliest opportunity.

When interrupts are disabled the hardware cannot get the attention of the CPU. If anything goes wrong, everything will stop and the keyboard cannot be used to break into the system; that is, the system has 'hung'.

The interrupts are disabled and enabled with two special instructions, CLI and STI respectively. The interrupt flag signals whether or not interrupts are currently enabled.

## Hardware interrupts

Interrupts fall into two distinct categories: hardware interrupts and software interrupts. The first type are generated by the hardware. These interrupts can break into your program at any time, unannounced, and are given priority by the CPU. For example, when a key is pressed the keyboard circuits generate a hardware interrupt; when part of memory fails another type of interrupt is generated.

The hardware interrupts are handled by the Programmable Interrupt Controller (PIC). The PIC on the 8086/8088 can cope with eight hardware interrupts; on the 80286 upwards, two linked PICs allow for up to fifteen hardware interrupts.

The hardware interrupts fall into two categories, signalled on separate lines.

### Maskable interrupts

Most hardware interrupts are signalled on the *interrupt required* (INTR) line. These are the *maskable interrupts*, and are overseen by the PIC. When the CPU finds an interrupt signalled on this line, it checks the interrupt flag. If the flag is set, the interrupt is processed; if the flag is clear (that is, the interrupts have been disabled), the interrupt is ignored.

The following maskable hardware interrupts are reserved by the system and exist as part of the ROM BIOS:

**00h** Divide by zero error. Signalled whenever the divisor in a DIV or IDIV expression is 0.

**01h** Used for tracing programs. When the trap flag is set, interrupt 01h is generated on the completion of each instruction in the program that is being traced. Control returns to the debugging program, which can check the contents of memory and registers before continuing with the next instruction. This allows you to single-step through the program, a process used by DEBUG's S command.

**03h** Sets break points in programs. The use is similar to 01h, except that execution continues until a break point is reached.

**04h** Handles overflows. This interrupt can also be generated indirectly from within a program by the INTO instruction; INTO generates an interrupt 04h if the overflow flag is set.

**05h** The Print-Screen facility (see Chapter 10 for details).

**06h** The User Mouse interrupt (see Chapter 7).

**08h** Used by the timer to generate clock ticks (see Chapter 5).

**09h** The keyboard interrupt (see Chapter 6).

Interrupts 07h and 0Ah to 0Fh are reserved for other hardware devices.

The 80286 upwards allow a further eight hardware interrupts, which are allocated to interrupts 70h-77h.

**The non-maskable interrupt**

The second interrupt line is used by the *non-maskable interrupt* (NMI). The difference is that the CPU *must* process this interrupt, regardless of the state of the interrupt flag. The NMI signals a major hardware failure: a RAM parity error, reduction in power, and so on. The NMI line is also connected to the maths co-processor and the expansion bus.

It is possible to disable the NMI by clearing the top bit of port A0h but it is extremely unwise to do so. (This is the only purpose of this port, the other seven bits being unused. Therefore the NMI can be disabled by setting the port to 00h and enabled by setting it to 80h.)

The NMI is allocated to interrupt 02h. When the interrupt occurs, a fatal error message is displayed and the computer must then be switched off. If a maths co-processor is installed, it inserts a replacement interrupt which deals with that chip's NMIs as well.

## Software interrupts

As described in Chapter 1, all data is transferred on the system bus between the various hardware ports, memory locations and registers. All devices are activated by moving specific data to their ports.

For example, to set the size of the hardware cursor, you must first specify the top and bottom lines in particular ports. Next, another value is placed in a third port, and this is the signal to activate the new cursor.

All programming instructions relating to the hardware are ultimately broken down into sequences of input and output to the ports. While it would be possible to write programs that access the ports directly, these would be very long-winded and troublesome to debug. Therefore, most of the time you will wish to use the ready-made routines, provided by the ROM BIOS, that handle all the hard work involved in communicating with the ports. These routines come in the form of *software interrupts*.

The main difference between hardware and software interrupts is that software interrupts are generated by an INT instruction in a program and are therefore predictable. For example, to generate interrupt 10h the instruction is: `INT 10h`. When this instruction is given, the CPU executes the routine pointed to by the interrupt vector; in other words, it treats it like any interrupt that is signalled by the hardware interrupt lines. A software interrupt is also very similar to an ordinary subroutine. However, it has the advantage that it can be located anywhere in memory and the code can be changed much more easily, possibly without even recompiling the program.

An interrupt routine can perform any operation but normally such routines relate to specific pieces of hardware. An interrupt routine must end with an IRET instruction rather than the normal RET.

All software interrupts are maskable; if you disable the interrupt flag, they have no effect at all.

Different groups of software interrupts are marked out for different purposes:

- Interrupts 10h to 1Fh are the BIOS interrupts. They exist as part of the computer's ROM and are all that is needed to operate the standard hardware devices. Theoretically, you could write a program based totally on these interrupts, with no reference to DOS; this would produce a program that is independent of the operating system but it is not usual to do so.
- Interrupts 20h to 3Fh are reserved for DOS (or any other operating system). Some provide alternative methods of accessing the hardware and work by calling the BIOS interrupts; others provide access to the DOS file-handling routines.
- Interrupts 40h to 5Fh are reserved for the ROM BIOS.
- Interrupts 60h to 6Fh are available to the programmer, though you should avoid 67h to 6Fh.
- Interrupts 70h to 7Fh are reserved for additional hardware interrupts.
- Interrupts 80h to FFh are reserved for BASIC.

Some of the DOS interrupts are not used, or are used but their services are not documented. It is as well to steer clear of the undocumented interrupts, since it cannot be guaranteed that their use will not be changed in future versions of DOS.

Most of the DOS functions are included in interrupt 21h, a massive interrupt that encompasses a large range of unrelated routines. A call to this interrupt is categorised by the *function number*, the number being supplied in register AH.

Bear in mind that the installation of particular programs or device drivers may result in new interrupts being added or some of the existing interrupts being redefined. You should also remember that some interrupts may vary from one machine to another. For example, interrupt 15h on the original IBM PC was used for the cassette drive; on the Amstrad PC it handles the battery-backed RAM.

## Interrupt replacements

If you want to create your own interrupts, these can be stored in the available vectors from 60h to 66h. Alternatively, you may want to modify an existing interrupt. While it is feasible to set up a new or modified interrupt manually – by storing the new interrupt in memory, calculating the interrupt vector, and storing the address of the new interrupt handler there – it is generally far simpler to use the functions provided by DOS. Using DOS is also considerably safer and less likely to interfere with other programs.

When modifying an existing interrupt, the replacement should normally end with a call to the original interrupt. This ensures that all possible outcomes are catered for and that the original interrupt routine is still available where needed. For example, if you want to activate a specific operation by a particular key press, you can replace the keyboard interrupt (interrupt 09h) with one that starts by checking for the required key press. If found, the new interrupt routine carries out its task and then ends with the IRET command. If the required key press is not found, the interrupt calls the original interrupt so that the key press is processed in the normal way.

In this way, you can effectively hijack an interrupt to make it perform some particular task, without having to totally redefine all its operations. This approach also has the advantage that if another program wants to use the same interrupt for its own purposes, that program will still work quite happily (as long as it does not use the same 'trigger' mechanism, of course).

The first stage in modifying an existing interrupt is to get the interrupt vector. This is done with DOS interrupt 21h, function 35h.

| | |
|---|---|
| *Interrupt:* | 21h |
| *Function:* | 35h |
| *Service:* | Get interrupt vector |
| *Entry values:* | AH=35h |
| | AL=interrupt number |
| *Exit values:* | ES:BX=interrupt vector |

All you have to do is tell DOS which interrupt you want and DOS will point to the vector for you. You can then save the existing address for when the new interrupt finishes.

The next stage in modifying an interrupt – and the main stage when creating a new interrupt – is to identify the location of the new interrupt routine. This can be done with interrupt 21h, function 25h.

| | |
|---|---|
| *Interrupt:* | 21h |
| *Function:* | 25h |
| *Service:* | Set interrupt vector |
| *Entry values:* | AH=25h |
| | AL=interrupt number |
| | DS:DX=pointer to interrupt handler |
| *Exit values:* | None |

You only need to specify where the new interrupt starts; DOS does the rest. Note that it may be necessary to change the data segment (DS) before calling this service. DS must be restored immediately afterwards.

You should always use the DOS services when modifying interrupt vectors, as this helps to ensure that your programs will operate satisfactorily in the OS/2 'DOS compatibility box'.

## Compatibility

The use of interrupts again brings up the question of compatibility. The higher the level of instruction that is used, the more likely it is to be compatible between versions of DOS and even between operating systems. The choice of instruction type is usually made in the following order:

- High level language
- DOS interrupt
- BIOS interrupt
- Direct access to port/memory

Moving higher up the list brings greater potential compatibility between operating systems and machines. On the other hand, moving down the list will generally give you greater speed and flexibility. Therefore, any program must find a satisfactory balance between compatibility and speed of operation.

# 5 The Clock

From the moment you switch on the computer its internal clock starts ticking. Everything the PC does is regulated by this tick, from the processing of simple additions to the production of sound. This chapter looks at the PC's clock and those operations that are dependent upon it. There is also a discussion of the battery-backed RAM that is included on many PCs and is used to keep track of time even when the computer is switched off.

## Timing processes

All timing processes are based on the 8284A system clock (or equivalent) which oscillates at a particular frequency. This frequency is measured in millions of cycles per second, or megahertz (MHz). For example, the standard PC runs at 4.77MHz while the average 80386 uses a 25MHz system clock. The frequency of the system clock is often quoted as the speed of the computer and, indeed, this frequency determines how quickly the PC can carry out basic operations. (It should be noted at this point that the speed of any part of a program may also be dictated by the hardware that is used. For example, the speed of disk access is determined not by the system clock but by the disk drive itself.)

Each oscillation of the system clock sets off a chain reaction. A pulse races through the entire computer system and causes the CPU to execute one part of an instruction. This is referred to as a *cycle*. Each process carried out by the computer takes a number of cycles to complete.

The number of cycles depends on the addressing mode and data size. Also, some instructions require fewer cycles to complete on the 80286 upwards.

When the CPU has completed the cycle, nothing happens until the next tick and the next pulse passes through the system.

The 8253 programmable interval timer (PIT) operates at a frequency of 1.19318 MHz. At each pulse the timer increments an internal word register. When this count reaches the maximum

(65535), the PIT issues a hardware interrupt 08h: this is the *clock tick*. This happens every 0.0549 seconds, giving about 18.2 ticks per second. The clock tick is the basis of many operations.

**Interrupt 08h**

The interrupt 08h routine in turn increments its own clock count in the double word at 046Ch. The next byte, at 0470h, holds a *midnight flag*. When the count in 046Ch reaches the value 001800Bh (the number of clock ticks in a day), it is reset to zero and the midnight flag is set to 1. If this happens again, no further change is made to the midnight flag. You can check the current clock count with function 00h of BIOS interrupt 1Ah.

---

*Interrupt:* 1Ah
*Function:* 00h
*Service:* Get clock count
*Entry values:* AH=00h
*Exit values:* AL= 00h (not yet midnight)
01h (past midnight)
CX=clock count (high order word)
DX=clock count (low order word)

---

Calling this interrupt clears the midnight flag, so if you do make this call, make sure that you use the data that is returned.

When the computer is first switched on (assuming it has no internal battery), the count is reset to 0. If you change the current time, the clock count is recalculated to match the new time of day. The count can be cleared at any time with function 01h of interrupt 1Ah.

---

*Interrupt:* 1Ah
*Function:* 01h
*Service:* Set clock count
*Entry values:* AH=01h
CX=clock count (high order word)
DX=clock count (low order word)
*Exit values:* None

---

This count is useful for timing (Figure 5.1) but not for keeping track of the current date and time.

```
TIMER:       ;Time an event in clock ticks
      ;The full version of this routine
      ;converts the clock ticks into
      ;seconds

      ;Limitations - this routine is slightly
      ;inaccurate in that is does not allow
      ;for the time taken to actually
      ;perform the calculations

      ;Program does not work if midnight has
      ;been passed before it starts, and is
      ;passed again during timing

      ;Calls TIMEROUT, any routine to be
      ;timed

      ;Exit values: TIMEHI=time high byte
      ;             TIMELO=time low byte
      ;             AX,BX,CX,DX changed

jmp timest

starthi      dw ?            ;Start time high word
startlo      dw ?            ;Start time low word
midflag      db ?            ;Midnight flag
timehi       dw ?            ;Time taken high word
timelo       dw ?            ;Time taken low word

timest:
      xor ah,ah
      int 1Ah                ;Get current clock
                             ;count
      mov [starthi],cx       ;Save count
      mov [startlo],dx
      mov [midflag],al
      call timerout          ;Call whatever
                             ;routine it is to be
                             ;timed
      xor ah,ah
      int 1Ah                ;Get clock count
                             ;again
      cmp al,[midflag]       ;Has midnight been
                             ;passed?
      jnz aftermid           ;If so, jump
      sub dx,[startlo]       ;Subtract low word
      sbb cx,[starthi]       ;Subtract high word
```

```
        mov [timehi],cx         ;Save time taken
        mov [timelo],dx
        jmp endtime

aftermid:
        sub [startlo],dx        ;Subtract low word
        sub [starthi],cx        ;Subtract high word
        xor bx,bx
        sub bx,[startlo]        ;Subtract from 0
        mov [timelo],bx
        xor bx,bx
        sbb [starthi],cx        ;Subtract from 0
        mov [timelo],bx

endtime:
        ret
```

*Figure 5.1*

One of the functions of interrupt 08h is also to issue an interrupt 1Ch, which is a BIOS interrupt that is used by many programs. It is also worth noting that interrupt 08h is used for the production of sound (see Chapter 9).

**AT-compatible timers**

The BIOS for the AT-compatibles (and PS/2s) includes an interrupt function for timing purposes.

| | |
|---|---|
| *Interrupt:* | 15h |
| *Function:* | 83h |
| *Service:* | Interval timer (AT only) |
| *Entry values:* | AH= 00h (start timer) |
| | 01h (stop timer) |
| | CX:DX=interval (microseconds) |
| | ES:BX=address of status byte |
| *Exit values:* | CF= 0 (success) |
| | 1 (failure) |

The status byte should be cleared before the function is called. This service runs in the background. When the required interval has elapsed, the status byte is set to 80h, so you need to check this byte from time to time.

For a more definite pause in a program, use function 86h.

---

| | |
|---|---|
| *Interrupt:* | 15h |
| *Function:* | 86h |
| *Service:* | Wait for interval (AT only) |
| *Entry values:* | AH=86h |
| | CX:DX=interval (microseconds) |
| *Exit values:* | CF= 0 (success) |
| | 1 (failure) |

---

**Reprogramming the PIT**

You can reprogram the PIT to generate ticks more frequently. However, some care needs to be taken. If you double the amount of ticks, for example, you must also change interrupt 08h to produce an interrupt 1Ch only every second time it is called.

This can cause problems with some programs. Microsoft's QuickBasic, for example, checks to see whether the time has been tampered with in this way. If so, it adapts to it. But if 1Ch has already been changed to account for the alteration (as happens with some mouse drivers, notably that of the Amstrad computers), the effect is that the clock is slowed down and, while working in QuickBasic, time passes very slowly!

## The Real Time Clock

All AT-compatibles and some PC-compatibles include a *Real Time Clock* (RTC). This device uses the interrupt 1Ch ticks to keep track of the time of day and current date. If the RTC is battery-backed, the time and date are maintained even when mains power is off. When the system is booted, the BIOS reads the RTC time and updates the clock tick count at 046Ch. DOS 3 also reads the RTC date and updates its own internal date when it is booted. The RTC also offers a little-used alarm feature. The address of the RTC data can be found by reading port 70h. The RTC also uses port 71H.

```
DEC2BCD:       ;Convert decimal value to BCD

      ;Entry values: DECINB holds decimal
      ;              value
      ;Exit values:  AX=BCD value
      ;              AX,BX,CX,DX,SI changed

      jmp bcdstart

decinb     db '    ',00  ;Decimal value to be
                         ;converted, as ASCII
                         ;string, terminated by
                         ;null character.
                         ;Maximum value 9999.
                         ;Routine does not
                         ;check that number
                         ;is valid.

bcdstart:
      xor ax,ax            ;Set AX=0 (AX will
                           ;hold hex value)
      xor bx,bx            ;Clear BX
      mov bl,10h           ;Move 10h into BX
      xor si,si            ;Clear SI (pointer
                           ;to next decimal
                           ;digit)

startbcon:
      xor cx,cx            ;Clear CX
      mov cl,decinb[si]    ;Get next decimal
                           ;digit
      cmp cl,00h           ;Check against 0
      jz endbcon           ;If 0, conversion is
                           ;complete
      mul bx               ;Otherwise, multiply
                           ;value in AX by 10
      sub cl,30h           ;Subtract
                           ;30h to convert
                           ;ASCII number to
                           ;actual value
      add ax,cx            ;Add new digit
      inc si               ;Increase SI, point
                           ;to next digit
      jmp startbcon        ;Jump to start of
                           ;loop
endbcon:
      ret
```

*Figure 5.2*

Note that the values used in the RTC functions are set and returned in binary coded decimal (BCD). A conversion routine is given in Figure 5.2.

**The date functions**

The DOS DATE command sets or displays the current date. For non-battery backed computers the date automatically starts at the PC's base date of 1st January 1980, whenever the computer is switched on.

You can check the current date in a program with DOS function 2Ah.

---

| | |
|---|---|
| *Interrupt:* | 21h |
| *Function:* | 2Ah |
| *DOS version:* | 1 |
| *Service:* | Get date |
| *Entry values:* | AH=2Ah |
| *Exit values:* | AL=day of week (0=Sunday) |
| | CX=year (1980-2099) |
| | DH=month (1=January) |
| | DL=day |

---

From this, you can see that the PC is able to cope with any date from the start of 1980 to the end of 2099.

In a similar way, the date is set with function 2Bh.

---

| | |
|---|---|
| *Interrupt:* | 21h |
| *Function:* | 2Bh |
| *DOS version:* | 1 |
| *Service:* | Set date |
| *Entry values:* | AH=2Bh |
| | CX=year (1980-2099) |
| | DH=month (1=January) |
| | DL=day |
| *Exit values:* | AL= 00h (date valid) |
| | FFh (date invalid) |

---

This function checks the validity of the date (making allowances for leap years, and so on) and returns FFh in AL if the date is invalid. This is illustrated in Figure 5.3.

```
DATEDOS:        ;Program to set new date with DOS
                ;function

        ;New date is included as command line
        ;parameters, DD MM YY (e.g. DATEDOS 07 05 91)

        ;Limitations: Must be one space between
        ;items and each must be 2 digits

        ;Calls PARSE (2.19), NEXTPARM (2.19),
        ;DEC2HEX (2.7), DISSTR (8.10)

        jmp datstart

errormes:    db 'Invalid date$'

datstart:
        call parse              ;Parse the command
                                ;line
        call nextvalue          ;Get a parameter and
                                ;convert to hex
        mov dl,al               ;DL=day
        push dx                 ;Save it
        call nextvalue
        pop dx                  ;Get day
        mov dh,al               ;DH=month
        push dx                 ;Save it
        call nextvalue
        mov cx,ax               ;CX=year
        add cx,076Ch            ;Add 1900 to year
        pop dx                  ;Get month & day
        mov ah,2Bh
        int 21h                 ;Set date
        cmp al,00h              ;Invalid date?
        jz okdate               ;Jump if not
        lea dx,errormes
        call disstr
okdate:
        int 20h

nextvalue:
        call nextparm           ;Read next PARAMETER
        cld
        xor cx,cx
        mov cl,04h
        mov al,00h
        lea di,decin
        rep stosb               ;Fill DECIN with
                                ;nulls
        lea si,parameter
```

```
        lea di,decin
        mov cl,02h                  ;Transfer contents
                                    ;of PARAMETER
        rep movsb                   ;to DECIN
        call dec2hex                ;Decimal-to-hex
                                    ;conversion
        ret
```

*Figure 5.3*

If the computer has a battery-backed RTC, this function will not necessarily reset it; this varies from one implementation of DOS to another.

On some machines, therefore, the new date remains in effect only until the computer is next booted.

Function 2Ah also returns the day of the week, so you can combine functions 2Ah and 2Bh to get the day of the week for any date in the 120-year period (see Figure 5.4).

```
DWEEK:          ;Program to return day of week

        ;Date to check is included as command line
        ;parameters, DD MM YY (e.g. DWEEK 07 05 91)

        ;Limitations: Must be one space between
        ;items and each must be 2 digits
        ;Calls DATEDOS (5.3), DISSTR (8.10)

        jmp dweekstart

days:           db 'Sunday   $Monday   $Tuesday  $'
                db 'Wednesday$Thursday $Friday   $'
                db 'Saturday $'

dweekstart:
       mov ah,2Ah                  ;Get current weekday
       int 21h
       push cx                     ;Save parameters
       push dx
       call datedos                ;Set date with
                                   ;parameters from
                                   ;command line
       cmp al,00h                  ;Was date valid?
       jnz abandon                 ;If not, give up
```

```
     mov ah,2Ah               ;Get date
     int 21h
     call showday             ;Display day of week
     pop dx                   ;Restore current
                              ;date parameters
     pop cx
     mov ah,2Bh               ;Reset date
     int 21h
abandon:
     int 20h

showday:                      ;Display day of week
     mov cl,0Ah               ;CL=10
     mul cl                   ;Multiply day code
                              ;by 10 to get offset
                              ;into table
     lea dx,days              ;DX points to table
                              ;of days
     add dx,ax                ;Add offset
     call disstr              ;Display day
     ret
```

*Figure 5.4*

**The RTC date functions**

Functions are available from the ROM BIOS to change the RTC. These are applicable to machines with battery-backed memory only. In general, this is the ATs and compatibles though some PCs (such as the Amstrad PC) also make use of this feature. The ROM BIOS routines provide a means of permanently changing the date and time. To read the current date from the RTC, use function 04h of interrupt 1Ah.

| | |
|---|---|
| *Interrupt:* | 1Ah |
| *Function:* | 04h |
| *Service:* | Get RTC date (AT-compatibles) |
| *Entry values:* | AH=04h |
| | CH=century (BCD) |
| | CL=year (BCD) |
| | DH=month (BCD) |
| | DL=day (BCD) |
| *Exit values:* | CF= 0 (RTC functioning) |
| | 1 (RTC not functioning) |
| | Other flags changed |

You can set the RTC date with function 05h of the same interrupt.

---

*Interrupt:* 1Ah
*Function:* 05h
*Service:* Set RTC date
*Entry values:* AH=05h (AT-compatibles)
CH=century (BCD) (19 or 20)
CL=year (BCD)
DH=month (BCD)
DL=day (BCD)
*Exit values:* CF= 0 (RTC functioning)
1 (RTC not functioning)
Other flags changed

---

This service does not carry out any validation of the date supplied. If an invalid date is given, an error message will be displayed when the system is next booted.

The service will be needed for those machines where the RTC date can only be set with a supplied set-up program and cannot be set via DOS.

When you use this function the DOS date in RAM is not affected; therefore, the new date only becomes effective when the computer is next booted. You may wish to use the DOS and BIOS functions together, to change both the current DOS date and the RTC date.

Since the location of the RTC data may not be the same on all computers, running the wrong version of the operating system (or a version for a different computer) on a PC with battery-backed RAM may result in the RTC date and time not being found; in this case the date and time is reset each time the computer is switched on.

## The time functions

Similar functions are provided for the current time. You can get the current time with function 2Ch of interrupt 21h.

| | |
|---|---|
| *Interrupt:* | 21h |
| *Function:* | 2Ch |
| *DOS version:* | 1 |
| *Service:* | Get time |
| *Entry values:* | AH=2C |
| *Exit values:* | CH=hours |
| | CL=minutes |
| | DH=seconds |
| | DL=hundredths of seconds |

Although this function returns the time in hundredths (0.01) of a second, remember that it is based on the clock ticks, which are produced every 0.054 seconds. Therefore, the value will jump by 1/20th of a second each time the clock ticks. If you are trying to use this function for timing purposes, it is more realistic to stick to tenths of a second for the results. Otherwise, for more accurate timing, you must access the PIT ports directly.

The current time is set with function 2Dh.

| | |
|---|---|
| *Interrupt:* | 21h |
| *Function:* | 2Dh |
| *DOS version:* | 1 |
| *Service:* | Set time |
| *Entry values:* | AH=2Dh |
| | CH=hours |
| | CL=minutes |
| | DH=seconds |
| | DL=hundredths of seconds |
| *Exit values:* | AL= 00h (time valid) |
| | FFh (time invalid) |

These functions are used by the DOS TIME command.

**The RTC time functions**

As for the date, you can also access the RTC time. The current time is obtained with function 02h of interrupt 1Ah.

---

| | |
|---|---|
| *Interrupt:* | 1Ah |
| *Function:* | 02h |
| *Service:* | Get RTC time (AT-compatibles) |
| *Entry values:* | AH=02h |
| | CH=hours (BCD) |
| | CL=minutes (BCD) |
| | DH=seconds (BCD) |
| *Exit values:* | CF= 0 (RTC functioning) |
| | 1 (RTC not functioning) |
| | Other flags changed |

---

Again, note that the figures must be given in BCD.

The current RTC time is set with function 03h.

---

| | |
|---|---|
| *Interrupt:* | 1Ah |
| *Function:* | 03h |
| *Service:* | Set RTC time (AT-compatibles) |
| *Entry values:* | AH=03h |
| | CH=hours (BCD) |
| | CL=minutes (BCD) |
| | DH=seconds (BCD) |
| | DL= 0 (GMT only) |
| | 1 (GMT and BST) |
| *Exit values:* | CF= 0 (RTC functioning) |
| | 1 (RTC not functioning) |
| | Other flags changed |

---

As for the RTC date, no validation is carried out by this service. The use of this function is illustrated in Figure 5.5.

This program is particularly useful, since it avoids the need to go through any complicated set-up program to adjust the RTC time. However, you should note that some AT-compatibles have variations in the interrupts and the way the RTC data is stored. Therefore, the routine given may not work on all machines.

```
TIMERTC:        ;Program to set new time with
                ;BIOS function

        ;New time is included as command line
        ;parameters, HH MM SS (e.g. TIMERTC 04 30 00)
        ;Validates time

        ;Limitations: Must be one space between
        ;items and each must be 2 digits

        ;Calls PARSE (2.19), NEXTPARM (2.19),
        ;DEC2HEX (2.7), DISSTR (8.10)

        jmp timstart

errormes2:   db 'Invalid time$'

timstart:
        call parse              ;Parse the command
                                ;line
        call nexttime           ;Get a parameter and
                                ;convert to BCD
        jc errortime            ;Jump if error
        mov ch,al               ;CH=hours
        cmp al,23h              ;Is hour valid?
        jg errortime            ;Jump if so
        push cx                 ;Otherwise, save it
        call nexttime
        jc errortime            ;Jump if error
        pop cx                  ;Get hours
        mov cl,al               ;CL=minutes
        cmp al,59h              ;Is minute valid?
        jg errortime            ;Jump if so
        push cx                 ;Otherwise, save it
        call nexttime
        jc errortime            ;Jump if error
        xor dx,dx
        mov dh,al               ;DH=seconds;GMT
        cmp al,59h              ;Is seconds valid?
        jg errortime            ;Jump if so
        clc
        pop cx                  ;Get hours & minutes
        mov ah,03h
        int 1Ah                 ;Set date
        jnc oktime              ;Jump if RTC not
                                ;functioning
errortime:
        lea dx,errormes2
        call disstr
oktime:
        int 20h
```

```
nexttime:
        call nextparm           ;Read next PARAMETER
        cld
        xor cx,cx
        mov cl,04h
        mov al,00h
        lea di,decinb
        rep stosb               ;Fill DECINB with
                                ;nulls
        lea si,parameter
        lea di,decinb
        mov cl,02h              ;Transfer contents
                                ;of PARAMETER
        rep movsb               ;to DECINB
        call dec2bcd            ;Decimal-to-BCD
                                ;conversion
        clc
        cmp al,00h              ;Is BCD value
                                ;positive or zero?
        jge timeend             ;Jump if so
        stc                     ;Otherwise, set
                                ;carry flag
timeend:
        ret
```

*Figure 5.5*

**GMT and BST**

Function 03h has an interesting feature, in that it allows you to switch between GMT and BST (in the UK). Note, however, that the date on which the switch takes place may change from one computer to another, depending upon which country the machine is intended for. For UK editions of this function the time is automatically changed on the last Sunday in April from 2 a.m. to 3 a.m., when this switch is set; similarly, on the last Sunday in October, the time is automatically set back from 2 a.m. to 1 a.m.

In the normal course of events, this special feature is not implemented, so a small program is necessary. However, for an event that occurs only twice a year, it may be felt that this is not really worth the effort.

## The alarm

If you have a battery-backed RTC, as found on AT-compatibles and some PCs, facilities are available to store an alarm time. This is done with function 06h of interrupt 1Ah.

| | |
|---|---|
| *Interrupt:* | 1Ah |
| *Function:* | 06h |
| *Service:* | Set RTC alarm (AT-compatibles) |
| *Entry values:* | AH=06h |
| | CH=hours (BCD) |
| | CL=minutes (BCD) |
| | DH=seconds (BCD) |
| *Exit values:* | CF= 0 (alarm now set) |
| | 1 (alarm was already set) |

Setting up an alarm is fairly simple; making use of it is a different matter. The ROM BIOS constantly checks the alarm time against the current time. When the alarm time is reached, the BIOS invokes interrupt 4Ah. Initially, this interrupt does nothing so you must insert your own interrupt routine.

You can switch the alarm off with function 07h.

| | |
|---|---|
| *Interrupt:* | 1Ah |
| *Function:* | 07h |
| *Service:* | Clear RTC alarm |
| *Entry values:* | AH=07h |
| *Exit values:* | None |

The alarm feature takes account of the current time only; the date is ignored. Therefore the alarm will go off at 24-hour intervals. With a little effort you can allow for the date as well as the time and make the program into a TSR.

# 6 The Keyboard

Almost all information originally makes it way onto the computer via the keyboard. This chapter looks at the keyboard hardware, the layout of the keys, the operation of the keyboard, the interrupts related to it, the special key combinations and the keyboard buffer.

## The keyboard hardware

The basic PC keyboard has 83 keys. Some AT-compatibles have 84 keys, providing an additional **Sys Req** key, but the majority of AT-compatibles and PS/2s have 101 or 102 keys. Some of these extra keys are also found on some 8086-based PC-compatibles. The operation is the same on all members of the PC family, though the positions of the special keys may be different.

The keyboard generally falls into three or four main sections:

- The central section of the keyboard holds the standard QWERTY typewriter keys. This includes the 26 letter keys, the numbers 0-9 and all the standard punctuation, arithmetic and other symbols. It also includes a number of special keys, such as **Ctrl**, **Alt** and **Caps Lock**.
- The number pad, on the right of the main keyboard, contains a set of keys that can be switched between two separate functions: cursor control or numeric.
- The function keys – 10 to the left on PC compatibles, 12 above the QWERTY keyboard on AT-compatibles – can be programmed within each application to perform specific processes.
- The cursor keypad, on AT-compatibles only, provides an alternative to the number pad for cursor operations.

## Operation of the keyboard

When a key is depressed, the keyboard circuits generate a *scan code*. This is a code in the range 00h to 7Fh. When the key is released, a *release code* is generated, with a value 80h more than the scan code (i.e. the MSB is set). The keyboard controller constantly checks for these codes. When any code is detected, the controller issues an interrupt 09h and puts the code in port 60h.

If there is a code already waiting in the port (usually when the interrupts are disabled), the code is stored in a special internal buffer. The controller can store a number of key presses ready to pass on to the main system. This buffer forms part of the keyboard hardware and is beyond the control of the program. It should not be confused with the main keyboard buffer, described below.

### AT keyboards

Most AT-compatibles and PS/2s have keyboards of 101 or 102 keys. The extra keys are duplicates of existing keys and produce scan codes of more than one byte. Usually, this is E0h followed by the scan code of the duplicate key. Some key combinations on these keyboard produce special scan codes (see Figure 6.4). The codes may also vary with the Shift status and variations will be found among some compatibles.

### The modifying keys

The first thing that interrupt 09h does is to check the code that has been received to see what type of key it is. Some keys modify the effect of other keys: **Shift**, **Ctrl**, **Alt**, **Caps Lock**, **Num Lock**, **Ins**, **Scroll Lock**. (Since it is possible to detect whether a key is still being depressed – by whether or not the release code has been sent – it would be possible to define other modifying keys; for example, you could instruct the routine to carry out a particular action only if two character keys were pressed together, the first of these keys acting like a **Shift** key.)

The current status of these special keys is held in the *keyboard status bytes*. These are two bytes of data, held at locations 0417h and 0418h, as shown in Figure 6.1. The first of these bytes is the most useful.

**Keyboard status bytes**

| First keyboard status byte (0417h) | | Second keyboard status byte (0418h) | |
|---|---|---|---|
| **Bit** | **Meaning if set** | **Bit** | **Meaning if set** |
| 7 | Insert on | 7 | Ins pressed |
| 6 | Caps Lock on | 6 | Caps Lock pressed |
| 5 | Num Lock on | 5 | Num Lock pressed |
| 4 | Scroll Lock on | 4 | Scroll Lock pressed |
| 3 | Alt pressed | 3 | Ctrl-Num Lock on |
| 2 | Ctrl pressed | 2 | Not used |
| 1 | Left Shift pressed | 1 | Not used |
| 0 | Right Shift pressed | 0 | Not used |

*Figure 6.1*

Some of the modifying keys are effective only while they are being pressed: the two **Shift** keys, **Ctrl** and **Alt**. When any of these keys is pressed, the corresponding bit in the status byte is set; when the key is released, the bit is cleared. Therefore, you can detect the status of any of these keys by inspecting the relevant bit.

The other modifying keys have a permanent effect on the keyboard each time they are pressed. These are the three locking keys – **Caps Lock**, **Num Lock** and **Scroll Lock** – and the **Ins** key. In these cases, releasing the key has no effect at all in the normal course of events. The relevant bits in 0417h show whether the particular function is on or off in each case. You can also tell whether the key is actually being depressed by checking particular bits in 0418h but, generally, this is of little interest.

The most important bit of 0418h is bit 3. This bit is set when **Ctrl-Num Lock** is being pressed (or **Pause** on AT-compatibles). This combination is used by many DOS programs to suspend the operation of a particular command. For example, with the TYPE command Ctrl-Num Lock interrupts the listing of a file. This key combination works like the other lock keys; press it again to resume normal operation.

The key combination **Ctrl-S** is often programmed to work in the same way as **Ctrl-Num Lock**.

The **Ins** and **Scroll Lock** keys do not modify other keys but do toggle bits in 0417h. Therefore, it can be useful to check their status. Many application programs use the **Ins** key to toggle between insert and overwrite modes, particularly when text is being entered. The **Scroll Lock** key is extremely under-used.

### Checking the key status

You can check the status of the modifying keys with function 02h of interrupt 16h.

| | |
|---|---|
| *Interrupt:* | 16h |
| *Function:* | 02h |
| *Service:* | Get keyboard status |
| *Entry values:* | AH=02h |
| *Exit values:* | AL=keyboard status byte |

Figure 6.2 shows a simple program that illustrates how the status may be checked and provides a display of the status bytes.

```
KEYTEST:        ;Tests KEYSTAT routine

        ;Calls DISSTR (8.10), NEWLIN (8.10),
        ;SCRENCLR (8.8), CUROFF (8.11)

        ;Cursor is switched off after program
        ;(badly behaved program!)

        jmp testst

message1        db '01234567$'
message2        db 'Press control keys to see'
                db 'effect or Ctrl-Break to end$'
message3        db 'Order of keys: 0 R-shift'
                db '1 L-shift  2 Ctrl       3 Alt$'
message4        db '4 Scroll Lock 5 Num Lock
                db '6 Caps Lock 7 Ins$'

testst:
        mov byte ptr status[08h],'$'  ;Store $ at
                                      ;end of STATUS
```

```
        call screnclr           ;Clear the screen
        call curoff             ;Switch off cursor
        call newlin
        lea dx,message1         ;Display instructions
        call dislin
        call newlin
        lea dx,message2
        call dislin
        lea dx,message3
        call dislin
        lea dx,message4
        call dislin
endlessloop:
        call keystat            ;Get status
        call newlin             ;Start new line
        call curstop            ;Move cursor to top
                                ;of screen
        lea dx,status
        call disstr             ;Display status
                                ;string
        jmp endlessloop         ;Program terminated
                                ;by Ctrl-Break

curstop:                        ;Move cursor to top
                                ;of screen
        mov ah,02h
        mov bh,00h
        mov dh,00h
        mov dl,00h
        int 10h
        ret

;-----------------------------------------

KEYSTAT:        ;Decode keyboard status

        ;Converts main keyboard status byte
        ;into individual characters for use
        ;by other routines
        ;Enhanced version stores characters to
        ;indicate which keys are pressed

        ;Entry values: None
        ;Exit values:  STATUS=8 bytes of status
        ;                             data
        ;              AX, CX, DI not saved

        jmp keyst

status        db 9 dup (?)  ;8 bytes for storing
                            ;results + space for
                            ;$
```

```
keyst:
        mov ah,02h
        int 16h                 ;Get keyboard status
        xor di,di
        xor cx,cx
        mov cl,08h              ;CL=8
getbit:
        rcr al,01h              ;Get next bit
        jc bitset               ;Jump if bit set
        mov status[di],00h      ;Otherwise, store 0
        jmp nextbit
bitset:
        mov status[di],01h      ;Store 1
nextbit:
        inc di                  ;Point to next byte
                                ;in STATUS
        loop getbit             ;Loop to get next bit
        ret
```

*Figure 6.2*

For full-sized keyboard (101 or 102 keys) there is an additional function to allow for the extra duplicates.

| | |
|---|---|
| *Interrupt:* | 16h |
| *Function:* | 12h |
| *Service:* | Get full-sized keyboard status (not early PCs) |
| *Entry values:* | AH=12h |
| *Exit values:* | AH=Second keyboard status byte<br>AL=First keyboard status byte |

The meaning of the two bytes is given in Figure 6.3. AL is identical to that for function 02h.

This function was not available on the earlier PCs.

**The key indicator lights**

Some keyboards (most, in fact, apart from the original IBM PC) have lights fitted into the key caps of the lock keys to indicate whether the status is on or off. These lights are a function of the hardware and come on or off automatically each time the key is pressed.

**Full-sized keyboard status bytes**

| First keyboard status byte (AL) | | Second keyboard status byte (AH) | |
|---|---|---|---|
| **Bit** | **Meaning if set** | **Bit** | **Meaning if set** |
| 7 | Insert on | 7 | Sys Req pressed |
| 6 | Caps Lock on | 6 | Caps Lock pressed |
| 5 | Num Lock on | 5 | Num Lock pressed |
| 4 | Scroll Lock on | 4 | Scroll Lock pressed |
| 3 | Alt pressed | 3 | Right Alt pressed |
| 2 | Ctrl pressed | 2 | Right Ctrl pressed |
| 1 | Left Shift pressed | 1 | Left Alt pressed |
| 0 | Right Shift pressed | 0 | Left Ctrl pressed |

*Figure 6.3*

The lights should reflect the current setting of the status bit. However, on PCs, it is possible to confuse the system by pressing the lock keys when interrupts are disabled, which is particularly easy during the system checks during booting. Once an indicator light gets out of step with the function of the key it remains so until the system is reset.

You may also find that the Shift status remains switched on occasionally, particularly if you manage to 'hide' the release code by some fast finger work. In this case, the letters will come out in capitals while all the symbols will produce the upper case characters even though no **Shift** key is being pressed. However, this problem will sort itself out the next time the **Shift** key is pressed.

On AT-compatibles and PS/2s you can change the status of the lock keys by updating the keyboard status bytes. On these machines, the indicator light is updated to match. This is useful if you want to turn **Num Lock** off when a program is started, for example.

## The special keys

When interrupt 09h detects a modifying key it adjusts the status bytes accordingly. No further action is taken.

If the key received is not one of the modifying keys, the interrupt routine first checks to see if the key that has been pressed, in combination with one of the modifying keys, produces one of the special key combinations. This will be the case when the status bits are set in a particular way.

### Ctrl-Break

When the **Scroll Lock/Break** key is pressed and the **Ctrl** key is being depressed, the routine issues a BIOS interrupt 1Dh. Initially, this is a dummy routine but DOS installs its own routine, pointed to by the interrupt vector. The routine address is also stored in DOS interrupt 23h. The Break key combination is used to interrupt the current operation.

When this key combination is detected, bit 7 of 0471h is also set. (Note that this byte is also used to store the boot status.) Its contents are not automatically cleared out, so if you want to make use of it in a program, you must make sure that you clear the byte at the beginning of the program and then clear it again after each Break combination has been detected.

The fact that the Break key combination has been pressed does not mean that action is taken immediately. As described below, the key combination is only effective if you are checking for it. Some DOS interrupts respond automatically to this key press, others ignore it.

The frequency with which DOS checks for the Break combination can be set in a variety of operations. Normally, DOS only checks for the Break key after any input or output but not during disk access. You can increase the frequency of checks either with the BREAK ON command or by inserting the `BREAK = ON` directive in CONFIG.SYS. Alternatively, you can increase the checks from within a program with function 33h of interrupt 21h.

| | |
|---|---|
| *Interrupt:* | 21h |
| *Function:* | 33h,00h |
| *Service:* | Get Ctrl-Break status |
| *Entry values:* | AH=33h |
| | AL=00h |
| *Exit values:* | AL=FFh (if entry code is invalid) |
| | DL= 00h (Ctrl-Break is off) |
| | 01h (Ctrl-Break is on) |

A variation of this interrupt turns the extra Break checking off.

| | |
|---|---|
| *Interrupt:* | 21h |
| *Function:* | 33h,01h |
| *Service:* | Set or clear Ctrl-Break operation |
| *Entry values:* | AH=33h |
| | AL=01h |
| | DL= 00h (Turn Ctrl-Break off) |
| | 01h (Turn Ctrl-Break on) |
| *Exit values:* | AL=FFh (if entry code is invalid) |

Many programs choose to treat **Ctrl-C** as having the same effect as **Ctrl-Break**.

**Shift-PrtSc**

When the **PrtSc** key is pressed, the interrupt 09h routine checks the **Shift** status. Here, the state of the **Caps Lock** key is ignored. If a **Shift** key is being pressed (or just **Print Screen** on the AT-compatibles), an interrupt 05h is generated.

| | |
|---|---|
| *Interrupt:* | 05h |
| *Service:* | Print screen |

The default interrupt 05h produces a screen dump if you are in a text screen mode. However, there are many programs that modify the effect of interrupt 05h; see Chapter 10 for further details.

**Ctrl-Alt-function key**

If either of the function keys **F1** or **F2** are pressed, the interrupt routine checks the **Ctrl** and **Alt** status. If both of these keys are also being depressed, the routine carries out a special action.

**Ctrl-Alt-F1** cancels the effect of the KEYBxx program. That is, the keyboard reverts to its natural state, producing the US key operations.

**Ctrl-Alt-F2** restores the standard KEYBxx action. For further details of the KEYBxx programs, see below.

### Ctrl-Alt-Del

This key combination is the really drastic one. If the **Del** key is pressed, the interrupt 09h routine checks the **Ctrl** and **Alt** status. If both of these are also being pressed, the program issues an interrupt 19h which reboots the computer. Further details can be found in Chapter 3.

### The Alt key

Interrupt 09h also includes a special routine for the **Alt** key. When the **Alt** key is pressed in combination with the keys on the number pad (but not the numeric keys at the top of the main QWERTY keypad), no immediate action is taken. However, the computer stores away the numeric keys as they are pressed, keeping the last three in a buffer. These last three numeric keys are treated as a three-digit decimal number and are stored in 0419h. When the **Alt** key is released, the three-digit code is treated as a standard ASCII code. For example, **Alt** with 1, 5 and 6 produces the hex value 9Ch (ASCII code 156), resulting in the £ symbol.

Since the data is stored in a single byte, the maximum is 255 (FFh) and any value above that is converted to a value mod 256. For example, **Alt-266** is the same as **Alt-010**. If less than three keys are pressed, the routine pads the ASCII code with leading zeros. In this way, you can produce the entire range of ASCII codes.

### Sys Req

When **Sys Req** is pressed on an 84-key keyboard, or **Alt-Sys Req** on the full-sized keyboard, the system sets AH=85h and then calls interrupt 15h. Initially this is a dummy routine.

## The keyboard translation table

As described above, the modifying keys adjust the status bytes, the special key combinations have routines of their own and any other release keys are thrown away. If the scan code makes it beyond this point, then it must be the code for a normal character key. The routine goes on to determine the ASCII character that corresponds to the key press. It does this by reference to the scan code and the first status byte (0417h). The result is shown in Figure 6.4, which shows the keyboard translation table that is used by the routine to produce an ASCII code from the various combinations of scan code and status bits.

The way in which the codes are treated is as follows:

- If the status byte is clear, the translated value can be found in the 'Unmodified' column.
- If the key is in the main QWERTY section and either the **Shift** key is pressed or **Caps Lock** is on (but not both), the result is found in the 'Shifted/Caps' column. If both **Shift** keys are pressed at the same time, the effect is that of a single **Shift** key; if either or both the **Shift** keys are pressed at the same time as **Caps Lock** is on, the keys cancel each other out and the key is effectively unmodified. For the QWERTY keys, the **Num Lock** key is irrelevant and therefore ignored.
- If the key is from the number pad, and either the **Shift** key is pressed or **Num Lock** is on (but not both), the 'Shifted/Num' column gives the result. If either of the **Shift** keys is pressed and the **Num Lock** is on as well, the modifying keys cancel each other out and the key is effectively unmodified. For the number pad keys, the status of the **Caps Lock** is irrelevant.
- If the **Ctrl** key is being pressed, the **Shift**, **Caps Lock** and **Num Lock** keys are ignored. **Ctrl** takes precedence over all of these. The results are

shown in the 'Ctrl' column of the translation table.

- If the **Alt** key is being depressed, the **Shift**, **Ctrl** **Caps Lock** and **Num Lock** keys are ignored; **Alt** takes precedence over everything. The results can be found in the 'Alt' column of the table.

The routine produces a two-byte word of data generally comprising the original scan code in the high byte and the corresponding ASCII code in the low byte. This has the advantage that two different results are produced for duplicate keys that produce the same ASCII value but have different scan codes (for example, the two asterisk (*) keys).

Where there is no ASCII code for the key, the low byte is 00h, or E0h for the extra keys on a full-sized keyboard. Therefore, if the word that is produced has a low byte of 00h or E0h, you know that a non-standard key is being pressed and you can find out which key it is by checking the high byte.

Note that the scan code in the high byte is modified in the following cases:

- Original scan code 01h to 0Dh when used in combination with **Alt**
- The function keys with **Shift**, **Ctrl** and **Alt**
- The keys of the number pad

This is because none of these keys has an ASCII equivalent, so each returns 00h in the low byte. The modification of the scan code allows you to distinguish between the different versions of these keys. Thus, if there is an ASCII code in the low byte, you can tell immediately what character key or control key has been pressed.

When **Alt** is used with a number pad combination, the system returns a single code word, regardless of the number of keys pressed. The high byte is 00h while the low byte is the ASCII code.

There may be some variations in the translation table for different machines, particularly for the additional keys on the full-sized keyboard.

**Keyboard translation table**

| Code | Key (UK) | Unmod-ified | Shifted /Caps | Shifted /Num | Ctrl | Alt |
|---|---|---|---|---|---|---|
| 01 | Esc | 011B | 011B | - | 011B | - |
| 02 | 1 ! | 0231 | 0221 | - | - | 7800 |
| 03 | 2 " | 0332 | 0340 | - | 0300 | 7900 |
| 04 | 3 # | 0433 | 0423 | - | - | 7A00 |
| 05 | 4 $ | 0534 | 0524 | - | - | 7B00 |
| 06 | 5 % | 0635 | 0625 | - | - | 7C00 |
| 07 | 6 ' | 0736 | 075E | - | 071E | 7D00 |
| 08 | 7 & | 0837 | 0826 | - | - | 7E00 |
| 09 | 8 * | 0938 | 092A | - | - | 7F00 |
| 0A | 9 ( | 0A39 | 0A28 | - | - | 8000 |
| 0B | 0 ) | 0B30 | 0B29 | - | - | 8100 |
| 0C | - _ | 0C2D | 0C5F | - | 0C1F | 8200 |
| 0D | = + | 0D3D | 0D2B | - | - | 8300 |
| 0E | ←Del | 0E08 | 0E08 | - | 0E7F | - |
| 0F | Tab | 0F09 | 0F00 | - | - | - |
| 10 | Q | 1071 | 1051 | - | 1011 | 1000 |
| 11 | W | 1177 | 1157 | - | 1117 | 1100 |
| 12 | E | 1265 | 1245 | - | 1205 | 1200 |
| 13 | R | 1372 | 1352 | - | 1312 | 1300 |
| 14 | T | 1474 | 1454 | - | 1414 | 1400 |
| 15 | Y | 1579 | 1559 | - | 1519 | 1500 |
| 16 | U | 1675 | 1655 | - | 1615 | 1600 |
| 17 | I | 1769 | 1749 | - | 1709 | 1700 |
| 18 | O | 186F | 184F | - | 180F | 1800 |
| 19 | P | 1970 | 1950 | - | 1910 | 1900 |
| 1A | [ { | 1A5B | 1A7B | - | 1A1B | - |
| 1B | ] } | 1B5D | 1B7D | - | 1B1D | - |
| 1C | Return | 1C0D | 1C0D | - | 1C0A | - |
| 1D | Ctrl | - | - | - | - | - |
| 1E | A | 1E61 | 1E41 | - | 1E01 | 1E00 |
| 1F | S | 1F73 | 1F53 | - | 1F13 | 1F00 |
| 20 | D | 2064 | 2044 | - | 2004 | 2000 |
| 21 | F | 2166 | 2146 | - | 2106 | 2100 |
| 22 | G | 2267 | 2247 | - | 2207 | 2200 |
| 23 | H | 2368 | 2348 | - | 2308 | 2300 |
| 24 | J | 246A | 244A | - | 240A | 2400 |
| 25 | K | 256B | 254B | - | 250B | 2500 |
| 26 | L | 266C | 264C | - | 260C | 2600 |
| 27 | ; : | 273B | 273A | - | - | - |
| 28 | ' @ | 2827 | 2822 | - | - | - |
| 29 | # ~ | 2960 | 297E | - | - | - |
| 2A | Left Shift | - | - | - | - | - |

| Code | Key (UK) | Unmod-ified | Shifted /Caps | Shifted /Num | Ctrl | Alt |
|---|---|---|---|---|---|---|
| 2B | \ \| | 2B5C | 2B7C | - | 2B1C | - |
| 2C | Z | 2C7A | 2C5A | - | 2C1A | 2C00 |
| 2D | X | 2D78 | 2D58 | - | 2D18 | 2D00 |
| 2E | C | 2E63 | 2E43 | - | 2E0F | 2E00 |
| 2F | V | 2F76 | 2F56 | - | 2F16 | 2F00 |
| 30 | B | 3062 | 3042 | - | 3002 | 3000 |
| 31 | N | 316E | 314E | - | 310E | 3100 |
| 32 | M | 326D | 324D | - | 320D | 3200 |
| 33 | , | 332C | 333C | - | - | - |
| 34 | . | 342E | 343E | - | - | - |
| 35 | / ? | 352F | 353F | - | - | - |
| 36 | Right Shift | - | - | - | - | - |
| 37 | PrtSc | 372A | PrtSc | - | 7200 | - |
| 38 | Alt | - | - | - | - | - |
| 39 | Space | 3920 | 3920 | - | 3920 | 3920 |
| 3A | Caps Lock | - | - | - | - | - |
| 3B | F1 | 3B00 | 5400 | - | 5E00 | 6800 |
| 3C | F2 | 3C00 | 5500 | - | 5F00 | 6900 |
| 3D | F3 | 3D00 | 5600 | - | 6000 | 6A00 |
| 3E | F4 | 3E00 | 5700 | - | 6100 | 6B00 |
| 3F | F5 | 3F00 | 5800 | - | 6200 | 6C00 |
| 40 | F6 | 4000 | 5900 | - | 6300 | 6D00 |
| 41 | F7 | 4100 | 5A00 | - | 6400 | 6E00 |
| 42 | F8 | 4200 | 5B00 | - | 6500 | 6F00 |
| 43 | F9 | 4300 | 5C00 | - | 6600 | 7000 |
| 44 | F10 | 4400 | 5D00 | - | 6700 | 7100 |
| 45 | Num Lock | - | - | - | Pause | - |
| 46 | Scroll Lock | - | - | - | Break | - |
| 47 | Key Pad 7 | 4700 | - | 4737 | 7700 | - |
| 48 | Key Pad 8 | 4800 | - | 4838 | - | - |
| 49 | Key Pad 9 | 4900 | - | 4939 | 8400 | - |
| 4A | Key Pad - | 4A2D | - | 4A2D | - | - |
| 4B | Key Pad 4 | 4B00 | - | 4B34 | 7300 | - |
| 4C | Key Pad 5 | - | - | 4C35 | - | - |
| 4D | Key Pad 6 | 4D00 | - | 4D36 | 7400 | - |
| 4E | Key Pad + | 4E2B | - | 4E2B | - | - |
| 4F | Key Pad 1 | 4F00 | - | 4F31 | 7500 | - |
| 50 | Key Pad 2 | 5000 | - | 5032 | - | - |
| 51 | Key Pad 3 | 5100 | - | 5133 | 7600 | - |
| 52 | Key Pad 0 | 5200 | - | 5230 | - | - |
| 53 | Key Pad . | 5300 | - | 532E | - | - |
| 54 | Sys Req | - | - | - | - | - |
| 55-7F | | Not used | | | | |

**Full-sized keyboards**

| Code | Key |
|---|---|
| 54 | Alt-Print Screen |
| 57 | F11 |
| 58 | F12 |
| E0 10 | Right Ctrl |
| E0 1C | Key Pad Enter |
| E0 36 | Key Pad / |
| E0 38 | Right Alt |
| E0 40 | Cursor Pad → |
| E0 47 | Cursor Pad Home |
| E0 48 | Cursor Pad ↑ |
| E0 49 | Cursor Pad Page Up |
| E0 4B | Cursor Pad ← |
| E0 4F | Cursor Pad End |
| E0 50 | Cursor Pad ↓ |
| E0 51 | Cursor Pad Page Down |
| E0 52 | Cursor Pad Insert |
| E0 53 | Cursor Pad Delete |
| E0 10 45 | Pause |
| E0 2A E0 37 | Print Screen |

(For interpretation of duplicates, see above)

*Figure 6.4*

**The keyboard buffer**

If the scan code/ASCII code word has made it through the system this far, it is stored in RAM in an area called the *keyboard buffer*. This buffer begins at 041Eh and is allocated 32 bytes of RAM, enough for 16 characters. The physical start of the buffer (as an offset from 0400h) is stored in 0480h. The physical end of the buffer is identified by 0482h. Therefore, you can increase the buffer size by changing the location of the buffer in 0480h and its finishing point in 0482h. This change can be made without having to alter interrupt 09h at all.

Each new character that is received from the keyboard controller is placed in the buffer in sequence. The byte at 041Ah points to the next character waiting in the buffer. 041Ch points to the next space to fill in the buffer. When a character is used, 041Ah is updated; when a new character is added, 041Ch is updated. The character remains in the buffer, of course, but can now be overwritten. The buffer is used on a rotational basis; when the last byte has been filled, the next keypress is stored back at the beginning of the buffer.

When the buffer is full any new character that is received before a gap has been created is discarded by interrupt 09h and the computer beeps.

You can force a keypress into the buffer with function 05h of interrupt 16h. Before calling the function place the scan code/ASCII code combination (as shown in Figure 6.3) in CX.

---

| | |
|---|---|
| *Interrupt:* | 16h |
| *Function:* | 05h |
| *Service:* | Put keypress in buffer (not early PCs) |
| *Entry values:* | AH=05h |
| | CH=Scan code |
| | CL=ASCII code |
| *Exit values:* | AL= 00h (success) |
| | 01h (failure) |

---

This function has no effect when the buffer is full. It is also ineffective on some of the earlier PCs and is not implemented on some PC-compatibles.

## The KEYB programs

The complications of the keyboard don't end here. Computers sold in different countries are provided with different keyboards. The number of keys and their positions is the same, but the operation of particular keys may vary from one keyboard to another. For example, on the UK keyboard the combination **Shift-2** (using the numeric key at the top of the keyboard) shows the " symbol (ASCII 22h); the same key on a US keyboard has an @ symbol (ASCII 40h).

In fact, all keyboards produce the same scan codes for the same keys. **Shift-2** gives the scan code 03h whether it is a US or UK keyboard. All that is different physically is the key caps. Therefore, you can expect to get the same result regardless of what keyboard is plugged into the PC.

To get different characters, you need a different translation table. This is the task of the KEYB programs. For example, KEYBUK (or KEYB UK) loads a translation table that converts **Shift-2** into a code of 0322h rather than 0340h. If there is no KEYB program installed, **Shift-2** produces the code 0340h, regardless of keyboard.

As a result, programs should not use the scan codes, unless absolutely necessary, as they may not have the desired effect. (If you are waiting for the user to press the @ key, you will have to check for different scan codes for different keyboards. If you test for the ASCII value of 40h, however, the result will be the same on all keyboards, provided the correct KEYB program is installed.)

Both the translation tables – the default (US) table and the KEYBxx table – are stored in memory. The user can switch between them with the **Ctrl-Alt-F1** and **Ctrl-Alt-F2** combinations.

A number of KEYB program exist and modify a varying number of keys. Some of the modifications produce the extended ASCII characters. For example, **Shift-3** on the US keyboard is 0423h (ASCII 23h = #); on the UK keyboard the same key produces 049Ch (ASCII 9Ch = £).

The combination of **Alt** with the number pad is unaffected by the KEYB programs. **Alt-35** (23h) always produces the # symbol while **Alt-156** (9Ch) always gives a £. Remember that you can tell whether an ASCII code is being produced by a normal key or an Alt code by whether or not the scan code is 00h.

What happens on the screen depends on the character table that is loaded (see Chapter 8). If you have not loaded the correct character table for the keyboard, the effect is still apparently wrong. The same can be said for the printer, which may produce different characters for the same codes, depending on the settings of dip switches.

## Duplicate keys

One of the uses for the scan codes is to detect duplicates. A number of keys – the **Shift** keys, **Return/Enter**, **Del** (on some machines), the arrow keys (on AT-compatibles), the arithmetic symbols, and so on – are duplicated on the keyboard. The duplicate keys produce the same ASCII code but *different* scan codes.

It is useful to know which physical key has produced an ASCII code in some circumstances, particularly when invoking TSRs (where you might want to specify that the user has pressed a particular **Shift** key). You can identify a specific key by reference to the scan code.

## Key repeats

When a key is pressed, a scan code is sent to the keyboard controller. The controller issues the corresponding translation code and then keeps track of the time until it receives either the key release code or another scan code. After half a second, if no other code is received, the original translation code is issued. Thereafter, on a standard PC keyboard, the translation code is sent ten times a second (nearly 11 on the PS/2s). The controller keeps this up until either the key is released or another key is pressed. In the event of a second key being pressed, the controller conveniently forgets the original key and repeats the new key if necessary.

The result is that a string of key codes is quickly placed in the buffer. For ordinary keys, these are treated as a string of normal key presses (since the release code is ignored in the normal course of events anyway). For the standard modifying keys, this string of repeats makes no difference; the status bit is set when a **Shift** key is depressed, for example, so repeating it makes no difference. For a lock key, on the other hand, the value is toggled each time the key is pressed.

On the PC, this repeat action is fixed. For AT-compatibles and PS/2s you can vary the delay before the repeat starts and the repeat frequency.

| | |
|---|---|
| *Interrupt:* | 16h |
| *Function:* | 03h |
| *Service:* | Set key repeat values (AT, PS/2) |
| *Entry values:* | AH=03h |
| | AL=05h |
| | BH=delay time |
| | BL=repeat rate |
| *Exit values:* | None |

The values for BX are shown in Figure 6.5.

**Repeat rates**

| BH (hex): | 00 | 01 | 02 | 03 |
|---|---|---|---|---|
| Delay (seconds): | ¼ | ½ | ¾ | 1 |

| BL (hex): | 00 | 01 | 02 | 03 | 04 | 05 | 06 | 07 |
|---|---|---|---|---|---|---|---|---|
| Repeats/sec: | 30.0 | 26.7 | 24.0 | 21.8 | 20.0 | 18.5 | 17.1 | 16.0 |
| BL (hex): | 08 | 09 | 0A | 0B | 0C | 0D | 0E | 0F |
| Repeats/sec: | 15.0 | 13.3 | 12.0 | 10.9 | 10.0 | 9.2 | 8.6 | 8.0 |
| BL (hex): | 10 | 11 | 12 | 13 | 14 | 15 | 16 | 17 |
| Repeats/sec: | 7.5 | 6.7 | 6.0 | 5.5 | 5.0 | 4.6 | 4.3 | 4.0 |
| BL (hex): | 18 | 19 | 1A | 1B | 1C | 1D | 1E | 1F |
| Repeats/sec: | 3.7 | 3.3 | 3.0 | 2.7 | 2.5 | 2.3 | 2.1 | 2.0 |

*Figure 6.5*

## Keyboard functions

Almost all data originates at the keyboard; even programs have to be input before they are stored on disk. Therefore, it is surprising perhaps that, unless you modify interrupt 09h to treat certain keys differently, there is really only one thing you can do: get a character from the buffer. BIOS interrupt 16h provides two alternatives.

DOS provides a little more variety in its keyboard functions, but they are essentially the same as the standard BIOS functions with a few extras thrown in. The BIOS functions are very pure, operating on only one item of hardware at a time. The DOS functions have no such scruples, and will happily mix calls to several devices in a single service routine. By including the code to display a character on the screen, the DOS keyboard functions provide the option to echo on the screen the character as it is collected from the keyboard buffer.

The DOS functions are split between those that respond to **Ctrl-Break** and those that ignore it.

## Getting a character

The next character in the keyboard can be extracted with function 00h of interrupt 16h.

| | |
|---|---|
| *Interrupt:* | 16h |
| *Function:* | 00h |
| *Service:* | Read character from keyboard |
| *Entry values:* | AH=00h |
| *Exit values:* | AH=scan code |
| | AL=ASCII code |

This function simply reads the code from the relevant part of memory, where the buffer is stored. At the same time, the routine updates the pointers so that the next time it is called, it will automatically pick up the next character in the buffer. (The character that has been read remains in memory, of course, until overwritten.)

If the buffer is empty, this function waits for a key press.

This function has the advantage that it returns the full word of data (including both the scan code and ASCII value). Therefore you can tell exactly which key has been pressed at any time. This allows you to distinguish between the **Ctrl**, **Alt**, **Alt**-keypad, function and cursor keys, as well as normal key presses.

To get a character but not wait when the buffer is empty, use the alternative reporting function described later.

**Full-sized keyboards**

For full-sized keyboards (with 101 or 102 keys), function 00h either ignores the extra keys or ignores the differences between duplicates. Later PCs have an additional interrupt 16h service which allows them to interpret these extra codes (as shown in the last section of Figure 6.3).

---

| | |
|---|---|
| *Interrupt:* | 16h |
| *Function:* | 10h |
| *Service:* | Read character from full-sized keyboard (not early PCs) |
| *Entry values:* | AH=10h |
| *Exit values:* | AH=scan code<br>AL=ASCII code |

---

**Getting a key (via DOS)**

The first DOS function to get a key press is 07h.

---

| | |
|---|---|
| *Interrupt:* | 21h |
| *Function:* | 07h |
| *DOS version:* | 1 |
| *Service:* | Keyboard input without echo (without Break) |
| *Entry values:* | AH=07h |
| *Exit values:* | AL=character |

---

Using this function is a two-stage process. The function initially returns the ASCII code for the key press. If this is greater than 0, the function reads and discards the scan code (so if you need to detect the difference between two keys with the same ASCII code, you must resort to the BIOS routine).

If the ASCII code is 0, however, the scan code is left in the buffer and you must follow on with a second call to the same function. This returns the scan code. You need to repeat this call following an ASCII 0 even if you don't want the scan code; otherwise, the buffer will be out of step.

The function waits for a key press but does not allow the wait to be interrupted by the **Break** key. It does not echo the character to the screen.

**Getting a key, with Break**

Function 08h is very similar to function 07h, the only difference being that you can interrupt this function by pressing **Ctrl-Break** while it is waiting for a key press.

---

*Interrupt:* 21h
*Function:* 08h
*DOS version:* 1
*Service:* Keyboard input without echo (with Break)
*Entry values:* AH=08h
*Exit values:* AL=character

---

**Getting a key, with echo**

The third function in this group waits for a key press, allows the **Break** key to be effective and has the added feature that it echoes the ASCII character on the screen.

---

*Interrupt:* 21h
*Function:* 01h
*DOS version:* 1
*Service:* Keyboard input with echo (with Break)
*Entry values:* AH=01h
*Exit values:* AL=character

---

Each of these functions is useful in particular circumstances. The program in Figure 6.6 illustrates the use of function 01h. Simply change the value being put into AH if you do not want the key press echoed or wish to switch off the **Break** key.

---

```
GETNUMKY:        ;Get a number from a key press

        ;Entry values: CL=max. number (0 - 9)

nexkey:
       mov ah,07h
       int 21h                   ;Get a key press
       cmp al,00h
       jg notspk                 ;Jump if not special
                                 ;code
```

```
     int 21h                 ;Otherwise, get scan
                             ;code for special
     jmp nexkey              ;and get another key

notspk:
     cmp al,30h              ;Is key before
                             ;numbers?
     jl nexkey               ;Jump if ASCII code
                             ; 30h ('0')
     sub al,30h              ;Get key value
     cmp al,cl               ;Is it less than Ch?
     jg nexkey               ;If not, get another
     ret

;-------------------------------------------------

GETYN:      ;Get Y or N after prompt

             ;Calls DISSTR (8.10)

             ;Entry values: None
             ;Exit values:  AL=0 for Y, 1 for N

     jmp ynst

prompt      db 'Are you sure (Y/N)?$'

ynst:
     lea dx,prompt
     call disstr
nexyn:
     mov ah,07h
     ;mov ah,08h             ;Alternative, if
                             ;break key allowed
     int 21h                 ;Get key press
     cmp al,60h              ;Is it upper case?
     jl ucase                ;If yes, skip
     sub al,20h              ;Else, convert to
                             ;upper case
ucase:
     sub al,59h              ;Is it Y?
     jz yes                  ;Jump if so (in
                             ;which case AL=0)
     add al,59h
     cmp al,4Eh              ;Is it N?
     jnz nexyn               ;If not, get another
     mov al,01h              ;If so, set AL=1
yes:
     ret
```

*Figure 6.6*

## Reporting the next character

A variation of the functions described so far reads a character from the keyboard but does not change the buffer. In effect, these functions tell you what key is waiting there but don't actually fetch it.

| | |
|---|---|
| *Interrupt:* | 16h |
| *Function:* | 01h |
| *Service:* | Read character if available |
| *Entry values:* | AH=01h |
| *Exit values:* | AH=scan code<br>AL=ASCII code<br>ZF= 0 (character available)<br>1 (buffer empty) |

With this BIOS function, the zero flag tells you whether or not there is a character; if there is, AX gives the complete word of data, including scan code and ASCII value.

This function is useful if you want to get a character from the keyboard but don't want the program tied up waiting if there isn't one; if the zero flag states that there is a character waiting, you can follow on immediately with a call to function 00h.

This function is also useful if you want to process some routine until a key is pressed.

### Full-sized keyboards

As for function 00h, there is another function available on all but the earliest machines which allows for the extra keys on the full-sized keyboard.

| | |
|---|---|
| *Interrupt:* | 16h |
| *Function:* | 11h |
| *Service:* | Read character from full-sized keyboard (not early PCs) |
| *Entry values:* | AH=11h |
| *Exit values:* | AH=scan code<br>AL=ASCII code<br>ZF= 0 (character available)<br>1 (buffer empty) |

**Reporting characters with DOS**

The DOS equivalent is function 0Bh of interrupt 21h.

---

*Interrupt:* 21h
*Function:* 0Bh
*DOS version:* 1
*Service:* Check keyboard buffer
*Entry values:* AH=0Bh
*Exit values:* AL= 00h (buffer empty)
FFh (character available)

---

You can set up a loop to test the keyboard buffer, which may be interrupted with **Ctrl-Break**.

## Combining keyboard and screen operations

DOS provides one rather odd function, which is used either for keyboard input or screen output, depending on how it is set up.

---

*Interrupt:* 21h
*Function:* 06h
*DOS version:* 1
*Service:* Keyboard input (see also Chapter 8)
*Entry values:* AH=06h
DL=FFh
*Exit values:* AL=input character
ZF= 0 (character available)
1 (buffer empty)

---

This peculiar hybrid reports the character waiting in the buffer if DL is set to FFh. The zero flag tells you whether or not there is a key; if there is, the ASCII code is in AL. If AL returns a value of 00h, indicating a specal key, you must repeat the call to the interrupt to get the scan code.

If DL is set to any value other than FFh, the corresponding ASCII character is displayed on the screen, as described in Chapter 8.

## Clearing the keyboard buffer

While a program is running, any key presses are added to the keyboard buffer. If you want to clear the buffer – for example, so that extra keys pressed while a menu is being drawn are ignored – you can use a routine that repeats functions 00h and 01h of interrupt 16h until the buffer is empty (see Figure 6.7).

Alternatively, you can use DOS function 0Ch.

| | |
|---|---|
| *Interrupt:* | 21 |
| *Function:* | 0Ch |
| *DOS version:* | 1 |
| *Service:* | Clear keyboard buffer, call interrupt 21h function |
| *Entry values:* | AH=0Ch<br>AL=function (01, 06, 07, 08, 0A) |
| *Exit values:* | (Various - as for selected function) |

This function is rather curious, in that it reads and discards the entire buffer, then waits for a key press by calling one of the other keyboard interrupts. The secondary function number is placed in AL. The results of that call are the same as before. If you don't want to wait for a key press, you can put a value in DL and request a call to function 06h.

```
BUFRCLR:        ;Clear the buffer

      ;Entry values: None
      ;Exit values: Flags changed

nextchar:
      mov ah,01h
      int 16h                    ;Check buffer
      jnz empty                  ;Jump if no character
                                 ;available
      mov al, 00h                ;Otherwise, read
                                 ;character
      int 16h
      jmp nextchar               ;and repeat loop
empty:
      ret
```

*Figure 6.7*

## String input

To get a string of text from the keyboard, using only the BIOS routines, you must devise a routine that repeats function 00h of interrupt 16h until the **Return** key is pressed. To be really useful, it must take account of the **Backspace** key being pressed. However, there is little point in re-inventing the wheel (though must programmers do so at least once in their careers!) and life is much easier if you use DOS function 0Ah.

---

| | |
|---|---|
| *Interrupt:* | 21h |
| *Function:* | 0Ah |
| *Service:* | Keyboard string input |
| *Entry values:* | AH=0Ah |
| | DS:DX=start of input buffer |
| *Exit values:* | None |

---

This does all the hard work for you. You must specify a data buffer to receive the incoming text in DS:DX. The first character of the buffer must hold the maximum length of text to be allowed, including one character for the carriage return. The maximum length is 255 characters, including the **Return** character. Since the input is terminated by **Return**, only one string is allowed at a time.

When the user types in the string, the **Backspace** or ← key can be used to rub out the last character. The entry is terminated by the **Return** key or can be abandoned by **Ctrl-Break**. If the full length is reached before **Return** is pressed, the computer beeps and the extra character is ignored.

When the entry is complete, DOS stores the length of the typed string (including the carriage return) in the second byte of the data buffer. The text itself starts at the third byte. Therefore, the space that needs to be set aside for this buffer is three characters more than the actual text length.

You cannot restrict the type of entry that can be made with this function (for example, you cannot insist on a numeric entry), except by validating the input afterwards and forcing the user to re-enter if necessary. If you want to validate text as it is typed in, you must design your own character-based input routine. The program in Figure 6.8 uses the standard routine to input a filename and extension.

```
GETFNAME:       ;Get a filename

      ;Limitations - no error checking
      ;Calls DISSTR (Fig 8.10)
      ;Entry values: None
      ;Exit values:  FNAME=filename
      ;              AX,DX,DI changed

      jmp getfnamest

entry:
inlen         db 0Dh
rtlen         db ?
fname         db ? dup 0Dh
fnmes         db 'Enter file name: $'

getfnamest:
      lea dx,fnmes            ;Point to FNMES
      call disstr             ;Display prompt
      lea dx,entry            ;Point to ENTRY
      mov ah,0Ah
      int 21h                 ;Get name from user
      ret
;-----------------------------------------------
FNAMETEST:       ;Test routine to get filename

      ;Calls GETFNAME, DISSTR, NEWLIN
      ;              (Figure 8.10)

      call getfname
      mov al,[rtlen]          ;Get length of name
      xor ah,ah
      mov di,ax
      mov fname[di],24h       ;Add '$' to name
      lea dx,fname            ;Point to name
      call newlin
      call disstr             ;Display name
      int 20h
```

*Figure 6.8*

# 7 Other Input Devices

This chapter looks at input devices other than the keyboard: the mouse, light pen and joystick. Of these, the mouse is by far the most widely used and has the greatest number of possibilities.

## The mouse

Most modern PCs are equipped with a mouse as standard. The device consists of a roller, the movement of which is converted into a set of co-ordinates that eventually result in the movement of a pointer on the screen. The mouse is fitted with two or more buttons, which can be treated like special key presses.

There are two types of mouse:

- The *bus mouse* comes with most of the components fitted onto a card, which fits into one of the PC's expansion slots. The data is transferred along the expansion bus.
- The *serial mouse* has everything fitted within the mouse itself, the cable from the mouse plugging into the serial socket.

There are many different types of mouse available but the principles are generally the same. This chapter concentrates on the industry-standard Microsoft-compatible features. There should be very few differences between these and most other breeds of mouse.

### Installing the mouse

In order to make use of a mouse, you must install the mouse driver in memory. To do this, include a directive in the CONFIG.SYS file in the form:

```
DEVICE = MOUSE.SYS
```

When the computer is booted, the device driver is installed in memory. You then need to run the MOUSE.COM program, which replaces two interrupts with special mouse interrupts.

Firstly, interrupt 08h is replaced with another interrupt that produces clock ticks every 0.018 seconds, three times the normal rate. The result is smoother movement of the mouse pointer on the screen. The programmable interrupt controller has counter 0 programmed to produce an interrupt at the same rate. This may cause timing problems with some applications.

Secondly, interrupt 06h is installed as the mouse button interrupt. Initially, this is a dummy routine but you can replace it with your own routine, as described later.

Once installed, you can use the DOS mouse interrupt 33h. Note that the mouse function is selected by the value in AL, not AH (which must always be 0).

**Initialising the mouse**

When the mouse is installed, it is automatically initialised. The various mouse parameters are set to their defaults, as shown in Figure 7.1.

**Mouse parameter defaults**

| Parameter | Default |
|---|---|
| X counter | 0 |
| Y counter | 0 |
| Mickey:pixel ratios: | |
| Horizontal | 8:8 |
| Vertical | 16:8 |
| Mode | Text |
| Text cursor | Reverse character |
| Cursor position | Centre of screen |
| Graphics cursor | Arrow |
| Cursor visibility | Hidden |
| Focal point | -1,-1 |
| Screen Mask | 0000 |
| Horizontal limits | 0,639 |
| Vertical limits | 0,199 |
| Light pen emulation | On |

*Figure 7.1*

The mouse can be re-initialised at any time so that the original defaults are restored, with interrupt 33h, function 00h.

| | |
|---|---|
| *Interrupt:* | 33h |
| *Function:* | 00h |
| *Service:* | Initialise mouse |
| *Entry values:* | AX=0000h |
| *Exit values:* | AL= FFh (mouse installed) |
| | 00h (no mouse found) |
| | BL=number of buttons |

## Mouse movement

When the mouse is moved, the roller turns three smaller wheels, which send values to the internal mouse circuits. From the values it receives, the mouse program is able to calculate the horizontal and vertical movement that has taken place. The movement relative to any starting point is stored as a pair of (x,y) co-ordinates. Of course, the mouse has no idea where the corresponding pointer is on the screen, so the co-ordinates are reset each time they are read by the PC. Therefore the co-ordinates represent the position relative to the last call. If you are programming for a mouse, you must make sure that the co-ordinates are read often enough for them to be cleared, otherwise the values will overflow.

The co-ordinates are integer counters, each unit representing movement of approximately 1/200th of an inch (1/8th millimetre) either horizontally or vertically. Unfortunately, this unit of movement is called the *mickey*. One mickey either horizontally or vertically changes the counter for that direction by 1. The counters are stored in words, so each may be in the range -32768 to +32767. This gives movement of over 13 inches in any direction; it sounds a lot but remember that picking up the mouse, moving it back to the start and then repeating the movement goes undetected by the mouse circuits; in this case, the count continues to increase.

The direction of movement affects the counters as follows:

| | |
|---|---|
| Move right | Increments X counter |
| Move left | Decrements X counter |
| Move forward | Increments Y counter |
| Move backwards | Decrements Y counter |

If you are holding the mouse the right way up, moving the mouse forward translates into pointer movement up the screen.

The counter values are stored in ports 78h (X) and 7Ah (Y). Reading the ports clears their values.

The best approach is to read the mouse counters with function 0Bh of interrupt 33h.

---

| | |
|---|---|
| *Interrupt:* | 33h |
| *Function:* | 0Bh |
| *Service:* | Read mouse counts |
| *Entry values:* | AX=000Bh |
| *Exit values:* | CX=X count |
| | DX=Y count |

---

This function gives the amount of movement in each direction since the interrupt was last called and clears the counters.

## The mouse cursor

The appearance of the mouse 'cursor' on screen depends upon the current display mode:

- In text modes, the pointer is an inverse character, which moves from character to character as you move the mouse.
- In graphics modes, the cursor defaults to an arrow-shaped pointer, the tip of which can be moved from pixel to pixel.

In the normal course of events, you don't need to worry about the movement of the pointer. When the mouse has been enabled, its movement is automatically translated into screen movement by the mouse driver.

The position of the pointer on the screen is determined by another set of co-ordinates, which give an absolute position on the screen. Horizontally, these co-ordinates run from 0 to 639, vertically from 0 to 199. This maximum range is always the same, regardless of the screen mode. You can convert the mouse co-ordinates ($x_m$,$y_m$) to the screen position ($x_s$,$y_s$) with the following formulae:

$$x_s = \frac{x_m \times m_c}{640} \qquad y_s = \frac{y_m \times m_r}{200}$$

where:

$m_c$ = maximum number of columns
$m_r$ = maximum number of rows

The result is always rounded down to the next integer. Note that the co-ordinates start at 0 in each case.

This formula works for both text and graphics modes. For example, in an 80 x 25 CGA text mode, with an 8x8 character matrix, the row = $y_m/8$ and column = $x_m/8$. Therefore, any pair of mouse co-ordinates from (632,192) to (639,199) translates to row 24, column 79: that is, the bottom right-hand character.

A similar conversion can be used to translate the original mouse counters to the mouse co-ordinates.

You can set the position of the cursor with mouse function 04h.

---

*Interrupt:* 33h
*Function:* 04h
*Service:* Set mouse cursor
*Entry values:* AX=0004h
CX=X co-ordinate
DX=Y co-ordinate
*Exit values:* None

---

**The mouse pointer window**

In some circumstances you will want to restrict the area of the screen within which the mouse pointer can move. Initially, the window for the mouse pointer is the whole screen. The window can be reduced with functions 07h and 08h.

---

| | |
|---|---|
| *Interrupt:* | 33h |
| *Function:* | 07h |
| *Service:* | Set mouse cursor horizontal limits |
| *Entry values:* | AX=0007h |
| | CX=minimum X co-ordinate |
| | DX=maximum X co-ordinate |
| *Exit values:* | None |

---

| | |
|---|---|
| *Interrupt:* | 33h |
| *Function:* | 08h |
| *Service:* | Set mouse cursor vertical limits |
| *Entry values:* | AX=0008h |
| | CX=minimum Y co-ordinate |
| | DX=maximum Y co-ordinate |
| *Exit values:* | None |

---

For each of these functions you must supply the mouse (not the screen) co-ordinates.

**The mickey:pixel ratio**

By default, each mickey of movement from left to right results in a change of 1 on the screen X co-ordinates. This is the mickey:pixel ratio. The ratio relates to the CGA screen so a 1:1 mickey:pixel ratio will give a different number of pixels for different screens.

The default vertical ratio is 2:1. You need to move the mouse two mickeys forward or backwards to move the pointer one pixel up or down the screen.

The mickey:pixel ratio can be changed with function 0Fh.

---

| | |
|---|---|
| *Interrupt:* | 33h |
| *Function:* | 0Fh |
| *Service:* | Set mickey:pixel ratio |
| *Entry values:* | AX=000Fh |
| | CX=X ratio (per 8 units) |
| | DX=Y ratio (per 8 units) |
| *Exit values:* | None |

---

Values are given here in terms of the number of mickeys per eight pixels. Therefore, the default ratio is 8:8 horizontally and 16:8 vertically. It is changed by setting the number of mickeys for each 8 pixels horizontally or vertically. For example, putting 4 in CX changes the horizontal ratio to 4:8 so that each four units of movement translate to 8 pixels and the cursor moves twice as fast across the screen.

**Mouse pointer speed**

As you move the mouse, the driver calculates its speed in terms of mickeys per second. When the mouse reaches a certain threshold value, the mouse driver doubles the speed at which the cursor moves across the screen. The default threshold is 64 mickeys per second but this can be changed with function 13h.

---

*Interrupt:* 33h
*Function:* 13h
*Service:* Set threshold for double speed
*Entry values:* AX=0013h
DX=threshold speed
(mickeys/second)
*Exit values:* None

---

A low value results in the pointer moving more rapidly at lower mouse speeds; setting the threshold very high results in a constant speed regardless of how quickly you move the mouse. There is a special case, when DX=0, whereby the threshold takes its default value.

## Mouse appearance

The appearance of the mouse cursor is affected by the values of two *masks*:

- The *screen mask* sets the shape of the cursor
- The *cursor mask* sets the relative attributes

The masks are each a word in length but the individual bits in each word have an important role to play.

**Text modes**

There are two options for the way in which the mouse cursor appears when in text mode. The first option is to use a *software cursor*. When the cursor is placed on the screen, the appearance is calculated for each byte of screen data as follows:

- First, a logical AND between the screen mask and data (both attribute and character) is carried out.
- Second, there is a logical XOR between the result and the cursor mask.

This sounds a great deal more complicated than it is. In fact, there are a limited number of options if you want a 'sensible' cursor. Each of the masks should be either 00h or FFh.

The second option is a *hardware cursor*. This simply consists of a flashing block, as for the normal hardware text cursor. The size of this block is determined by the raster lines that are covered, as for the normal cursor (see Chapter 8).

You can set the masks or cursor size with function 0Ah of interrupt 33h.

---

| | |
|---|---|
| *Interrupt:* | 33h |
| *Function:* | 0Ah |
| *Service:* | Define mouse text cursor |
| *Entry values:* | AX=000Ah |
| | BL= 00h (Software cursor) |
| | 01h (Hardware cursor) |
| | CX= Screen mask (BL=0) |
| | First scan line (BL=1) |
| | DX=Cursor mask (BL=0) |
| | Last scan line (BL=1) |
| *Exit values:* | None |

---

Note that the cursor type is set in BL.

**Graphics modes**

In screen graphics modes, the mouse cursor consists of a pointer that covers a 16 x 16 block of pixels. The screen mask and cursor mask are each 16 words in length, with one word corresponding to each line of the cursor block. The words correspond to the lines of pixels from top to bottom; the bits in each word relate to the pixels from left to right along the line.

When creating the cursor, the same logical operations are carried out as for the text cursor: there is a logical AND between the existing screen data and the screen mask, followed by an XOR between the result and the cursor mask. From this, you can deduce that a 1 in the screen mask means that the pixel is included in the cursor shape, a 0 excludes it. Within the cursor shape, the colour is set to either logical colour 0 or 1 by the corresponding value in the cursor mask. Outside the cursor shape, the pixel stays the same if the corresponding bit in the cursor mask is 0, otherwise its colour is inverted.

Although this may appear to give great flexibility, there is actually very little leeway if the pointer is not to become a complete mess. The shape of the pointer is set by the screen mask; the colour of the pointer and background rectangle on which it sits are set by the cursor mask. There are therefore only four main options for the cursor mask:

- A mask of all 0s results in a black pointer on an invisible box.
- A mask of all 1s gives a white pointer, with the background inverted.
- If the cursor mask is identical to the screen mask, the result is a white pointer on an invisible box.
- If the cursor mask is the inverse of the screen mask, the pointer is black and the background is inverted.

With care, you can combine these options to produce a more varied result but make sure that the cursor does not become too untidy.

**The focal point**

The pointer in graphics modes covers a very large area. Therefore, you must define which of the 256 pixels covered by the rectangle is the one actually being pointed to. This is the *focal point*. The default is the top left-hand corner of the pointer block; thus for the default arrow pointer, the focal point is the tip of the arrow.

Any new focal point is calculated as an offset from the top-left corner, measured to the right and down.

### Defining the graphics cursor

The complete cursor is defined with function 09h. Before calling this function, you must point to the 64 bytes of the mask with ES:DX.

---

| | |
|---|---|
| *Interrupt:* | 33h |
| *Function:* | 09h |
| *Service:* | Define mouse graphics cursor |
| *Entry values:* | AX=0009h |
| | BX=X co-ordinate offset |
| | CX=Y co-ordinate offset |
| | ES:DX=address of screen and cursor masks |
| *Exit values:* | None |

---

### Turning the mouse cursor on and off

The display of the mouse cursor (in either text or graphics modes) is turned on with function 01h.

---

| | |
|---|---|
| *Interrupt:* | 33h |
| *Function:* | 01h |
| *Service:* | Show mouse cursor |
| *Entry values:* | AX=0001h |
| *Exit values:* | None |

---

Similarly, you can turn the mouse cursor off with function 02h.

---

| | |
|---|---|
| *Interrupt:* | 33h |
| *Function:* | 02h |
| *Service:* | Hide mouse cursor |
| *Entry values:* | AX=0002h |
| *Exit values:* | None |

---

Although the mouse cursor is invisible when turned off, the device driver still keeps track of the current cursor position. Therefore, if you move the mouse and turn the cursor back on, the cursor will have moved.

The normal text cursor (in text modes) is handled independently of the mouse cursor. The two cursors can be in different positions and are affected by different interrupts. Normally, therefore, the text cursor is turned off when the mouse cursor is active and vice versa. For more information on the text cursor, see Chapter 8.

**Updating the screen**

When the screen is being updated, you must turn the mouse cursor off first; otherwise, you are likely to end with a very messy screen display. This is done with function 10h.

| | |
|---|---|
| *Interrupt:* | 33h |
| *Function:* | 10h |
| *Service:* | Hide mouse cursor while updating |
| *Entry values:* | AX=0010h |
| | CX=top left X co-ordinate |
| | DX=top left Y co-ordinate |
| | SI=bottom right X co-ordinate |
| | DI=bottom right Y co-ordinate |
| *Exit values:* | None |

This function defines the area that is to be updated, then turns off the cursor. It is much faster than function 02h. After the update, you must turn the cursor back on with function 01h.

## The mouse buttons

The Microsoft-compatible mouse has two buttons; some other mice have three buttons. These buttons are used to send signals to the computer. They are linked into the keyboard controller, so act like ordinary keys. When the left and right buttons are pressed, they generate scan codes 7Dh and 7Eh respectively. Releasing the buttons generates the codes FDh and FEh. Normally, all these codes translate to ASCII FFh.

Although it is possible to check for the scan codes and act accordingly, the easiest method is to work via the standard interrupts, which do all the decoding for you. To get the current mouse information, use function 05h of interrupt 33h. You must supply the mouse button in which you are interested (0-left, 1-right).

---

| | |
|---|---|
| *Interrupt:* | 33h |
| *Function:* | 05h |
| *Service:* | Get mouse button press |
| *Entry values:* | AX=0005h |
| | BL= 00h (left button) |
| | 01h (right button) |
| *Exit values:* | AX= 00h (button not pressed) |
| | 01h (button pressed) |
| | BX=number of presses since last call |
| | CX=X co-ordinate at last press |
| | DX=Y co-ordinate at last press |

---

The interrupt tells you all you need to know about the mouse: whether or not the selected button is currently pressed, how many times it has been pressed since the last call, and the (x,y) screen co-ordinates – using the mouse scale – of the cursor when the button was last pressed.

Function 06h gives button release information.

---

| | |
|---|---|
| *Interrupt:* | 33h |
| *Function:* | 06h |
| *Service:* | Get mouse button release |
| *Entry values:* | AX=0006h |
| | BL= 00h (left button) |
| | 01h (right button) |
| *Exit values:* | AX= 00h (button not pressed) |
| | 01h (button pressed) |
| | BX=number of presses since last call |
| | CX=X co-ordinate at last release |
| | DX=Y co-ordinate at last release |

---

If you are not interested in the number of button presses, you can obtain most of this information with a single interrupt, using function 03h.

| | |
|---|---|
| *Interrupt:* | 33h |
| *Function:* | 03h |
| *Service:* | Get mouse information |
| *Entry values:* | AX=0003h |
| *Exit values:* | BX=button status |
| | CX=X co-ordinate |
| | DX=Y co-ordinate |

Note that BX, not AX, is used for the button status. (CX,DX) are the *current* mouse co-ordinates.

## The user mouse interrupt

Hardware interrupt 06h is a user-defined interrupt for the mouse. When the interrupt is invoked, DOS passes it the current button status and mouse co-ordinates.

| | |
|---|---|
| *Interrupt:* | 06h |
| *Service:* | Mouse interrupt |
| *Entry values:* | BX=button status |
| | CX=X co-ordinate |
| | DX=Y co-ordinate |
| *Exit values:* | (Defined by programmer) |

This gives an application the ability to react to mouse movement or the buttons, regardless of whatever else may be going on. The mouse is checked for an event at each clock tick.

Initially this is a dummy routine but it can be replaced by any other routine. Function 0Ch of interrupt 33h sets up the new interrupt.

| | |
|---|---|
| *Interrupt:* | 33h |
| *Function:* | 0Ch |
| *Service:* | Set mouse interrupt |
| *Entry values:* | AX=000Ch |
| | CX=event mask |
| | ES:DX=address of new interrupt |
| *Exit values:* | None |

This routine installs the new interrupt vector and determines the conditions under which the interrupt will next be invoked (the *event mask*). For more than one event, add the corresponding values together. After this, the interrupt will be invoked whenever one of the specified events occurs. For example, to act only when the right-hand button is pressed or released, the mask value is 06h.

It is also worth noting that the mouse can be made to emulate a light pen (see below).

## The light pen

A light pen consists of a small light-emitting diode (LED) and a switch. The light pen plugs into the system board, from which it gets its power. When the light switch is depressed, the LED lights up. If it is touching the screen, the screen hardware can detect its presence and calculate its position. Use of the light pen is dealt with by a single interrupt.

---

| | |
|---|---|
| *Interrupt:* | 10h |
| *Function:* | 04h |
| *Service:* | Get light pen information |
| *Entry values:* | AX=0004h |
| *Exit values:* | AH= 01h (Switch set) |
| | 00h (Switch clear) |
| | DH=character row |
| | DL=character code |
| | CX=pixel row (EGA/Hercules) |
| | CH=pixel row (CGA) |
| | DX=pixel column |

---

CX and DX only return values if AH=0 (the switch is on) and the light pen is touching the screen. The pen position is returned both as a character position (based on the units of the current screen mode) and a pixel position. The pixel row number will fit into CH only if you are working in a CGA mode; otherwise it is returned in CX.

### Mouse emulation

If you don't have a light pen, the mouse can emulate it. This rather dubious function is turned on with function 0Dh of the mouse interrupt.

---

*Interrupt:* 33h
*Function:* 0Dh
*Service:* Turn light pen emulation on
*Entry values:* AX=000Dh
*Exit values:* None

---

Now any calls to interrupt 10h function 04h return the mouse screen co-ordinates, so routines that rely on the light pen can still be used. You can turn off this rarely-used facility with function 0Eh.

---

*Interrupt:* 33h
*Function:* 0Eh
*Service:* Turn light pen emulation off
*Entry values:* AX=000Eh
*Exit values:* None

---

## The joystick

Even less useful on a PC is the joystick attachment. While popular with many home computers, it is rarely used with a PC and very few programs account for it.

A measure of the joystick's perceived importance is the fact that there are no standard interrupts on the PC to deal with this function.

The way in which the joystick is programmed varies from one computer to another. In some cases the joystick is treated as an extension of the keyboard, with the joystick movement being translated into scan codes.

The AT and some compatibles, on the other hand, use function 84h of interrupt 15h to gather information.

| | |
|---|---|
| *Interrupt:* | 15h |
| *Function:* | 84h |
| *Service:* | Get joystick information (not PCs) |
| *Entry values:* | AH=84h |
| | DX=00h (digital data) |
| | 01h (analogue values) |
| *Exit values:* | AL=digital settings (bits 4 to 7) |
| | AX, BX, CX, DX = analogue values |

A considerable amount of effort is required to make really usable code.

# 8 The Video Display

The screen is the computer's main means of communicating with its human masters. The computer uses the screen to inform, instruct, warn and admonish. The screen is used by applications to present anything from a simple list of options to a complex, moving picture. There is a huge variety of options and, consequently, a vast array of tools for handling this device.

## Screen components

The video display hardware is composed of three separate parts:

- The monitor, which produces the display itself.
- The video RAM, where the data to be displayed is stored.
- The display adaptor or gate array: the card or chip that translates the data from the video RAM into the information required by the monitor to produce the display.

## The monitor

The major component of the screen display is the cathode ray tube (CRT). All the other hardware of the monitor is dedicated to producing the necessary signals for the CRT to be effective. The display consists of a rectangular grid of phosphorous dots, called *pixels*. The maximum *resolution* of the screen is determined by the number of such dots.

The actual display is created by an electron beam. This beam scans along each row of dots in turn. The CRT controller receives data from the display adaptor/gate array which has converted the original data into the pattern of dots needed for the display. From the pattern of data that is received, the CRT controller determines whether the beam should be turned on or off. When the beam is on, a pixel is lit for an instant.

Each line of pixels is called a *raster* line. Each raster line is scanned from left to right. The beam is switched off when it reaches the end of the line and moves back to the left and down a line. This period, when the beam is switched off, is called the *horizontal retrace*. When the beam reaches the end of the last line, it is moved diagonally back to the beginning of the first line again. This period is the *vertical retrace* and takes a little longer.

To allow for the fact that the beam will overshoot, it is always left switched on for a little while at the end of each line and turned on early at the beginning. Extra lines of pixels are also illuminated at the top and bottom of the screen. This results in a screen *border*. Nothing can be written on the border as data but in some modes you can set the border colour.

The pixels fade very quickly. Therefore, the screen is refreshed about 60 times a second. At each refresh, the entire set of data is read from video RAM and displayed on the screen. Theoretically, therefore, you could change the display up to 60 times a second. Unfortunately, the time taken to write the necessary data to the video RAM greatly reduces the frequency with which the screen can be updated.

For example, it can take several seconds to fill the screen with a high-resolution graphics display where each pixel is uniquely defined. However, you can change small portions of the display and get the appearance of smooth movement.

Most of the display operations are carried out automatically. All you need to do is put the necessary data into video RAM and the display hardware will take care of the rest, converting the data into the necessary pattern, transferring it to the monitor and illuminating the pixels. No further intervention is necessary. This opens the way for some very simple, yet effective programming of the display.

**Monitor types**

Monitor types tend to fall into three broad categories:

- Pure monochrome monitors, able to produce just a single colour (usually white, green or amber), in either normal or high-intensity, on a black background.

- Grey-scale monitors, able to produce a range of grey shades at each pixel.
- Colour monitors, with a wide range of capabilities, from limited, 16-colour monitors to the more advanced models with an almost unlimited choice of colours.

Each type of monitor expects to receive information in a certain format. Therefore, the monitor must be matched with the appropriate type of display adaptor or gate array.

## Video RAM

The 128K of address space from A0000h to BFFFFh is reserved for the *video RAM*. This is the location in which programs store data before it is transferred to the CRT controller for display.

Physically, the video RAM is positioned on the display adaptor card, the expansion card or within the gate array chip. However, it is treated by the CPU as normal RAM. Therefore, you can read from and write to the video RAM just like any other part of memory. You do need to be aware of the limitations, however. It takes slightly longer to write to video RAM and writing to it directly may result in 'snow'. These problems are covered later.

Video RAM is *memory-mapped*; that is, each pixel or block of pixels directly corresponds to a bit, byte or word of data in video RAM. The way in which the data is used depends on the display mode. The methods of storing data are described later.

## Adaptors and gate arrays

The link between the video RAM and the CRT is the display adaptor card or gate array chip. This device takes the data in video RAM and converts it into a pattern of instructions that the CRT can understand. The type of translation is determined by the display mode: for example, in text modes, the adaptor changes each word of data into a pattern corresponding to the pixels needed to reproduce that character; in graphics modes, one or more bits are converted into a colour code for each individual pixel.

**MDA**

The first display adaptor, supplied with the original IBM PC in 1981, was the Monochrome Display Adaptor (MDA). This adaptor is capable of producing only text, with no graphics. The display consists of 25 rows, each of 80 characters. Each character can be white, intense white, underlined or reversed (black on white). This leads to rather restricted programming opportunities.

**Hercules adaptor**

The Hercules company came to the rescue of those who wanted a graphics capability. The Hercules Card adds the ability to plot individual pixels in either normal or intense white. The resolution of a Hercules screen is 748 pixels across the screen by 350 vertically.

**CGA**

IBM's first attempt at a colour monitor was the Colour Graphics Adaptor (CGA). This adaptor combines a graphics capability with the traditional text mode. In graphics mode, the resolution is 640 pixels horizontally by 200 vertically, each pixel being displayed in one of sixteen colours. The number of characters in text modes is the same as MDA (25 x 80) but each character can be displayed in up to sixteen colours, with any of eight background colours, and an option for the character to blink. The trade-off for this increase in colour is that the quality of text is considerably reduced in comparison with the sharpness of the MDA.

The CGA adaptor is also used for many grey-scale monitors, where the sixteen colours are represented by sixteen shades of grey. It is important to realise that most adaptors do not know what sort of monitor they are talking to. They will send the information in what they believe to be the correct format;

there will be no problem at the other end as long as the correct type of monitor is attached.

**EGA**

The next stage in improving graphics resolution resulted in the Enhanced Graphics Adaptor (EGA). Again, this yields a maximum of 16 colours but these can be selected from a choice of 64. The graphics displays have a resolution of 640 by 350 pixels, so although they are not quite up to the Hercules standard they come very close and have the advantage of full colour.

In text modes, the same 80 characters per row are allowed, but with displays of either 25 or 43 rows per screen. At 25 rows, the readability of the text is greatly enhanced; the 43-row mode tends to be somewhat hard on the eyes.

**MCGA**

The Multi-Colour Graphics Array (MCGA) arrived with the PS/2 models 25 and 30. The MCGA supports all the standard CGA functions but also has a 320x200 mode that allows up to 256 colours on the screen at a time. Additionally, there is a high-resolution 640x480 mode but with only two colours. It is called an *array*, rather than adaptor, because most of the components are contained in a single chip rather than being stored on a board; *gate array* is a jargon term for particular types of complex chip.

**VGA**

The next in this line of developing devices is the Virtual Graphics Array (VGA). The VGA allows up to 256 different colours on the screen at any one time, selected from 65,536 possible variations. Graphics resolution exceeds any of the other standards described above, at 720 by 480 pixels. Text modes are similar to those of the EGA, but there is an added option of up to 50 rows of text on the screen; however, with this number of rows it is the sheer physical size of the text that makes it hard to read, rather than the clarity of the individual characters.

**XGA**

The latest display standard, suppied with the PS/2 model 90, is the Extended Graphics Array (XGA). This monitor offers resolutions up to 1024 x 768, with 256 colours displayed.

**Compatibility**

The advantage of these better monitors over their earlier, more basic counterparts is that the text is clearer and the graphics are better defined. The disadvantage is that a great deal more memory must be used (with the possibility of much slower programs because of the extra work that has to be done shifting data around) and there are also potential compatibility problems. A program written for the CGA can be adapted for EGA and VGA very easily. The reverse is not necessarily true. The compatibility problem can be overcome by adopting one of these approaches:

- Specify a minimum monitor requirement.
- Write the program for the most basic of adaptors (and therefore do not make the most of the sophisticated options provided by the later adaptors).
- Write separate routines for each type of adaptor, so that no matter what machine the program is run on, you will make the most of the equipment available.

In fact, writing separate routines for different monitors is not as complex as it sounds and is often a realistic alternative.

Some boards are able to mimic more than one of the standards; in these cases it is often possible to set the default mode by dip switches. Information about the adaptor installed on the PC can be found in memory location 0487h.

## The video ports

A great many ports are dedicated to transferring data to and from the video adaptors. Although you can program these ports directly it is not generally advisable to do so. Programming the video ports requires a considerable amount of experience; apart from anything else, it is possible to do some quite serious damage to the display hardware by reckless experimentation. Even reading a port can have unexpected consequences.

Perhaps most importantly, the majority of effects can be accomplished without recourse to the ports anyway. Almost anything you might want to do can be achieved with either the ROM BIOS interrupts or through direct access to the video RAM.

A full discussion of this massive subject is beyond the scope of this book. For the overwhelming majority of programs access to the ports is irrelevant; programming at this level is only necessary if you are intending to produce high speed, complex graphic displays.

The screen operations that form part of the ROM BIOS are handled by interrupt 10h. DOS provides some of these operations with its own interrupts but the operating system is suprisingly limited in this respect.

## Pixel components

The way in which pixels are constructed depends upon the monitor type.

### *Monochrome monitors*

For monochrome monitors each pixel can only be either on or off. When switched on, a pixel can be at one of two intensities. This give a maximum of three options for each individual pixel.

### *CGA*

On CGA monitors each pixel is comprised of three separate components. These are the primary video colours – red, green and blue – from which the term 'RGB' is derived. In addition, the entire pixel can either be at normal or high intensity. The three components must all be at the same intensity level. The high intensity option results in colours that are lighter and brighter. Not all monitors offer this choice of two intensities; those that do are sometimes referred to as IRGB monitors.

Each character or pixel is colour coded in memory. The possible range of colours is represented by four bits of data. The first bit represents the intensity (the bit being set for high intensity), the other three are for the red, green and blue components respectively. The sixteen possible colour combinations are listed in Figure 8.1.

**The IRGB colours**

| No. | Colour | Intensity | Red | Green | Blue |
|---|---|---|---|---|---|
| 0 | Black | 0 | 0 | 0 | 0 |
| 1 | Blue | 0 | 0 | 0 | 1 |
| 2 | Green | 0 | 0 | 1 | 0 |
| 3 | Cyan | 0 | 0 | 1 | 1 |
| 4 | Red | 0 | 1 | 0 | 0 |
| 5 | Magenta | 0 | 1 | 0 | 1 |
| 6 | Brown | 0 | 1 | 1 | 0 |
| 7 | White | 0 | 1 | 1 | 1 |
| 8 | Grey | 1 | 0 | 0 | 0 |
| 9 | Light Blue | 1 | 0 | 0 | 1 |
| 10 | Light Green | 1 | 0 | 1 | 0 |
| 11 | Light Cyan | 1 | 0 | 1 | 1 |
| 12 | Light Red | 1 | 1 | 0 | 0 |
| 13 | Light Magenta | 1 | 1 | 0 | 1 |
| 14 | Yellow | 1 | 1 | 1 | 0 |
| 15 | Intense White | 1 | 1 | 1 | 1 |

*Figure 8.1*

An inspection of this chart shows that the order o the colours in numerical sequence is in fact logical and not random as appears at first glance. Thi numbering system, where each bit directly repre sents a colour component, means that there is direct map between the data byte in RAM and th pixel components. No further coding is needed an the data can be interpreted directly by the monito hardware when producing the colour display.

*High resolution colour*

For EGA monitors, each of the three colours has two separate components: low and high intensity. Each of these can be either on and off, thus giving four options for each colour's intensity: off, low, high, low+high. The intensity of each colour can be set independently so the result is that there are 64 (4x4x4) separate colours available. This type of monitor is sometimes referred to as an rgbRGB monitor.

## Video state

Various options of the display hardware combine to form the *video state*. This is comprised of the following:

- Whether the display is text or graphics based
- The number of colours that are available
- The number of lines of text
- The number of characters per line
- The number of display pages

The values assigned to each of these options is determined by the *display mode*. Each mode is given a number, in the range 0-15.

The display modes fall into two quite separate categories: text and graphics. Within each group of modes, there are options that are suitable for each of the video standards that have been developed and, for each one, usually several options for the way in which the adaptor is used.

## Text modes

One set of modes is used for displaying text only: modes 0, 1, 2, 3 and 7. These modes are character-based, so can display any of the standard or extended ASCII characters. They cannot display lines or other shapes, however. The only way of producing any sort of resemblence of a graphic display is to combine the box-drawing characters that form part of the extended ASCII set. Correctly combined, these can draw many types of line and rectangle.

In text modes, the screen is divided into a limited number of non-overlapping character blocks. For each block, which is of fixed size for the mode, you can determine the character colour and background colour. Each character block can have its colours set independently of the rest of the screen.

Each character on the screen is represented by two bytes of data in the video RAM. Text modes use the video RAM that starts at B8000h. A 25 x 80 screen takes 4,000 bytes. In this case, 4K is allocated to the screen display (the data in video RAM always beginning at a 1K boundary). As a result, there are 96 unused bytes at the end of the display data. The table in Figure 8.2 gives information

**Maximum values for text modes**

| Mode | Characters | | Colours | | | Palettes | |
|---|---|---|---|---|---|---|---|
| | Rows | Cols | Foregr | Backgr | Blink? | | Pages |
| 0 | 40 | 25 | 16* | 16* | No | 1 | 8 |
| 1 | 40 | 25 | 16 | 8 | Yes | 1 | 8 |
| 2 | 80 | 25 | 16* | 16* | No | 1 | 4 |
| 3 | 80 | 25 | 16 | 8 | Yes | 1 | 4 |
| 7 | 80 | 25 | 3** | 2** | No | 1 | 1 |

* Colour suppressed modes: the 'colours' are shades of grey

** Monochrome styles: only 4 combinations allowed

**Memory requirements in text modes**

| Mode | Bytes Per Char. | Chars Per page | Page size | Allocated Memory | Pages | Location |
|---|---|---|---|---|---|---|
| 0 | 2 | 1000 | 2K | 16K | 8 | B8000 |
| 1 | 2 | 1000 | 2K | 16K | 8 | B8000 |
| 2 | 2 | 2000 | 4K | 16K | 4 | B8000 |
| 3 | 2 | 2000 | 4K | 16K | 4 | B8000 |
| 7 | 2 | 2000 | 4K | 4K | 1 | B8000 |

*Figure 8.2*

about video RAM memory usage. (Display 'pages' are described later in this chapter.)

The first byte of each pair stores the ASCII code for the character; the second byte holds the characters *attribute*.

The ROM holds a table of data for the standard 256 ASCII codes. For each ASCII character, the ROM stores the corresponding pixel pattern. When the character needs to be displayed, there is a direct translation into this pattern. The ASCII code provides the offset to the start of the relevant pattern in the table. You cannot change the contents of this table, as it is stored in ROM, but in some modes you can substitute a table of your own (see below).

The attribute byte stores a code for the colour of the character and its background. In CGA modes,

**Encoding character attributes**

| Bit | 7 | 6 | 5 | 4 | 3 | 2 | 1 | 0 | |
|---|---|---|---|---|---|---|---|---|---|
| | Blink | Background colour (0-7) | | | | Foreground colour (0-15) | | | |
| **CGA Modes** | | | | | | | | | |
| Examples: | | | | | | | | | |
| 17h | 0 | 0 | 0 | 1 | 0 | 1 | 1 | 1 | White on blue |
| CFh | 1 | 1 | 0 | 0 | 1 | 1 | 1 | 1 | Bright white on red, blink |
| **Monochrome modes** | | | | | | | | | |
| Sensible values | | | | | | | | | |
| 07h | 0 | 0 | 0 | 0 | 0 | 1 | 1 | 1 | White on black |
| 70h | 0 | 1 | 1 | 1 | 0 | 0 | 0 | 0 | Reverse |
| 01h | 0 | 0 | 0 | 0 | 0 | 0 | 0 | 1 | Underline |
| 00h | 0 | 0 | 0 | 0 | 0 | 0 | 0 | 0 | No character |

(Add blink (bit 7, 80h) and/or intensity (bit 3, 04h) to any of these combinations.)

*Figure 8.3*

the low 4 bits store the *foreground* colour (the colour of the character itself). The next 3 bits give the background colour for the character; hence only 8 background colours are allowed. Finally, the top-bit is set when you want the character to blink. This is summarised in Figure 8.3. For MDA displays, the options are more limited.

When the blink bit is set, the character block alternates between displaying the character and just a blank background. The blink occurs about four times a second. This is a feature of the hardware so is not changeable.

**Character tables**

In CGA graphics modes (4 to 6), the appearance of the standard ASCII display characters is fixed. The pixel maps for extended ASCII characters are held in a table pointed to by interrupt 1Fh. Therefore a different set of characters in the range 80h to FFh can be implemented by storing a new character table in RAM and changing the interrupt vector (a procedure adopted by GRAPHICS.COM).

For EGA, MCGA, VGA and XGA you can change the character tables – in both text and graphics modes – with function 11h of interrupt 10h. This function is split into two parts, with subfunctions for text modes and graphics modes.

Part of RAM is set aside for character tables: four tables on the EGA and MCGA, eight on the VGA. These can be loaded with character tables from the ROM BIOS or user-defined tables. You can also adjust the character height to fit more lines on the screen.

---

*Interrupt:* 10h
*Function:* 11h (text modes)
*Service:* Load/select character table
*Entry values:* AH=11h
AL= 00h (Load user-defined chars)
01h (Load ROM 8x14 characters) (not MCGA)
02h (Load ROM 8x8 characters)
03h (Select character table)
04h (Load ROM 8x16 characters) (not EGA)

10h (User-defined, adjust height)
11h (ROM 8x14, adjust height) (not MCGA)
12h (ROM 8x8, adjust height) (not MCGA)
14h (ROM 8x16, adjust height) (VGA)
BL=table number
*If AL=00h or 10h*:
BH=bytes per character
CX=number of characters
DX=start character
ES:BP points to character table

*Exit values:* None

---

*Interrupt:* 10h
*Function:* 11h (graphics modes)
*Service:* Load/select character table
*Entry values:* AH=11h
AL= 20h (Load extended ASCII 8x8 characters)
21h (Load user-defined chars)
22h (Load ROM 8x14 characters) (not MCGA)
23h (Load ROM 8x8 characters)
24h (Load ROM 8x16 characters) (not EGA)
BL= 00h (Variable number of rows)
01h (14 rows)
02h (25 rows)
03h (43 rows)
(Not used for AL=20h)
CX=bytes per character (if AL=21h)
DL=number of rows (if BL=00h, AL>20h)
ES:BP points to character table (if AL=20h or 21h)

*Exit values:* None

---

*Interrupt:* 10h
*Function:* 11h, 30h
*Service:* Get character table information
*Entry values:* AH=11h
AL=30h
BH=00h (Interrupt 1Fh table)

| | |
|---|---|
| | 01h (Interrupt 43h table) |
| | 02h (ROM 8x14 table) |
| | 03h (ROM 8x8 table, upper half) |
| | 04h (ROM 8x8 table, lower half) |
| | 05h (ROM 9x14 table) |
| | 06h (ROM 8x16 table) |
| | 07h (ROM 9x16 table) |
| *Exit values:* | CX=character height |
| | DL=number of rows -1 |
| | ES:BP points to character table |

## Writing directly to memory

The fastest way to write characters to the screen in text modes is to put them directly into the video RAM. Every time the screen is refreshed, the contents of the video RAM are read and translated directly into the video display. Therefore, if you place the pairs of bytes in memory, at the appropriate point, they will be almost instantly converted into the required display. This is illustrated by the program in Figure 8.4.

This is one of the few occasions when you can work directly with the hardware, rather than through the interrupts, without having to worry too much about compatibility problems. This method is adopted by very many programs, so there should be no problems with compatibility in the future.

```
WRITETST:       ;Test text-writing program

                ;Calls WRITETEX
                ;Registers changed

        jmp testst

testdata:
    db 'Text is placed here',0Dh
    db 'with ',01h,94h,'attributes',01h,07h
    db ' inserted',0Dh,'in the text',0Dh
    db 01h,3Dh,'as required',01h,07h,00h
    ;Must not exceed 100 bytes
```

```
dataend:      db ?            ;End of data marker

testst:
      xor cx,cx
      mov cx,dataend          ;Calculate length of
                              ;text
      sub cx,testdata
      lea di,text             ;ES:DI points to
                              ;TEXT
      lea si,testdata         ;DS:SI points to
                              ;TESTDATA
      cld
      rep movsb               ;Move TESTDATA into
                              ;TEXT
      call writetex
      int 20h

;------------------------------------------------

WRITETEX:      ;Write block of text to screen

         ;Takes text from memory
         ;Attributes defined by special codes
         ;embedded in text. Special codes
         ;consist of 01h followed by
         ;attribute byte, 0Dh for carriage
         ;return. Text terminated by
         ;null character.

        ;Entry values: TEXT=text to be
        ;displayed
        ;Exit values: AX,BX,CX,DX,SI,DI changed

      jmp writest

text:         db 64h dup (?)  ;Allow 100 bytes

        ;Insert text here. Use 0Dh for CR-LF
        ;sequence. Make sure attribute is
        ;returned to normal at end of text.

attrib:       db ?      ;Current attribute
linestrt:     dw ?      ;Start of current line
                        ;(as no. bytes from top
                        ;left)
lineno:       db ?      ;Next line number

writest:
      lea bx,0b800h           ;BX points to
                              ;display RAM
      mov es,bx               ;ES points to
                              ;display RAM
```

```
        lea bx,text             ;BX points to TEXT
        mov si,bx               ;SI points to TEXT
        lea dx,attrib           ;DX points to ATTRIB
        mov ah,00h
        mov al,03h
        int 10h                 ;Set mode 3 and
                                ;clear screen
        mov byte ptr [attrib],07h
                                ;Initialise attribute
                                ;(white on black)
        mov word ptr [linestrt],0000h
                                ;Point to top left-
                                ;corner of string
        mov byte ptr [lineno],01h
                                ;Next line is
                                ;initially line 1
        xor di,di               ;DI is offset to
                                ;display RAM
                                ;so ES:DI points to
                                ;display position
                                ;and DS:SI points to
                                ;text to write
nextchar:
        cld
        lodsb                   ;Get byte
        dec si
        cmp al,01h              ;Is it attribute?
        jz nextattr             ;Jump if it is
        cmp al,0Dh              ;Is it CR?
        jz creturn              ;Jump if so
        cmp al,00h              ;Is it end of text?
        jz endwrite             ;If so, jump
        cld
        movsb                   ;Otherwise, display
                                ;character
        push si
        mov si,dx               ;SI points to ATTRIB
        cld
        movsb                   ;Store current
                                ;attribute in next
                                ;byte
        pop si                  ;Restore SI to
                                ;position in TEXT
        jmp endloop
nextattr:
        inc si
        cld
        lodsb                   ;Get attribute
        mov [attrib],al         ;Save attribute
        jmp endloop
```

```
creturn:
      mov di,[linestrt]      ;DI points to start
                             ;of line
      add di,0A0h            ;Add 160 to DI
                             ;i.e. point to start
                             ;of next line
      mov [linestrt],di      ;Save start of new
                             ;line
      mov bl,[lineno]        ;BL points to this
                             ;line
      inc bl                 ;BL points to next
      mov [lineno],bl        ;Save next line
      inc si
endloop:
      jmp nextchar
endwrite:
      xor bx,bx              ;Set up cursor
                             ;parameters
      mov dh,[lineno]
      xor dl,dl
      mov ah,02h
      int 10h                ;Put cursor on line
                             ;below text
      ret
```

*Figure 8.4*

**Snow**

While the method described above is fast, it is not always totally successful. On monitors such as the original IBM PC's CGA, writing directly to the screen in this way may result in *snow*. What happens is that if you write to the video RAM at the same time that it is being read – something which will happen extremely frequently on slower 8086 machines – the value that is read by the adaptor hardware is indeterminate. The result is that that particular character will not be displayed correctly. The effect over the screen as a whole is that, as it is being updated, specks of colour will flash across the screen.

Many monitors and adaptors have been developed in such a way that they automatically cut out snow. However, if snow does become a problem, it can be overcome by changing the screen-writing routines so that they only write to the display RAM during the relatively long period of the vertical retrace.

The principle is this: When you are ready to write something to the screen, check to see if you are in a vertical retrace period (this is done by inspecting the vertical synchronisation signal of the adaptor I/O port). If this is not a vertical retrace period, wait until it is. On the other hand, if it is a vertical retrace period, wait until the next one starts. (Since you don't know how far into the vertical retrace you are, it is not safe to start writing; you must wait until you have a complete vertical retrace period at your disposal.) When a retrace period begins, you can write a group of characters to RAM; as soon as you have done this, you must wait until the next retrace period starts before writing the next section. This takes longer when writing a full screen of data but, since most of the time you are only rewriting a part of it, it shouldn't make that much difference in most applications. This should clear up any problems with snow.

If you are really keen, you can use the horizontal retrace period as well, though these periods are considerably shorter and therefore not much can be written in each one.

## Graphics modes

The remaining modes – modes 4, 5, 6 and 13 onwards – are the graphics modes (modes 8-12 are reserved). In these modes, the adaptor works entirely with individual pixels rather than characters. Any individual pixel can be set to any of the available colours, completely independently of all other pixels. In some respets this gives a great deal of flexibility. However, it does have its drawbacks. Graphics modes take a lot more memory and require far more by way of programming in order to produce reasonable displays. The data to create each pixel is stored in one or more bits of memory, depending on the mode. In graphics modes, display data starts at B8000h for CGA and at A0000h for EGA, MCGA and VGA modes. The available modes are:

| | |
|---|---|
| CGA: | 4-6 |
| EGA: | 4-6, 13-16 |
| MCGA: | 4-6, 17,19 |
| VGA: | 4-6, 13-19 |
| XGA: | 4-6, 13-19 |

The number of bits used for each pixel depends upon the number of colours required; if only a two-colour display is needed, each pixel is represented by 1 bit, four colours take 2 bits and so on.

**Memory banks**

The storage of display data in graphics modes is not quite so straightforward as that of text modes. In CGA modes, the display RAM is divided into 8K *banks*. The data for the first row of screen pixels is stored in the first bank but the second row of pixels is derived from the second bank. If two banks of data are in use, the third row resumes from the end of the first row in the first bank, the fourth row comes from the second bank, and so on. In this way, the data alternates between the two banks.

If four banks are used, the first bank has the data for rows 0, 4, 8, ..., the second bank represents rows 1, 5, 9, ..., and so on.

**EGA modes**

In 16-colour EGA modes, things become even more complex. The data appears to start at A0000h but is not stored in the way you might expect. Each pixel is represented by 4 bits, and each bit is stored on a different bank. Thus bank 0 holds bit 0 for each pixel. Within the bank, the bits are stored sequentially.

Writing data directly to memory for EGA modes is generally not very successful and it is far safer to use the interrupts described below.

Figure 8.5 shows the number of colours, pixel resolution and memory requirements for each of the graphics displays.

**Maximum values for graphics modes**

| Mode | Rows | Columns | Colours | Palettes | Pages | Memory |
|---|---|---|---|---|---|---|
| 4 | 200 | 320 | 4 | 2 | 1 | 16K |
| 5 | 200 | 320 | 4* | 2 | 1 | 16K |
| 6 | 200 | 640 | 2 | 1 | 1 | 16K |
| 13 | 200 | 320 | 16 | 1 | 1 | 32K |
| 14 | 200 | 640 | 16 | 1 | 1 | 64K |
| 15 | 350 | 640 | 2 | 1 | 1 | 28K |
| 16 | 350 | 640 | 16 | 1 | 1 | 112K |
| 17 | 480 | 640 | 2 | 1 | 1 | 40K |
| 18 | 480 | 640 | 16 | 1 | 1 | 60K |
| 19 | 200 | 320 | 256 | 1 | 1 | 64K |

* Colour suppressed mode: the 'colours' are shades of grey.

**Memory requirements for graphics modes**

| Mode | Colours | Pixels/ byte | Pixels/ row | Bytes/ row | Rows | Page size | Location |
|---|---|---|---|---|---|---|---|
| 4 | 4 | 4 | 320 | 80 | 200 | 16K | B8000 |
| 5 | 4 | 4 | 320 | 80 | 200 | 16K | B8000 |
| 6 | 2 | 8 | 640 | 80 | 200 | 16K | B8000 |
| 13 | 16 | 2 | 320 | 160 | 200 | 32K | A0000 |
| 14 | 16 | 2 | 640 | 320 | 200 | 64K | A0000 |
| 15 | 2 | 8 | 640 | 80 | 350 | 28K | A0000 |
| 16 | 16 | 2 | 640 | 320 | 350 | 112K | A0000 |
| 17 | 2 | 8 | 640 | 80 | 480 | 40K | A0000 |
| 18 | 16 | 2 | 640 | 120 | 480 | 60K | A0000 |
| 19 | 256 | 1 | 320 | 320 | 200 | 64K | A0000 |

*Figure 8.5*

## Working with pixels

Each pixel on the screen sits on a rectangular grid and its position can be defined absolutely by a pair of co-ordinates, starting from (0,0) in the top left-hand corner. The first co-ordinate is the distance along the row while the second gives the distance from the top of the screen. The upper limits for the co-ordinates depend upon the screen mode that has been selected.

Note that DOS is not really interested in pixel-based operations or, indeed, graphics of any type. Being a character- and file-based operating system, it has no room for operations of this type. Therefore, there are no DOS equivalents to the interrupts described here.

In many respects this is a pity, since it means that there is no guaranteed way of ensuring compatibility from one machine to another. However, the interrupts described below will be effective on all true PC compatibles.

**Writing pixels**

If you are producing graphics rather than character-based displays, assuming that you are intending to write directly, the easiest way of changing the colour of an individual pixel is to use interrupt 10h, function 0Ch. The co-ordinates must be placed in the CX and DX registers. The colour of the pixel should be placed in AL.

---

*Interrupt:* 10h
*Function:* 0Ch
*Service:* Display pixel
*Entry values:* AH=0Ch
AL=colour (add 80h for XOR)
CX=pixel column
DL=pixel row
*Exit values:* None

---

As an alternative, you can add 80h to the colour in AL. The effect of this is that the routine carries out an XOR operation between the value in AL and the existing pixel. The pixel will therefore always change colour (unless the new colour is 00h). If you put a number of pixels of a particular colour on an object of the same colour, they will still show up. If you put a line of pixels across a multi-coloured object, the line should still be obvious in most circumstances (except where the screen is already many-coloured). Another advantage is that if you repeat the call to the interrupt, using the same colour, the original colour is restored. The disadvantage of the XOR operation is that it can be very difficult to work out what the screen will end up like.

Many objects consist entirely of straight lines. A straight line is approximated by a sequence of pixels. It is simple to draw a straight line that is either horizontal, vertical or diagonal, but lines at other angles can be a little more complex. A number of algorithms exist for calculating the pixels that are needed to most closely approximate a straight line.

### Reading pixels

You will sometimes know the colour of each individual pixel but this is not always obvious, especially when a great many drawing operations have been carried out. The quickest way to check the colour of a particular pixel is to use function 0Dh of interrupt 10h.

---

*Interrupt:* 10h
*Function:* 0Dh
*Service:* Read pixel colour
*Entry values:* AH=0Dh
CX=pixel column
DL=pixel row
*Exit values:* AL=colour

---

## Palettes

Although there are many colours available for use on the EGA and VGA monitors, not all of them can appear at the same time. The more colours that are available, the greater the memory requirements for storing an entire screen display. For practical reasons, most modes limit you to just a selection of the available colours, called a *palette*.

Each of the colours in the palette is given a *logical* number, the numbers ranging from 0 upwards. Each of these logical colours is mapped onto a *physical* colour. For example, a palette of 16 colours will have logical numbers from 0 to 15, but each one of these may represent any one of the available physical colours (in any order).

All ROM BIOS functions work with logical colours, rather than physical colours; of course, on CGA screens, where the full selection of colours is always available (in most modes), the logical and physical colours always coincide.

For example, any reference to colour 2 will always mean the third logical colour, regardless of the physical colour that this represents. One of the advantages of this system is that you can have a complete change in the colours used in the program simply by changing the palette; there is no need to change the program itself at all.

When a character attribute is stored in RAM, it is always the logical colour that is used. Palettes are only used for graphics modes.

For CGA modes, the palettes are fixed. In modes 4 and 5, two palettes are available, each of four colours (see Figure 8.6).

**CGA palettes**

| Mode(s) | Palette | Logical No. | Colour | Bit pattern |
|---|---|---|---|---|
| 4/5 | 0 | 0 | Black | 00 |
| | | 1 | Green | 01 |
| | | 2 | Red | 10 |
| | | 3 | Brown | 11 |
| | 1 | 0 | Black | 00 |
| | | 1 | Cyan | 01 |
| | | 2 | Magenta | 10 |
| | | 3 | White | 11 |
| 6 | 0 | 0 | Black | 0 |
| | | 1 | White | 1 |
| 10 | 0 | 0 | Black | 00 |
| | | 1 | Cyan | 01 |
| | | 2 | Magenta | 10 |
| | | 3 | White | 11 |

*Figure 8.6*

This means that only two bits are required in memory to represent each pixel. Logical colour 0 can be set to any physical colour, providing some variety. When displaying text in these graphics modes, logical colour 3 is used for the foreground and colour 0 for the background. The palette for modes 4 and 5 is selected with interrupt 10h, function 0Bh. The physical colour for logical colour 0 is changed by making BH=0 and placing the physical colour (in the range 0-15) in BL. The palette is selected by making BH=1 and putting the palette number (0 or 1) in BL.

---

| | |
|---|---|
| *Interrupt:* | 10h |
| *Function:* | 0Bh |
| *Service:* | Select colour palette |
| *Entry values:* | AH=0Bh |
| | BH=palette |
| | BL=colour |
| *Exit values:* | None |

---

*Mode 6*

Mode 6 has only one palette, consisting of two colours, and therefore requires only one bit per pixel in memory.

*Mode 10*

Mode 10 has just a single palette, identical to palette 0 in mode 4.

*Colour 0*

In text modes, colour 0 is used for the border. In graphics modes, colour 0 is used for the border and the background to any text.

**EGA modes**

In the EGA modes, 16 colours can be displayed on the screen at any one time, out of the 64 that are available. In this case, the 16-colour palette can be chosen to be any selection of colours. The default is to select the first eight and last eight physical colours: that is, the high bits of the colour byte are all the same (see Figure 8.7).

**The EGA default palette**

| Log No. | Colour | Low Red | Low Grn | Low Blue | High Red | High Grn | High Blue | Phys No. |
|---|---|---|---|---|---|---|---|---|
| 0 | Black | 0 | 0 | 0 | 0 | 0 | 0 | 0 |
| 1 | Blue | 0 | 0 | 0 | 0 | 0 | 1 | 1 |
| 2 | Green | 0 | 0 | 0 | 0 | 1 | 0 | 2 |
| 3 | Cyan | 0 | 0 | 0 | 0 | 1 | 1 | 3 |
| 4 | Red | 0 | 0 | 0 | 1 | 0 | 0 | 4 |
| 5 | Magenta | 0 | 0 | 0 | 1 | 0 | 1 | 5 |
| 6 | Brown | 0 | 0 | 0 | 1 | 1 | 0 | 6 |
| 7 | White | 0 | 0 | 0 | 1 | 1 | 1 | 7 |
| 8 | Grey | 1 | 1 | 1 | 0 | 0 | 0 | 56 |
| 9 | Light Blue | 1 | 1 | 1 | 0 | 0 | 1 | 57 |
| 10 | Light Green | 1 | 1 | 1 | 0 | 1 | 0 | 58 |
| 11 | Light Cyan | 1 | 1 | 1 | 0 | 1 | 1 | 59 |
| 12 | Light Red | 1 | 1 | 1 | 1 | 0 | 0 | 60 |
| 13 | Light Magenta | 1 | 1 | 1 | 1 | 0 | 1 | 61 |
| 14 | Yellow | 1 | 1 | 1 | 1 | 1 | 0 | 62 |
| 15 | Intense White | 1 | 1 | 1 | 1 | 1 | 1 | 63 |

*Figure 8.7*

The palettes and border colour are changed (for both EGA and VGA) with the first four subfunctions of interrupt 10h, function 10h.

---

*Interrupt:* 10h
*Function:* 10h, 00h
*Service:* Set EGA/VGA palette colour
*Entry values:* AH=10h
AL=00h
BH=physical colour value
BL=logical colour number
*Exit values:* None

---

*Interrupt:* 10h
*Function:* 10h, 02h
*Service:* Set whole EGA/VGA palette
*Entry values:* AH=10h
AL=02h
ES:DX points to 17-byte table of colour values plus border colour
*Exit values:* None

---

| | |
|---|---|
| *Interrupt:* | 10h |
| *Function:* | 10h, 01h |
| *Service:* | Set EGA/VGA border colour |
| *Entry values:* | AH=10h |
| | AL=01h |
| | BH=border colour value |
| *Exit values:* | None |

| | |
|---|---|
| *Interrupt:* | 10h |
| *Function:* | 10h, 03h |
| *Service:* | Select intensity/blink for attribute bit 7 (EGA/VGA) |
| *Entry values:* | AH=10h |
| | AL=01h |
| | BL= 00h (intense background) |
| | 01h (blink) |
| *Exit values:* | None |

**VGA modes**

The VGA palette registers are read/write registers (as opposed to the EGA's write-only registers). Therefore, you can check the current palette colours.

| | |
|---|---|
| *Interrupt:* | 10h |
| *Function:* | 10h, 07h |
| *Service:* | Get VGA palette colour |
| *Entry values:* | AH=10h |
| | AL=07h |
| | BL=logical colour number |
| *Exit values:* | BH=physical colour value |

| | |
|---|---|
| *Interrupt:* | 10h |
| *Function:* | 10h, 09h |
| *Service:* | Get whole VGA palette |
| *Entry values:* | AH=10h |
| | AL=09h |
| | ES:DX points to 17-byte table of colour values plus border colour |
| *Exit values:* | None (table updated) |

*Interrupt:* 10h
*Function:* 10h, 08h
*Service:* Get VGA border colour
*Entry values:* AH=10h
AL=08h
*Exit values:* BH=border colour value

---

**Video DAC registers**

The MCGA and VGA have a video Digital-to-Analogue Convertor (DAC), that holds 256 colour registers. Each of these can be programmed to hold any one of the 256K (=64x64x64) possible colours. Each of the three red/blue/green components for each register can take any of 64 different values. The registers are used like the palettes described above.

For 16-colour modes, only the first 16 registers are used on the MCGA. In these modes, the VGA has a palette of 16 registers, that select any set of 16 DAC registers.

Unless you specify otherwise, the default colours on the MCGA and VGA match those of the CGA.

A number of services affect the DAC registers.

---

*Interrupt:* 10h
*Function:* 10h, 10h
*Service:* Set DAC register
*Entry values:* AH=10h
AL=10h
BX=register number
CH=green component (00h-3Fh)
CL=blue component
DH=red component
*Exit values:* None

---

*Interrupt:* 10h
*Function:* 10h, 15h
*Service:* Get DAC register
*Entry values:* AH=10h
AL=15h
BX=register number

| | |
|---|---|
| *Exit values:* | BX=register number<br>CH=green component (00h-3Fh)<br>CL=blue component<br>DH=red component |

| | |
|---|---|
| *Interrupt:* | 10h |
| *Function:* | 10h, 12h |
| *Service:* | Set block of DAC registers |
| *Entry values:* | AH=10h<br>AL=12h<br>BX=first register number<br>CX=number of registers<br>ES:DX points to table of RGB values (3 bytes each) |
| *Exit values:* | None |

| | |
|---|---|
| *Interrupt:* | 10h |
| *Function:* | 10h, 17h |
| *Service:* | Get block of DAC registers |
| *Entry values:* | AH=10h<br>AL=17h<br>BX=first register number<br>CX=number of registers<br>ES:DX points to table of RGB values (3 bytes each) |
| *Exit values:* | None (table updated) |

The VGA palette, by default, selects from the first 64 DAC registers (called DAC page 0). You can change to a different group (page) of registers. You can also reduce the 'page size' to 16 registers.

| | |
|---|---|
| *Interrupt:* | 10h |
| *Function:* | 10h, 13h |
| *Service:* | Set VGA DAC page |
| *Entry values:* | AH=10h<br>AL=13h<br>BH= 00h (4 pages, if BL=00h)<br>01h (16 pages, if BL=00h)<br>page number (if BL=01h)<br>BL= 00h (select number of pages)<br>01h (select page number) |
| *Exit values:* | None |

---

| | |
|---|---|
| *Interrupt:* | 10h |
| *Function:* | 10h, 1Ah |
| *Service:* | Get VGA DAC page |
| *Entry values:* | AH=10h |
| | AL=1Ah |
| *Exit values:* | BH=page number |
| | BL= 00h (4 pages) |
| | 01h (16 pages) |

---

Finally, you can convert any block of colour DAC registers to their grey-scale equivalents.

---

| | |
|---|---|
| *Interrupt:* | 10h |
| *Function:* | 10h, 1Bh |
| *Service:* | Convert DAC to greys |
| *Entry values:* | AH=10h |
| | AL=1Bh |
| | BX=first register number |
| | CX=number of registers |
| *Exit values:* | None |

---

## Display modes

As described above, the PC supports a number of different display modes. The BIOS provides two routines for setting and checking the current display mode.

### Setting the display mode

The current display mode can be changed with function 00h of interrupt 10h.

---

| | |
|---|---|
| *Interrupt:* | 10h |
| *Function:* | 00h |
| *Service:* | Set video mode |
| *Entry values:* | AH=00h |
| | AL=new video mode |
| *Exit values:* | None |

---

This function sets the new mode to that held in AL. It also clears the screen in the process.

```
SCRENCLR:        ;Clears the screen

        ;Can be called from any routine
        ;All registers preserved

        push ax
        push bx
        mov ah,0fh
        int 10h                 ;Get current mode
        mov ah,00h
        int 10h                 ;Set mode, same as
                                ;before
        pop bx
        pop ax
        ret
```

*Figure 8.8*

**Clearing the screen**

The function to change the mode always clears the screen, regardless of whether the mode is actually being changed. It is essential that the screen should be cleared when changing modes. The fact that the screen is cleared even if the mode is staying the same means that the function can be used as a simple 'clear screen' procedure. This is illustrated in Figure 8.8.

This method has the added advantage that it will work on any monitor and in any mode, so provides a clear-screen routine that is truly compatible across all PCs and all monitors.

For MCGA, EGA and VGA modes, add 80h to the new mode number if you do *not* want the screen cleared.

Note that this service also resets any palette to its default colours.

You can also clear the screen with function 06h, described below, by defining the entire screen as a window and setting AL=00h.

**Reading the current mode**

You can identify the current display mode at any time with function 0Fh of the screen interrupt.

| | |
|---|---|
| *Interrupt:* | 10h |
| *Function:* | 0Fh |
| *Service:* | Get video mode |
| *Entry values:* | AH=0Fh |
| *Exit values:* | AH=width (characters) |
| | AL=video mode |
| | BH=page |

This function is particularly useful for memory-resident programs, where the mode is set by some other application program.

**Mode information in memory**

You can also check the current mode by inspecting system variable 0449h. The number of columns on the current display is stored in 044Ah while the number of rows (less 1) is held in 0484h.

## Display pages

Where memory requirements are low (for example, in text modes), there is room in the video RAM for more than one screenful of data at a time. The BIOS makes use of this fact by dividing the video RAM into *display pages*. Each one of these can hold all the information needed to create the screen display.

One of these is the *active* display page: that is, the page that holds the information currently being displayed on the screen. If you change the active display page, the display changes instantly. This means that a new screen can be built up in another display page; the second page can be made active once the new screen is ready. This removes the need to worry about using the vertical retrace to avoid snow. On slower PCs, it also means that the user does not have to watch the screen being updated, though there will inevitably be a delay while the new screen is being built.

Display pages are numbered from 0, and there can be up to eight pages, depending on the display mode. When you change display mode, page 0 always becomes the active display page.

Display pages always begin at 2K boundaries in memory. The size of a single page (in units of 1K) is given at 044Ch. The start of the active display page, as an offset from the start of video RAM, is stored at 044Eh. The number of the active display page is held at 0462h.

### Display page functions

A new active display page can be selected with function 05h of interrupt 10h.

---

| | |
|---|---|
| *Interrupt:* | 10h |
| *Function:* | 05h |
| *Service:* | Select active display page |
| *Entry values:* | AH=05h |
| | AL=page |
| *Exit values:* | None |

---

As soon as this interrupt is invoked, the new display will appear.

There is no function specifically to check on the current active page but the active page number is returned as part of function 0Fh (described above).

## Windows

If a program is to use any form of windows on the screen, it is generally up to the programmer to construct suitable routines for handling them. Putting a new window on the screen is simple; taking it off again is not quite so straightforward. Unless you want to redraw the screen in its entirety every time a window is removed, your program must include the following steps:

- Save the existing contents of the window area.
- Draw a blank window on the screen. Fill the window with the necessary text or graphics.
- When the window is no longer required, rewrite that area with the previously saved data.

Figure 8.9 is a routines to display a coloured box on screen, the first step in creating a window.

```
BOX:        ;Draw filled box

            ;Entry values: BX=pointer to box data
            ;Exit values:  None

      push ax
      push cx
      push dx
      call block
      pop dx
      pop cx
      pop ax
      ret

block:                          ;Fill block of colour
      push bx
      mov al,[bx]                  ;Get first row no.
      cbw
      mov si,ax
      xor cx,cx
      mov cl,[bx+2]
      sub cl,[bx]
      inc cl
reprow:
      mov dx,si                    ;Set up cursor
                                   ;position at start
                                   ;of row
      mov dh,dl
      mov dl,[bx+01]
      push bx
      xor bx,bx
      mov ah,02
      int 010                      ;Move cursor to
                                   ;start of row
      pop bx
      push cx
      xor cx,cx
      mov cl,[bx+3]                ;Calculate line
                                   ;length
      sub cl,[bx+1]
      inc cx
      push bx                      ;Set up display
                                   ;characteristics
      mov al,[bx+4]                ;Get background
                                   ;colour
      xor bh,bh
      mov bl,al                    ;Set backgr colour
      mov al,0db                   ;Block character
      mov ah,09
      int 010                      ;Display string in
                                   ;background colour
```

```
pop bx
pop cx
inc si
loop reprow
pop bx
ret
```

*Figure 8.9*

**Scrolling text in windows**

Although the BIOS – and indeed DOS – does nothing to help you create windows on the screen, there are two useful functions that will allow you to scroll the text within a window. Before invoking either of these routines, you must place the co-ordinates of the top left and bottom right-hand window corners in the registers.

| | |
|---|---|
| *Interrupt:* | 10h |
| *Function:* | 06h |
| *Service:* | Scroll window up |
| *Entry values:* | AH=06h |
| | AL=number of lines to scroll |
| | BH=attribute for new line |
| | CH=top row |
| | CL=left column |
| | DH=bottom row |
| | DL=right column |
| *Exit values:* | None |

| | |
|---|---|
| *Interrupt:* | 10h |
| *Function:* | 07h |
| *Service:* | Scroll window down |
| *Entry values:* | AH=07h |
| | AL=number of lines to scroll |
| | BH=for new line filler attribute |
| | CH=top row |
| | CL=left column |
| | DH=bottom row |
| | DL=right column |
| *Exit values:* | None |

These functions are not particularly clever in the way that they work. As soon as the function is invoked, all text within the window area is moved up or down one line. The line at the top or bottom is lost and the new line that is created is filled with blanks. Since you have specified the background colour, the blank line matches the rest of the window.

This is a fairly fast function. It is up to the program to keep track of what is currently displayed at the window and fill in the blank lines; the program must also control the position of the cursor, if any.

Set AL=00h to clear the window.

## Writing characters to the screen

For such a complex device, the ROM BIOS – and indeed DOS – provides very few functions for displaying text and graphics. There are, in fact, three BIOS functions that will write text to the screen, while DOS provides a few others with slightly more sophisticated – and therefore less flexible – facilities.

### Writing characters

BIOS interrupt 10h provides a number of screen-handling routines. The first of these is function 0Ah.

---

*Interrupt:* 10h
*Function:* 0Ah
*Service:* Display character
*Entry values:* AH=0Ah
AL=character
BH=page (text modes)
BL=colour (graphics modes)
CX=repeat count (0 for continuous repeat)
*Exit values:* None

---

This function displays a single character one or more times on the screen. The number of times is specified in CX. Writing begins at the current cursor position and continues to the end of the line. If the end of the line is reached, in text modes, the remaining characters are written at the start of the next line. In graphics modes, the extra characters are ignored. If the text is written beyond the last character of the last line, the whole screen scrolls up to accomodate the additional text.

There is a special case, specified by CX=0, when the same character is written to the screen repeatedly until the Break key is pressed.

In text modes, the attribute for the character is the same as the last character written. If no character has yet been written to the screen, the attribute defaults to a white character on black background. For graphics mode, the foreground colour must be given in BL and the background colour is logical colour 0 (the physical colour of which depends upon the palette that has been selected).

Under this function, the cursor does not move.

**Writing characters with an attribute**

A slightly different version of the above is provided by function 09h.

---

| | |
|---|---|
| *Interrupt:* | 10h |
| *Function:* | 09h |
| *Service:* | Display character |
| *Entry values:* | AH=09 |
| | AL=character |
| | BH=page |
| | BL=attribute (text modes) |
| | CX=repeat count (0 for continuous repeat) |
| *Exit values:* | None |

---

The only difference here is that the attribute must be specified in AH. This byte specifies the blink, background and foreground attributes, as described earlier.

**Writing characters in teletype mode**

Function 0Eh provides the most useful of the BIOS single-character facilities.

---

| | |
|---|---|
| *Interrupt:* | 10h |
| *Function:* | 0Eh |
| *Service:* | Display teletype character |

*Entry values:* AH=0E
AL=character
BH=page
BL=colour (graphics modes)
*Exit values:* None

---

This function displays only one character, advancing to the next line or scrolling the screen, where necessary. For text modes, the attribute is the same as the last character written; while in graphics modes the foreground colour must be specified.

The most important feature, however, is that the cursor automatically advances to the next position.

This function is often referred to as the *teletype* function, since repeated calls to the interrupt result in a string of characters being written across the screen, with ends of line and screen automatically taken care of. If you need to change the text attribute part of the way through, this can be achieved by a call to function 09h.

Perhaps the most frustrating aspect of this function is that writing a character to the last position on the screen results in the screen automatically scrolling, since the cursor is moved to the start of the next line. This is fine if you are typing a file to the screen but makes the function unsuitable for filling any static display where text has to be written along the full length of the bottom line. The problem can be resolved by calling function 0Ah (above) when the final character is reached.

**Control characters**

When any of the functions above encounters an ASCII character in the range 00h to 1Fh (the control codes), a special symbol is usually displayed. The pattern for these symbols is stored in the ROM ASCII table. For example, displaying ASCII 01h results in the 'happy face' character. However, the teletype function (0Ah) treats the following control characters slightly differently:

**07h** BELL. The computer beeps.

**08h** BS (Backspace). The cursor moves back one character and the previous character is deleted.

**0Ah** LF (Line Feed). The cursor moves down one line.

**0Dh** CR (Carriage Return). The cursor moves to the beginning of the current line.

This further enhances the teletype function.

**The DOS teletype function**

DOS uses the BIOS function 0Ah to produce its own teletype function.

---

| | |
|---|---|
| *Interrupt:* | 21h |
| *Function:* | 02h |
| *DOS version:* | 1 |
| *Service:* | Display character |
| *Entry values:* | AH=02h |
| | DL=character |
| *Exit values:* | None |

---

This function works in a similar way to BIOS function 0Ah, except that ASCII 08h moves the cursor to the left but doesn't delete the existing character. DOS also checks for the **Ctrl-Break** key after each character is displayed.

There is an identical function as part of DOS function 06h.

---

| | |
|---|---|
| *Interrupt:* | 21h |
| *Function:* | 06h |
| *DOS version:* | 1 |
| *Service:* | Display character (see also Chap 6) |
| *Entry values:* | AH=06h |
| | DL=character other than FFh |
| *Exit values:* | None |

---

This function has already been described in Chapter 6. If DL is given any value other than FFh, the function is used for output and the character in DL is displayed on the screen. The advantage of this function is that it can be called automatically by another of the group of DOS keyboard interrupts.

**Displaying strings of text**

DOS includes a routine to display an entire string of text. Using this function is often easier than writing your own routine.

| | |
|---|---|
| *Interrupt:* | 21h |
| *Function:* | 09h |
| *DOS version:* | 1 |
| *Service:* | Display string |
| *Entry values:* | AH=09h |
| | DS:DX=start of string |
| *Exit values:* | None |

The string must be pointed to by DS:DX before the function is called. In memory, the string of text must be terminated by the '$' character (ASCII 36h). Everything up to but not including the $ is displayed.

The text is displayed with the current attributes, starting at the current cursor position, and the cursor is advanced to the end of the string. In most respects, therefore, it acts just like the teletype function.

This function is fine for any string of text that does not include the $ character. There is no equivalent BIOS function.

Figure 8.10 includes a selection of useful display routines.

```
DISBYT:          ;Display byte in AL as hex
                 ;All registers preserved

      push ax
      push cx
      push ax
      mov cl,04h
      shr al,cl              ;Get first 4 bits
      call dis4              ;Display as character
      pop ax
      and al,0fh             ;Get last 4 bits
      call dis4              ;Display as character
      pop cx
      pop ax
      ret
```

```
dis4:                           ;Display single hex
                                ;character
      cmp al,0ah                ;Check for value=0Ah
      jge letter
      add al,30h           ;Convert to ASCII 0 to 9
      jmp disch

letter:
      add al,37h           ;Convert to ASCII A to F

disch:
      mov ah,0eh
      int 10h
      ret

;-----------------------------------------------

DISWRD:       ;Display word in AX as hex

      ;Entry values: AX=word to display
      ;Exit values: All registers preserved

      push ax
      mov al,ah
      call disbyt               ;Display high byte
      pop ax
      call disbyt               ;Display low byte
      ret

;-----------------------------------------------

DISSTR:       ;Display string

   ;Entry values: DX=offset address of message
   ;Exit values: All registers preserved

      push ax
      mov ah,09h                ;Call interrupt to
                                ;display text at DX
      int 21h
      pop ax
      ret

;-----------------------------------------------

NEWLIN:       ;Print CR,LF to start new line

      ;Entry values: None
      ;Exit values:  All registers preserved
```

```
     push ax
     mov al,0Dh               ;AL=Carriage Return
                              ;(0Dh)
     mov ah,0Eh               ;Print CR
     int 10h
     mov al,0Ah               ;AL=Line Feed (OAh)
     mov ah,0Eh               ;Print LF
     int 10h
     pop ax
     ret

;---------------------------------------------------

DISLIN:       ;Display a line of text

  ;Entry values: DX = offset address of message
  ;Exit values:  All registers preserved

     call disstr              ;Displaying string
     call newlin              ;Move to new line
     ret
```

*Figure 8.10*

**Displaying characters on the EGA**

For the EGA, MCGA and VGA, the ROM BIOS provides a service to write a string of text. This service was not available on early PCs, so should be used with care.

| | |
|---|---|
| *Interrupt:* | 10h |
| *Function:* | 13h |
| *Service:* | Display EGA string (EGA etc., not early PCs) |
| *Entry values:* | AH=13h |
| | AL= 00h (attribute fixed, do not move cursor) |
| | 01h (attribute fixed, move cursor) |
| | 02h (attribute not fixed, do not move cursor) |
| | 03h (attribute not fixed, move cursor) |
| | BL=attribute (if AL=00h or 01h) |
| | BH=page |
| | CX=string length |

| | |
|---|---|
| | DX=cursor position |
| | ES:BP points to text string |
| *Exit values:* | None |

For AL=02h or 03h each character in the string should be followed by an attribute.

**Reading a character from the screen**

Sometimes it is easier to find out from the system what character is displayed at a particular position rather than trying to work it out within a program, particularly for a memory-resident program. The BIOS provides a function to read the character at the current cursor position.

| | |
|---|---|
| *Interrupt:* | 10h |
| *Function:* | 08h |
| *Service:* | Read character |
| *Entry values:* | AH=08h |
| | BH=page |
| *Exit values:* | AH=attribute |
| | AL=character |

If necessary, you must first set the cursor position with function 02h.

This function works in both text and graphics modes. It is particularly useful for graphics screens, since in those modes you cannot check the contents of the screen by inspecting the video RAM. In graphics modes the function works by comparing the pattern of dots in memory with that stored for the characters in the BIOS. However, if the pattern cannot be recognised – even if only one corner of the character block is the wrong colour – the function does not attempt to guess what character it may be; rather, it returns the value 00h in AL. Therefore, if you draw a line that touches a character block, that character becomes unreadable to this function. For normal text areas, however, it is extremely useful.

## The hardware cursor

The system keeps track of the cursor position at all times. The cursor position consists of a character row and column number, measured from the top left-hand corner, with each of the co-ordinates starting at 0. Separate cursors are maintained independently for each display page, the co-ordinates being stored in memory at locations 0450h to 045Fh. These sixteen bytes hold the cursor co-ordinates for up to eight display pages.

### The text cursor

In text modes, the cursor consists of a flashing block. The width of the cursor is the same as the width of the character block and cannot be changed. The height of the cursor, by default, is two pixels but this can be varied. This cursor is a feature of the hardware, and therefore you are limited in what you can do. The advantage is that much of the hard work is already done for you.

### The graphics cursor

In graphics modes, the system still maintains the cursor position in memory and adjusts it for the various functions automatically. However, the cursor itself is always invisible. You can use the same functions as for the text modes (described below) to move the cursor to a new position, find out where the cursor is and so on. If you want the cursor to actually appear on the screen, you must write a routine to display it.

## Cursor functions

Various BIOS functions exist to adjust the size and position of the cursor, and to report its current status.

### Cursor size

The size of the hardware cursor in text modes is measured in terms of *raster lines*. The raster lines are the horizontal lines of pixels that make up the character block. These are numbered from 0 at the top of the character block down to 7 (CGA), 13 (EGA) or 15 (VGA).

By default, the cursor uses raster lines 6 and 7 (CGA), 11 and 12 (EGA) or 12 and 13 (VGA). This is changed with function 01h of interrupt 10h.

---

| | |
|---|---|
| *Interrupt:* | 10h |
| *Function:* | 01h |
| *Service:* | Set cursor size |
| *Entry values:* | AH=01h |
| | CH=first raster line (20h no cursor) |
| | CL=last raster line |
| *Exit values:* | None |

---

For this function, all you need to do is set the first and last raster lines; the cursor consists of the area between (and including) these limits. There are a few special points to note:

- To produce a block cursor that fills the entire character block, set CH=0 and CL equal to the maximum raster line number.
- For a cursor that consists of a single raster line make CH and CL the same.
- To make the cursor 'wrap around' the block, so that it appears at both the top and bottom of the character, set CL to be less than CH.
- Finally, there is a special case where CL=20h, in which the cursor is turned off altogether.

While you can have a different cursor position for each display page, the cursor size is the same for all pages. Therefore, you may need to change the cursor size when you change the display page.

The first and last raster lines are held in memory at locations 0461h and 0460h respectively.

**Turning the cursor on and off**

Turning the cursor off (with CL=20h) can be particularly useful. To turn it back on again, you simply need to call the same function and reset the raster lines. Figure 8.11 illustrates two short routines to turn the cursor off and then on again, restoring the cursor to its original size.

```
      ;This listing includes two routines -
      ;one to turn the cursor off and
      ;one to turn it on again. These
      ;routines should be used as a pair

CUROFF:       ;Turn cursor off

      ;AX and CX must be pushed onto stack
      ;before call, and popped after CURON

      jmp curst

cursz         dw ?                   ;Cursor size

curst:
      mov ah,03h
      int 10h                 ;Get current cursor
                              ;characteristics
      mov [cursz],cx          ;Save cursor size
      mov ch,20h
      xor cl,cl
      mov ah,01h
      int 10h                 ;Turn cursor off
      ret

;-----------------------------------------------

CURON:       ;Turn cursor on

      mov cx,[cursz]          ;Recover cursor size
      mov ah,01h
      int 10h                 ;Restore cursor
      ret
```

*Figure 8.11*

**Moving the cursor**

Some of the display interrupt functions described above automatically move the cursor when they are called; changing the display mode resets the cursor to (0,0). On other occasions, you can move the cursor with BIOS interrupt 10h, function 02h.

| | |
|---|---|
| *Interrupt:* | 10h |
| *Function:* | 02h |
| *Service:* | Set cursor position |
| *Entry values:* | AH=02h |
| | BH=page (0 for graphics modes) |
| | DH=row |
| | DL=column |
| *Exit values:* | None |

Remember that the row and column numbers are counted from 0 in the top left-hand corner.

For graphics modes, the page number must always be set to 0 when this function is called (since only one display page is allowed in these modes).

**The cursor status**

The cursor location is given by function 03h. This function also returns the current cursor size, in terms of the first and last raster lines.

| | |
|---|---|
| *Interrupt:* | 10h |
| *Function:* | 03h |
| *Service:* | Get cursor information |
| *Entry values:* | AH=03h |
| | BH=page |
| *Exit values:* | CH=first raster line |
| | CL=last raster line |
| | DH=row |
| | DL=column |

# 9 Sound

The production of sound is very basic on the IBM PC and compatibles. The sound-producing device is a single speaker, which is physically capable of two things only: the speaker can be pushed out and it can be pulled in. When a current is generated, the speaker is pushed out; when the current is turned off, the speaker returns to its original position. This simple action creates a wave of movement in the air surrounding the speaker which, when it reaches us, is interpreted as a sound. Each time this happens, we hear a single click.

When there are many clicks close together, this is heard as a continuous tone. The *frequency* of the clicks – how often they are being generated – determines the *pitch* of the sound that is heard. The higher the frequency, the higher the pitch.

Therefore, the production of sound, at its most basic, involves nothing more than making the speaker pulse in and out at a specific frequency. Each pulse in and out of the speaker is a single *cycle*. The frequency of any sound is measured in cycles per second, or hertz (Hz).

On the PC, the frequency is the only thing that can be changed. The volume cannot be varied, although sounds of different frequencies may be slightly louder or softer. By changing the frequency at which the speaker pulses, it can be made to issue any audible note; this single note can be made to last for any length of time. Therefore, it is possible to produce very simple music, though this has a rather tinny sound to it.

## Programming for sound

Since the production of sound is generally regarded as somewhat frivolous, and certainly unnecessary for business applications, there are no interrupts dedicated to the production of sound. Therefore, all sound production has to be achieved at the most basic hardware level.

Producing any sound involves two things. First, the timer must be programmed to produce pulses at the required rate. Second, the speaker must be turned on or off.

The programmable interrupt timer (PIT), or equivalent, has three counters, the third of which is dedicated to sound production. This counter has an associated two-byte register, in which a value can be stored. The timer counts the clock ticks as they are generated and when the total number of ticks reaches the value stored in the register, a pulse is emitted. The counter is reset to 0 and starts again. This pulse arrives at the speaker and, if the speaker is ready to receive, results in a single click. Therefore, the value put in the PIT register determines the frequency of the sound that is produced.

Timer 2 operates at a frequency of 1.193180 MHz. The register value can be calculated from:

$$\text{Register value} = \frac{\text{timer frequency}}{\text{sound frequency}}$$

The sound frequencies that are required to produce standard notes and are available within the limits of the PC are shown in Figure 9.1. For example, you can produce a note that is close to middle C with:

```
Register value = 1193180/261.6
               = 4561.09
```

**Sound frequencies (Hz)**

| Note | Octave 1 | 2 | 3 | 4 | 5 | 6 | 7 |
|---|---|---|---|---|---|---|---|
| C | | 32.7 | 65.4 | 130.8 | **261.6*** | 523.3 | 1046.5 |
| C# | | 34.7 | 69.3 | 138.6 | 277.2 | 554.4 | 1108.7 |
| D | 18.4 | 36.7 | 73.4 | 146.8 | 293.7 | 587.3 | 1174.7 |
| D# | 19.5 | 38.9 | 77.8 | 155.6 | 311.1 | 622.3 | 1244.5 |
| E | 20.6 | 41.2 | 82.4 | 164.8 | 329.6 | 659.3 | 1328.5 |
| E# | 21.8 | 43.7 | 87.3 | 174.6 | 349.2 | 698.5 | 1396.9 |
| F | 23.1 | 46.3 | 92.5 | 185.0 | 367.0 | 740.0 | 1480.0 |
| G | 24.5 | 49.0 | 98.0 | 196.0 | 392.0 | 784.0 | 1568.0 |
| G# | 26.0 | 51.9 | 103.8 | 207.7 | 415.3 | 830.6 | 1661.2 |
| A | 27.5 | 55.0 | 110.0 | 220.0 | 440.0 | 880.0 | 1760.0 |
| A# | 29.1 | 58.3 | 116.5 | 223.1 | 466.2 | 932.3 | 1864.7 |
| B | 30.9 | 61.7 | 123.5 | 246.9 | 493.9 | 987.8 | 1975.5 |

*middle C

*Figure 9.1*

Therefore, putting 4561 in the PIT register will produce clicks about 262 times a second, the frequency required for middle C. The table shows the minimum and maximum frequencies that can reasonably be obtained by the PC.

**Setting the PIT register**

The first stage in the production of any sound is to store the required value in the PIT register. Because you are working directly with the ports, this is more complicated that may at first be anticipated.

Channel 2 of the PIT uses ports 42h and 43h. Setting up the register is a two-stage process. First, you must tell the PIT that a new value for the register is expected, by putting the value B6h in port 43h. Second, the required register value must be sent to port 42h. The register value is a word but port 42h can only accept a byte at a time. Therefore, the value must be sent as two separate bytes, the low byte being transmitted first.

As soon as the second byte arrives, the counter starts working and pulses are emitted to the entire system at the required rate.

**Turning the speaker on and off**

By this stage, the PIT is busy broadcasting pulses to any part of the system that is willing to listen but as yet, no one can hear them. The second stage is to turn on the speaker.

Port 61h is used for a variety of purposes. Bits 0 and 1 are reserved for the speaker.

When bit 0 is clear, this indicates that the speaker is being programmed directly; when bit 0 is set, the speaker is being controlled by the timer.

Bit 1 must be cleared when no sound is to be emitted or set when a sound is to be generated. Therefore, to turn the speaker on and program it via the timer, both bits must be set. This can be done with an OR instruction between the existing value and 03h. You need to use OR so that bits 3 to 7 are not changed; these higher bits are used for different purposes.

As soon as the speaker is turned on, the pulses being emitted by the PIT will be interpreted as the required note. To change the frequency of the note,

all you need to do is change the value of th
register.

The advantage of this method of producing soun
is that the timer does most of the hard work for you
Once the sound has been generated, you can let th
timer get on with producing the pulses, leaving th
CPU free to carry on with other processing. You onl
need to involve the CPU again when the note is t
change. If a note is maintained for even a fraction c
a second, quite a bit of other processing can b
done in between. The disadvantage of this proce
dure is the inflexibility of the sounds that can b
produced.

Figure 9.2 demonstrates three methods c
producing sound: the DOS screen-writing functio
with the BELL character, programming the PIT an
speaker, and writing directly to the ports (a
described below).

```
BEEP1:          ;Sound the speaker once

   ;Uses the standard DOS interrupt to
   ;display a character - in this case ASCII 07

      mov dl,07h              ;DL = BEL
      mov ah,02h
      int 21h                 ;Display character
      int 20h

;-----------------------------------------------

TUNE:          ;Plays a tune

      ;Entry values: None
      ;Exit values:  AX, CX, SX, SI changed

      jmp timest

freq          dd 1193180     ;Timer frequency
music         dw 294,1000h,330,1000h,262,1000h
              dw 131,1000h,196,2000h,0000h
              ;Music data: frequency,duration
              ;terminated by nulls

timest:
      in al,61h               ;Get port 61h values
      push ax
      or al,03h               ;Set bits 0 and 1
      out 61h,al              ;Send to port 61h
```

```
     xor si,si
note:
     mov ax,word ptr [freq]
           ;Move Timer frequency into DX:AX
     mov dx,word ptr [freq+2]
     cmp byte ptr music[si],0000h ;Is note 0?
     jz endtune              ;If so, end
     div music[si]           ;Divide Timer
                             ;frequency by note
     add si,02h              ;Point to duration
     push ax
     mov al,0B6h
     out 43h,al              ;Tell Timer to
                             ;expect value
     pop ax
     out 42h,al              ;Send low byte
     mov al,ah
     out 42h,al              ;Send high byte
     mov cx,music[si]        ;Put duration in CX
     add si,02h
     call waitloop           ;Call delay loop
     jmp note                ;Repeat
endtune:
     pop ax
     out 61h,al              ;Switch speaker off
     int 20h

waitloop:                    ;Delay loop
         ;Delay value should be placed in CX
     push cx                 ;Save current CX
     xor cx,cx
     mov cl,20h              ;Loop 32 times
noploop:
     nop                     ;Loop to do nothing
     loop noploop
     pop cx                  ;Get CX back
     loop waitloop           ;decrement and loop
     ret

;-------------------------------------------

SOUND:   ;Generate sound by direct write to port

     jmp soundst

portin:      db ?            ;Port value on entry

soundst:
     cli                     ;Disable interrupts
     xor cx,cx
soundloop:
     in al,97                ;Get port 97h value
     mov [portin],al         ;Save value
```

```
        mov al,79
        out 97,al               ;Output to port
        mov bx,cx
wait2:                          ;Wait for shorter
                                ;time each time
        dec bx
        jnz wait2
        mov al,[portin]     ;Get original port value
        out 97,al           ;Send to port
        inc cx
        cmp cx,0300h
        jnz soundloop
        sti                     ;Enable interrupts
        int 20h
```

*Figure 9.2*

## Programming the ports for sound

The alternative to the above method is to write directly to the relevant ports. If you clear bit 0 of port 61h (with an AND operation between the existing value and FCh), the speaker is directly under your control. From then on, all you need to do is set bit 1 to push the speaker out, and clear bit 1 to pull the speaker back in. The bit can be set with the command `OR 02h`. It can be cleared with `AND FDh` Alternatively, the current setting can be switched with `XOR 02h`.

The type of sound that is produced depends not only on the frequency with which the speaker is pushed out and in but also the regularity of the speaker movement. By applying a varying pattern, you can produce a totally different sound.

You can produce almost any sound by pushing and pulling the speaker with the required pattern. The disadvantages are that this method requires the permanent attention of the CPU; CPUs with different speeds will generate different sounds; and a great deal of experience is required before you can judge what sound will be produced by a particular pattern of codes.

Nevertheless, using these various methods, you should be able to produce a selection of basic sounds.

# 10 The Serial and Parallel Ports

Apart from the standard devices connected to specific parts of the system – the keyboard, screen, mouse and disk drives – all other communication has to be done with either the expansion slots or the serial and parallel ports. Programming of the expansion slots depends upon the particular card that has been attached. For the serial and parallel ports, however, the range of options is limited. Therefore programming can be quite straightforward yet produce apparently complex results.

These external ports are standard points to which any suitable device can be connected, allowing data to be transferred in one or both directions. This means that all devices must conform to the standards laid down by the PC hardware, which is common across all true compatibles.

Note that there is no real connection between these *external* hardware ports, which are simply places to plug some device into the system, and the *internal* ports used for data transfer on the system bus. However, when data is transferred to and from the external hardware ports, it *is* passed through the internal ports. The ports used are those with addresses from 0400h to 040Dh.

### DOS functions

The DOS functions described below all relate to the *standard* serial and parallel ports. By default the standard port is the first port in each case but the functions can be directed to work with a different port with the DOS MODE command. Any program based on the DOS interrupts will work with the standard ports; it is up to the user to set this up before the application is run.

## The serial port hardware

The serial port allows transfers of data in both directions. Although it is used for some printers and plotters (where one-way transfer only is needed) the main use is for devices such as digitisers and modems, where the two-way transfer of data is essential. Although the original IBM PC allowed for seven serial ports, on the PS/2 up to three ports are catered for. The ports are numbered from 0 onwards.

Data is sent out as a stream of individual bits. Only two pins in the port are required for the actual transfer of data, the other lines being used for sending and receiving various signals. Serial ports on PCs and compatibles are either 25-pin or 9-pin. The uses of the pins on the 25-pin RS-232C asynchronous serial port are shown in Figure 10.1.

**The serial connector**

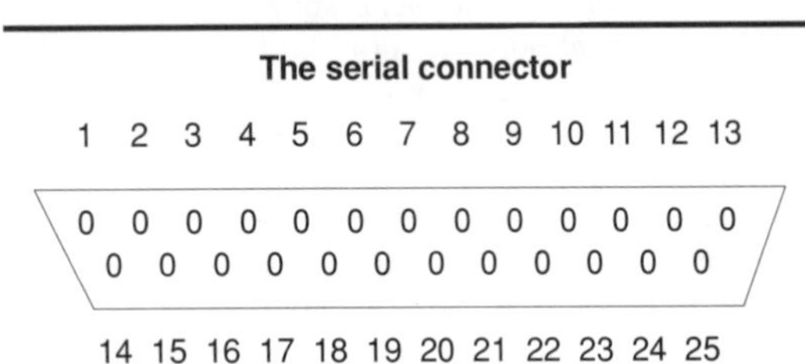


| Pin | Use |
|---|---|
| 1 | Not used |
| 2 | TXD (Data output) |
| 3 | RXD (Data input) |
| 4 | RTS (Request To Send) |
| 5 | CTS (Clear To Send) |
| 6 | DSR (Data Set Ready) |
| 7 | Signal ground |
| 8 | DCD (Data Carrier Detect) |
| 9-19 | Not used |
| 20 | DTR (Data Terminal Ready) |
| 21 | Not used |
| 22 | RI (Ring Indicator) |
| 23-25 | Not used |

*Figure 10.1*

**The protocol**

The serial port can be used to transmit data at various speeds, and with a variety of data formats and error-checking methods. The way in which data is transferred is called the *protocol*. Before any data can be transferred, the computer and the device to which it is connected must be set up to operate with the same protocol.

## Programming the serial port

Although serial communications may seem complex, in fact there are very few commands that can be given. These are all covered by interrupt 14h. Note that the PS/2 offers two further services (04h and 05h), which are not covered here.

### Setting the protocol

The first stage of setting up a program to work with a serial port should always be to initialise the port with the protocol to be used. This is done with function 00h.

| | |
|---|---|
| *Interrupt:* | 14h |
| *Function:* | 00h |
| *Service:* | Initialise serial port |
| *Entry values:* | AH=00h |
| | AL=protocol code |
| | DX=port number |
| *Exit values:* | AH=main status code |
| | AL=modem status code |

Register AH holds the following information:

- The baud rate: the speed at which data is transferred
- The parity: the type of error checking
- The stop bit: the number of bits sent after each item of data
- The data length: the number of bits transferred at a time

The way in which AH is divided up and the possible values it may take are shown in Figure 10.2.

The interrupt returns the serial port status in AH, the meaning of which is shown in Figure 10.3.

**Serial data transfer byte**

| Bit | Use |
|---|---|
| 7 | ) |
| 6 | ) Baud rate |
| 5 | ) |
| 4 | ) Parity |
| 3 | ) |
| 2 | Stop bits (0=1 stop bit,1=2 stop bits) |
| 1 | ) Data size |
| 0 | ) |

**Baud rate codes (bits 7,6,5)**

| Code | Bit 7 | Bit 6 | Bit 5 | Baud rate |
|---|---|---|---|---|
| 0 | 0 | 0 | 0 | 110 |
| 1 | 0 | 0 | 1 | 150 |
| 2 | 0 | 1 | 0 | 300 |
| 3 | 0 | 1 | 1 | 600 |
| 4 | 1 | 0 | 0 | 1200 |
| 5 | 1 | 0 | 1 | 2400 |
| 6 | 1 | 1 | 0 | 4800 |
| 7 | 1 | 1 | 1 | 9600 |

**Parity codes (bits 4,3)**

| Code | Bit 4 | Bit 3 | Parity |
|---|---|---|---|
| 0 | 0 | 0 | None |
| 1 | 0 | 1 | Odd |
| 2 | 1 | 0 | None |
| 3 | 1 | 1 | Even |

**Data size (bits 1,0)**

| Code | Bit 1 | Bit 0 | Size |
|---|---|---|---|
| 0 | 0 | 0 | Not used |
| 1 | 0 | 1 | Not used |
| 2 | 1 | 0 | 7-bit |
| 3 | 1 | 1 | 8-bit |

*Figure 10.2*

**Serial port main status codes (AH)**

| Code (hex) | Meaning |
|---|---|
| 1 | Data ready |
| 2 | Overrun |
| 4 | Parity error |
| 8 | Framing error |
| 10 | Break detected |
| 20 | Holding buffer empty |
| 40 | Shift buffer empty |
| 80 | Timeout |

*Figure 10.3*

Function 00h also returns in AL the *modem status*, a set of errors specifically designed for modem communications (see Figure 10.4).

**Serial port modem status codes (AL)**

| Code (hex) | Meaning |
|---|---|
| 1 | Delta CTS |
| 2 | Delta DSR |
| 4 | Trailing-edge RI |
| 8 | Delta line signal detect |
| 10 | CTS |
| 20 | DSR |
| 40 | RI |
| 80 | Line signal detect |

*Figure 10.4*

### Sending data

After initialising the port you can start sending data. You must send one character at a time, using function 01h.

*Interrupt:* 14h
*Function:* 01h
*Service:* Send character to serial port
*Entry values:* AH=01h
AL=character to send
DX=port number
*Exit values:* AH=main status code

---

You can send the data to any of the serial ports.

DOS provides a similar service, function 04h of interrupt 21h.

---

*Interrupt:* 21h
*Function:* 04h
*DOS version:* 1
*Service:* Send character to serial port
*Entry values:* AH=04h
DL=character to send
*Exit values:* None

---

In this case you cannot specify the port, since the function always refers to the *standard* port, as set by the MODE command. The other disadvantage of this service is that it does not return the status.

**Receiving data**

You can get a character from the serial port with function 02h.

---

*Interrupt:* 14h
*Function:* 02h
*Service:* Get character from serial port
*Entry values:* AH=02h
DX=port number
*Exit values:* AH=main status code
AL=character received

---

If there is a character waiting, the ASCII value is returned in AL. If an error occurs, the status code is returned in AH. If there is no character waiting and no error, both registers will be 0. Therefore, if you are expecting data, you must keep checking until AX is non-zero.

DOS provides a similar service with function 03h.

| | |
|---|---|
| *Interrupt:* | 21h |
| *Function:* | 03h |
| *DOS version:* | 1 |
| *Service:* | Get character from serial port |
| *Entry values:* | AH=03h |
| *Exit values:* | AL=character |

**Checking the status**

After every action – either sending or receiving data – the serial port status is set. You can check the status to see if all is well with BIOS function 03h.

| | |
|---|---|
| *Interrupt:* | 14h |
| *Function:* | 03h |
| *Service:* | Check serial port status |
| *Entry values:* | AH=03h |
| *Exit values:* | AH=main status code |
| | AL=modem status code |

The status code takes the same values as for the other functions (see Figures 10.3 and 10.4).

## Parallel port hardware

The parallel port allows data transfer in one direction only. Control information can travel both ways, but the standard parallel port will not receive incoming data. The parallel ports are used mainly for parallel printers. Up to three parallel ports are allowed, numbered 0, 1 and 2.

Unlike the serial port, the parallel port can be used to send a complete byte at a time, along eight parallel wires. The result is must faster transmission. The other wires on the standard centronics 25-pin connector are used for control data, as shown in Figure 10.5.

The other advantage of using parallel ports is that the data is always sent at the same speed and in the same format, so there are no protocol problems.

**The parallel printer connector**

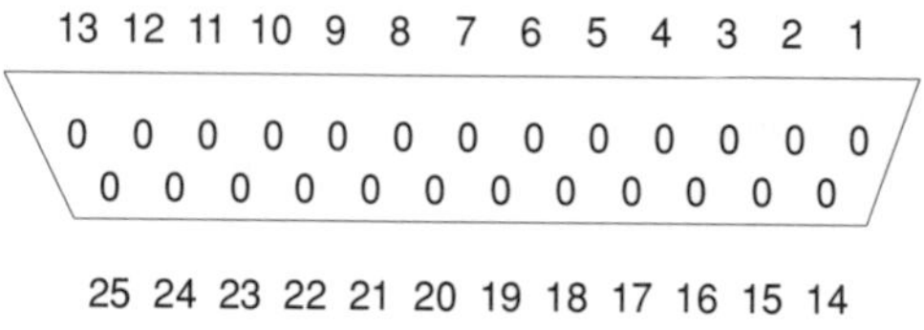

```
13 12 11 10  9  8  7  6  5  4  3  2  1
 0  0  0  0  0  0  0  0  0  0  0  0  0
   0  0  0  0  0  0  0  0  0  0  0  0
25 24 23 22 21 20 19 18 17 16 15 14
```

| Pin | Use |
|---|---|
| 1 | - (Data strobe) |
| 2 - 9 | Data bits 0-7 |
| 10 | - (Printer acknowledge) |
| 11 | Printer busy |
| 12 | Paper out |
| 13 | Select printer |
| 14 | - (Auto feed Select) |
| 15 | - (Printer error) |
| 16 | - (Reset printer) |
| 17 | - (Printer on-line) |
| 18 -25 | GND |

*Figure 10.5*

## Programming the parallel ports

Programming one of the parallel ports is very straightforward. First you must initialise the printer (and check that the status code that is returned is all right); then you can send the data. The BIOS parallel port services form interrupt 17h.

**Initialising the parallel port**

There is no need to set the protocol but you do need to tell the printer or other device that you are about to send data. This is done with function 01h.

| | |
|---|---|
| *Interrupt:* | 17h |
| *Function:* | 01h |
| *Service:* | Initialise parallel port |
| *Entry values:* | AH=01h |
| | DX=port number |
| *Exit values:* | AH=status code |

**Parallel printer status byte**

| Bit | Meaning if set |
|---|---|
| 7 | Printer not busy |
| 6 | Printer acknowledge |
| 5 | Paper out |
| 4 | Printer on-line |
| 3 | Printer error |
| 2 | Not used |
| 1 | Not used |
| 0 | Time-out error |

*Figure 10.6*

This function returns a status code, the meaning of which is shown in Figure 10.6.

Obviously, you should check that no error status has been returned before attempting to send data. The initialisation routine that performs this service sends the bytes 08h and 0Ch to the printer control port, 02FAh.

**Sending parallel data**

A single byte can be sent to the parallel port with function 00h.

| | |
|---|---|
| *Interrupt:* | 17h |
| *Function:* | 00h |
| *Service:* | Send character to parallel port |
| *Entry values:* | AH=00h |
| | AL=character |
| | DX=port number |
| *Exit values:* | AH=status code |

The character to send must be specified in AL. Once this function has been invoked, nothing else can be done until the printer either acknowledges that the byte has been received successfully or notifies an error in the status code. When the data is transmitted, it is actually placed in internal port 0378h, where the parallel device collects it.

DOS also has its own service, function 05h of interrupt 21h.

| | |
|---|---|
| *Interrupt:* | 21h |
| *Function:* | 05h |
| *DOS version:* | 1 |
| *Service:* | Send character to parallel port |
| *Entry values:* | AH=05h |
| | DL=character |
| *Exit values:* | None |

In this case, no status code is returned.

**Checking the parallel port status**

You can check the status of a parallel port at any time with BIOS function 02h.

| | |
|---|---|
| *Interrupt:* | 17h |
| *Function:* | 02h |
| *Service:* | Check parallel port status |
| *Entry values:* | AH=02h |
| | DX=port number |
| *Exit values:* | AH=status code |

The data returned in the status code is also stored in internal port 0379h. This is a read-only port which holds the status in a slightly different format (see Figure 10.7).

**Parallel print status port (0379h)**

| Bit | Use |
|---|---|
| 7 | Not Printer busy |
| 6 | Not Printer acknowledge |
| 5 | Paper out |
| 4 | Printer on-line |
| 3 | Not printer-error |
| 2 | Not used |
| 1 | Not used |
| 0 | Not used |

*Figure 10.7*

Various printer conditions may be notified as part of the status:

- Printer busy: indicates whether or not the device is ready for more data
- Printer acknowledge: this bit is set when data has been received satisfactorily
- Paper out: the bit is set when the printer's paper-out detector is activated
- Printer selected: the bit is set when the printer is on-line, clear when the printer is off-line
- Printer error: this indicates some other, undefined error

**Printer control**

The system uses bit 4 of port 037Ah to decide how to react to an acknowledgement signal from the printer. If this bit is set, the 'printer acknowledge' signal results in hardware interrupt 07h being issued. Initially, this is a dummy routine but can be replaced with any other. Usually the interrupt routine is set up by the device driver for the printer or other parallel device.

If bit 4 of the port is clear, the printer acknowledge signal is ignored. This bit is sometimes referred to as the Enable Interrupt and Acknowledge flag.

Note that the other bits of this port are used for other hardware purposes.

## Time-out errors

Once the instruction to send data has been given, the PC tries to execute the command immediately. It starts by checking the RTS line to see if the device is ready to receive. If it is, the data is sent. If not, the PC waits, and keeps on trying until the line is ready. However, the PC only keeps trying for a specific length of time. If there is still no success – for example, because the device is not switched on – the result is a *time-out error*.

The main problem with this is that the CPU is tied up the whole time while waiting for the device to respond and cannot be interrupted. This can be very frustrating. If you are trying to print and realise that the printer is not ready, there is nothing to be done until the PC has established that fact for itself and responds with the time-out message. This delay can be anything up to a minute.

The obvious solution would be to reduce the time that the PC waits. However, some operations may take several seconds to complete even when the device is ready. For example, if the printer buffer is full, you have to wait until some characters have been printed before the next characters are accepted. If the characters waiting to be printed consist of form feeds, this may take some time. As a result, if the time the PC is prepared to wait is set too low, the printer will time-out whenever it does a form feed. This is even more annoying than having to wait for a proper time-out. Therefore, a program must choose a sensible middle way.

Different devices need different waiting times, so allowing for the worst possible case will result in a program that is frustrating to use with many devices. The best approach is to allow the user to change the time-out period as part of the device configuration.

### Time-out period

The time-out period is calculated from the value in ports 0478h to 047Ah (for parallel ports 0-2), and 047Ch and 047Dh (serial ports 0 and 1). The value stored in these ports represents the number of half-second intervals to wait. The default value for parallel ports is 20: i.e. ten seconds before the time-out; for serial ports, the default is 1: a half-second wait only.

## The Print Screen function

On most PCs, pressing Shift-PrtSc (or just Print Screen on AT-compatibles) results in a hardware interrupt 05h being issued. By default, this results in a copy of the screen (in text modes only) being sent to the standard parallel port; that is, it produces a screen dump. This is one of the ROM BIOS routines.

At any time, you can check how the dump is progressing by inspecting the contents of memory location 0500h. The value returned is as follows:

**00h** Print screen has been completed

**01h** Print screen is still in progress

**FFh** Time-out error

Interrupt 05h ties up the CPU while the dump is in progress.

This interrupt is fairly simple to redirect and there are many small programs available to do this. One of the most common, GRAPHICS.COM, is usually supplied with DOS and extends the routine to allow for the printing of the extended ASCII characters as well as the standard ASCII set. Other routines are used to produce screen dumps for graphics screens or to store the current contents of the screen display in a file on disk.

With EGA, MCGA and VGA adapters a routine is provided that allows for screens of more than 25 rows. This is put into effect with a subfunction of interrupt 10h, function 12h.

---

| | |
|---|---|
| *Interrupt:* | 10h |
| *Function:* | 12h |
| *Service:* | Multi-line print-screen (not CGA) |
| *Entry values:* | AH=12h |
| | BL=20h |
| *Exit values:* | None |

---

# 11 Disks and Disk Drives

This section looks at disks and disk drives and how they are accessed. Most of the routines described here are part of the ROM BIOS and are independent of the operating system. The next chapter looks at the disk file structure imposed by DOS.

It should be noted that the original IBM PC also offered a port for connecting a cassette recorder. Functions 00h to 03h of interrupt 15h provide facilities for handling this device. However, the cassette has rarely been used and these functions are often used for other purposes on PC-compatibles.

The BIOS disk functions form interrupt 13h. In each case, the carry flag is set if an error occurs.

## Floppy disk drives

The operation of the floppy disk drives is controlled by the 765A floppy disk controller (or equivalent). All data transfer is via the DMA controller.

On power-up, the system checks the links or dip switches on the system board to see what floppy drives are installed. It updates memory location 0410h with the relevant data.

The ROM contains data relating to the operation of the drives. This is called the *disk parameter table*. The location of the table is stored as an address at interrupt 14h; this is not an interrupt as such, merely a pointer to the table. The disk parameter table is shown in Figure 11.1.

Port 0352h is used for floppy disk control, as illustrated in Figure 11.2. Bits 0 and 1 select the drive. There may be up to four floppy drives, numbered 0 to 3. The motor for any one of these drives can be switched on with bits 4 to 7.

When one of these bits is set, the disk drive starts and the drive light comes on. Data can be read or written almost immediately. Memory location 043Fh indicates which of the drives are running.

After the completion of any disk operation, the time-out value from the disk parameter table is

**Disk parameter table**

| Byte | Use | Value (hex) |
|---|---|---|
| 00 | 2nd byte of disk controller command | DF |
| 01 | 3rd byte of disk controller command | 02 |
| 02 | Motor timeout | 64 |
| 03 | Sector size code (default = 512 bytes) | 02 |
| 04 | Last sector or track | 09 |
| 05 | Gap length for read and write | 2A |
| 06 | Data length | FF |
| 07 | Gap length for formatting | 50 |
| 08 | 'Blank' character for formatting | F6 |
| 09 | Head settling delay | 0F |
| 0A | Motor on delay | 04 |

*Figure 11.1*

**Port 0352h**

| Bit | Use | |
|---|---|---|
| 7 | Switch on drive 3 motor and enable selection of drive | |
| 6 | Switch on drive 2 motor and enable selection of drive | |
| 5 | Switch on drive 1 motor and enable selection of drive | |
| 4 | Switch on drive 0 motor and enable selection of drive | |
| 3 | Set to enable request to DMA | |
| 2 | Reset Controller (by clearing, waiting, then setting bit) | |
| 1 | ) Select drive | (00=drive A) |
| 0 | ) | (01=drive B) |

*Figure 11.2*

transferred to memory location 0440h. The value is decremented at each clock tick. When it reaches 0, the disk drive is switched off and the corresponding bit in 043Fh is cleared. The light will go off at this stage. The default time-out is 64h.

You can have two drives running at once, particularly when transferring data between drives. However, as a rule only one drive light is on at a time; this indicates the drive that is currently being accessed or the last drive to have been used.

The interrupts use a table of floppy disk information, which is pointed to by the vector for interrupt 1Eh.

## Disks

Disks are circular pieces of plastic or metal, coated with a magnetic substance. The disk is gripped at the hub in the centre and the drive spins it at very high speed. The read/write heads can be moved from the centre of the disk to the outside and can be positioned over any individual track. The heads either touch the surface or float just above it, depending on the type of drive. Each head can either read or write data.

Floppy disks are flexible, and are held in a plastic case. There is a read/write slot in the cover, which allows the heads to transfer data to and from the disk; an index hole, which identifies the start of the tracks; and a write-protect notch, which is used to indicate whether or not a disk may be written to. On PCs, you may find either 3½" or 5¼" disk drives. PS/2s are fitted with 3½" disks as standard, though provision for 5¼" drives is also made.

**The DRIVPARM directive**

DRIVPARM d /F:f /H:h /S:s /T:t /NONREMOVABLE /CHECKDOOR

where:

| | |
|---|---|
| `d` | Drive number (0=A, 1=B, etc.) |
| `f` | Disk format (see below) |
| `h` | Number of heads |
| `s` | Number of sectors |
| `t` | Number of tracks |
| `/NONREMOVABLE` | Non-removable device |
| `/CHECKDOOR` | Checks to be carried out on door lock before any access |

N.B. Only the drive number must be specified. All other parameters optional.

*Figure 11.3*

Hard disks are rigid and held in a vacuum, which allows them to be spun at much higher speeds. Data can be packed much more tightly, giving the advantage of a higher capacity and faster access times. Usually, a hard disk unit consists of at least two separate disks, giving a total of four or more sides.

Each PC is set up for a specific number of drives. Others can be specified through DOS by giving the relevant information in a DRIVPARM directive in CONFIG.SYS, as shown in Figure 11.3.

## Drive numbers

Most of the ROM BIOS interrupts described below require the drive number to be specified. The floppy drives are numbered from 0 (for drive A). The hard disk drives are counted from 80h. Thus the second hard disk drive is 81h.

### Logical drives

If there is only one floppy disk drive, this is allocated two *logical drives*, A and B. This allows you to perform such operations as copying a file from one disk to another using a single drive.

Similarly, the hard disk may be split into a number of *partitions*, each of which is given its own drive letter.

You can also install a device driver (such as RAMDRIVE.SYS) that sets aside part of memory to act like a disk drive. This *RAM drive* is also given its own drive letter.

Finally, any drives on other machines that are accessed via a network are allocated logical drive letters that follow on from those described above.

### DOS drive numbers

The DOS interrupts use a drive numbering system that relates to the logical drives (rather than the physical units). As a general rule 0 represents drive A, 1 is drive B, etc. However, some functions use 0 for the current drive, in which case drive A is 1, and so on.

## Disk architecture

An understanding of the way in which a disk is divided up for data storage is of vital importance when writing programs to transfer data to and from disk.

*Platters*

Each hard disk consists of two or more physical disks, called *platters*.

*Sides*

Data can usually be stored on either side of a floppy disk or platter. On floppy disks the sides are numbered 0 and 1; some drives only allow access to one side of a floppy disk (side 0). Hard disks generally have four or more sides, also numbered from 0.

*Heads*

The sides of a disk are often referred to by the read/write *heads*, particularly on hard disks. When programming, the terms 'side' and 'head' are synonymous.

*Tracks*

Each side of the disk is marked out with a number of concentric circles, where data is to be stored. These are *tracks*. On floppy disks there are either 40 or 80 tracks, numbered from 0. The number of tracks on a hard disk varies.

*Sectors*

Each track is divided into *sectors*, which form the basic unit of data storage. The number of sectors depends on the type of disk and the operating system. Unlike the other units, sectors are numbered from 1.

*Clusters*

For data transfer, the sectors are grouped into *clusters*. Typically there are two or four sectors per cluster. DOS always allocates and transfers data a cluster at a time.

*Cylinders*
The tracks are grouped vertically into *cylinders*. Cylinders are particularly used when referring to hard disks. They are numbered from 0 so, for example, cylinder 0 includes track 0 from each of a standard hard disk's four or more sides.

*Partitions*
Hard disks may be subdivided into *partitions*. Each partition includes a number of consecutive cylinders.

**Physical access to data**
A disk drive has one read/write head for each side. All the heads are moved together. Therefore, for efficiency, the disk is filled one cylinder at a time, starting at cylinder 0 and moving in towards the centre. When changing from one track to another within a cylinder, all that is involved is selecting a different head to read or write the data; this is achieved through the software. When moving to a track in a different cylinder, however, the heads must be physically moved. This takes a relatively long time. Therefore, head movement is kept to a minimum to make disk access as fast as possible.

As data is stored on the disk it inevitably spreads over many cylinders; after changes have been made, a file can easily be split over several cylinders, and access to that file becomes slower. This problem can be overcome by using a utility program that reorganises files on a disk so that data is once more consecutive in each file.

## Sector numbering

All disk organisation is based on the numbering of individual sectors. There are two systems in common use: one for the BIOS, the other for DOS.

**BIOS disk references**
The sector is the smallest unit of data for disk-handling purposes. For the BIOS routines, any sector on a floppy disk can be identified by quoting its track, side and sector number. For hard disks the

reference is the cylinder, head and sector number. The track/cylinder is usually referenced first, to match the order in which the disk is filled.

**DOS disk references**

DOS, which always has to be different, has its own numbering system, based purely on sector numbers. Each sector is given a unique reference number. The sectors are counted through from Track 0 Side 0 Sector 1 in the same order that the disk is filled. These *logical* sector numbers start at 0 and work through to the maximum number.

**Sector number conversions**

You can convert from the BIOS Track:Side:Sector system to DOS sectors with this formula:

DOS sector = (Track x Sectors per track x No. sides)
+ (Side x Sector per track)
+ Sector -1

Similarly, the BIOS reference can be extracted from the DOS sector number with the formula:

Track = INT((DOS Sector)/(No. sides x Sectors per track)
Side = INT(DOS Sector/Sectors per track)mod(No. sides)
Sector = (DOS Sector) mod (Sectors per track) + 1

'INT' represents the integer part of the number.

DOS 4 uses double-word sector numbers, providing access to more than 65,536 sectors.

## Formatting floppy disks

Before a disk can be used it must be *formatted*. This process marks out the tracks and sectors on each side and fills them with blank data. Since each byte is written to, any existing data is destroyed.

Any error, even if it affects only a single byte, results in the whole sector being marked as 'bad.' If there is a bad sector on a floppy disk it should be reformatted; a repeat of the problem usually means that the disk should be regarded as unsafe. For hard disks, bad sectors are a common occurrence and, as long as they do not exceed 1% of the total capacity, should be not be a cause for concern.

**AT-compatibles**

On AT-compatibles (and all PS/2s) you should precede any floppy disk format with calls to functions 17h and 18h of interrupt 13h, which remind the system of the disk type.

---

| | |
|---|---|
| *Interrupt:* | 13h |
| *Function:* | 17h |
| *Service:* | Set floppy disk type |
| *Entry values:* | AH=17h |
| | AL= 01h (5¼" double-density drive) |
| | 02h (5¼" high density drive, DD disk) |
| | 03h (5¼" high density drive and disk) |
| | 04h (3½" drive) |
| *Exit values:* | AH=error code (if CF=1) |

---

| | |
|---|---|
| *Interrupt:* | 13h |
| *Function:* | 18h |
| *Service:* | Set disk parameters |
| *Entry values:* | AH=18h |
| | CH=number of tracks |
| | CL=sectors per track |
| | DL=drive |
| *Exit values:* | AH=error code (if CF=1) |
| | ES:DI points to disk parameter table |

---

The second function returns the address of a copy of the 11-byte disk parameter table (see Figure 11.1).

**The format function**

Formatting is carried out by the BIOS – there is no DOS equivalent – with function 05h of interrupt 13h.

---

| | |
|---|---|
| *Interrupt:* | 13h |
| *Function:* | 05h |
| *Service:* | Format disk track |

*Entry values:* AH=05h
CH=track
DH=head
DL=drive
ES:BX=location of list of address marks
*Exit values:* AH=error code (if CF=1)

This service formats a single track only, a flexibility that can be useful for unusual applications or copy-protection purposes.

**Address marks**

During formatting the BIOS places a four-byte *address mark* at the start of each sector. This identifies the sector and defines the number of bytes of data in the sector (not counting the address mark). The sector size is defined by a code. The construction of the address mark is shown in Figure 11.4.

Before calling the interrupt, a string of address marks must be placed in memory, one for each sector on the track, pointed to by ES:BX.

**Sector address mark**

| Byte | Meaning | Normal Range | |
|---|---|---|---|
| | | Hard disk | Floppy disk |
| 1 | Track/cylinder | 0 - *nn* | 0 - 79 |
| 2 | Side/Head | 0 - 3 | 0 - 1 |
| 3 | Sector | 1 - *nn* | 1 - 9 |
| 4 | No. bytes (code) | 0 - 3 | 0 - 3 |

N.B *nn* = Number varies

**Byte 4: number of bytes code**

| Code | Bytes/sector |
|---|---|
| 0 | 128 |
| 1 | 256 |
| 2 | 512 |
| 3 | 1024 |

*Figure 11.4*

The address mark is needed when the sector is read or written. The interrupt routine searches the marks for a matching value when instructed to read or write a particular sector.

**Writing a blank track**

The BIOS writes an address mark followed by the number of blank bytes specified. The start of the first sector is determined by the position of the index hole.

On floppy disks, there is room for about 5120 bytes of data on each track (ten 512-byte sectors). Usually, therefore, the standard 9-sector format leaves some unused space at the end of each track.

On the PC and most compatibles, the disk drive stays at a constant speed, regardless of the track it is on. Therefore the amount of space physically taken by each byte gets progressively smaller as the heads move towards the centre. For this reason, attempting to format a double density disk as high density will often produce errors in the inner tracks (where the quality of the surface is not good enough to take the high density data).

**DOS formats for floppies**

DOS 1 was only able to handle 5¼" floppies, and these were formatted with eight 512-byte sectors per track, and 40 tracks per side. Drives were either single- or double-sided (SS or DOS), giving capacities of 160K or 320K. Machines that cannot cope with any higher capacity than this are now extremely rare. (Note that DOS 1 was also able to handle 8" disks, which are now obsolete.)

DOS 2 increased disk capacity by allowing nine sectors per track, giving 180K or 360K per disk. This inevitably led to some compatibility problems, though it is now safe to assume that the vast majority of machines are able to cope with these capacities. A disk can be formatted for single-sided machines with the DOS FORMAT command by adding the /1 parameter. To format at eight sectors per track, use /8.

All of these disks are referred to as *double-density* (DD). The *single-density* format became obsolete before the first PCs arrived on the scene.

DOS 3 introduced support for 3½" disks. Double-sided, double-density disks format at 720K (with 9 sectors per track), while high-density (HD) drives give 1.44M (18 sectors per track). At the same time, 5¼" high-density drives were catered for, giving a capacity of 1.2M (with 15 sectors per track).

DOS 5 supports extended-density (ED) 3½" disks, giving a capacity of 2.88M (with 36 sectors per track).

The disk formats supported by DOS are given in Figure 11.5.

Note that 5¼" high-density drives require a level of fine-tuning which often means that a disk formatted as *double* density on one such machine is unreadable on another.

**Floppy Disk Formats**

| Size | Name | Sides | Tracks | Sectors | Capacity | DOS ver |
|---|---|---|---|---|---|---|
| 5¼" | SS DD (8)* | 1 | 40 | 8 | 160K | 1.0 |
| | DS DD (8)* | 2 | 40 | 8 | 320K | 1.25 |
| | SS DD (9)* | 1 | 40 | 9 | 180K | 2.0 |
| | DS DD (9) | 2 | 40 | 9 | 360K | 2.0 |
| | HD | 2 | 80 | 15 | 1.2M | 3.0 |
| 3½" | SS DD (8)* | 1 | 80 | 8 | 320K | 3.2 |
| | DS DD (8)* | 2 | 80 | 8 | 640K | 3.2 |
| | SS DD (9) | 1 | 80 | 9 | 360K | 3.2 |
| | DS DD (9) | 2 | 80 | 9 | 720K | 3.2 |
| | HD | 2 | 80 | 18 | 1.44M | 3.2 |
| | ED | 2 | 80 | 36 | 2.88M | 5.0 |

*Now obsolete

*Figure 11.5*

**Disk Parameter Block (DPB)**

Information relating to the organisation of a disk (bytes per sector, root directory entries, etc.) is held in the BIOS Parameter Block (BPB), which is accessed by the disk driver (see Figure 14.6).

DOS 5 allows you to access a Disk Parameter Block (DPB), where similar information is held. There are two functions: one for the current drive, thet other for any specified drive.

| | |
|---|---|
| *Interrupt:* | 21h |
| *Function:* | 1Fh |
| *DOS version:* | 5 |
| *Service:* | Get current DPB |
| *Entry values:* | AH=1Fh |
| *Exit values:* | AL= 00h (Success) |
| | FFh (Failure) |
| | DS:BX=address of DPB |

| | |
|---|---|
| *Interrupt:* | 21h |
| *Function:* | 32h |
| *DOS version:* | 5 |
| *Service:* | Get DPB |
| *Entry values:* | AH=32h |
| | DL=drive (0=current, 1=A, etc.) |
| *Exit values:* | AL= 00h (Success) |
| | FFh (Failure) |
| | DS:BX=address of DPB |

The layout of the DPB is given in Figure 11.6

**Disk Parameter Block (DPB)**

| Offset | Bytes | Meaning |
|---|---|---|
| 00h | 2 | Drive number (0=A) |
| 02h | 2 | Unit number for driver |
| 04h | 4 | Bytes per sector |
| 08h | 2 | Sectors per cluster – 1 |
| 0Ah | 2 | Sectors per cluster as power of 2 |
| 0Ch | 4 | Sector number of start of FAT |
| 10h | 2 | Number of FATs |
| 12h | 4 | Number of root directory entries |
| 16h | 4 | First sector number of first cluster |
| 1Ah | 4 | Number of clusters + 1 |
| 1Eh | 4 | Total sectors for FAT |
| 22h | 4 | First directory sector |
| 26h | 8 | Address of device driver |
| 2Eh | 2 | Media descriptor |
| 30h | 2 | Access indicator |
| 32h | 8 | Address of next DPB |
| 3Ah | 4 | Last allocated sector number |
| 3Eh | 4 | Number of free sectors |

*Figure 11.6*

## Formatting hard disks

Preparing a hard disk is a little more complex, and requires three stages:

- A *hard format* routine marks out the tracks and writes data to every byte, in the same way as for a floppy disk.
- The disk must be *partitioned*, splitting the cylinders into one or more consecutive groups.
- A *soft format* routine prepares an individual partition for data.

### Hard format

A hard format program blanks out an entire hard disk, overwriting every byte. The number of sides (heads), tracks (cylinders) and sectors per cylinder varies from one hard disk to another. For this reason, each make of PC will have its own hard format program.

The hard format routines may use several of the interrupt 13h functions.

### Partitioning the disk

A partition consists of a number of consecutive cylinders and follows on directly from the previous partition. Each partition is treated as a separate *logical* drive. It is given its own drive letter and the operating system behaves as if it is a separate physical drive. Therefore, the partitions do not even have to be soft formatted with the same operating system.

Note that the first sector of cylinder 0 is used by DOS for storing disk partition information. This table of information identifies the start and end of each partition, the operating system and whether or not the partition is bootable. The first sector also holds a boot program that loads and runs the boot program on the bootable partition.

DOS 2 allows only a single DOS partition. DOS 3 increases this to four partitions but with only one 'active' at a time; to change from one to another the user must run the FDISK program. Each partition has a maximum capacity of 32M.

DOS 3.3 provides for *primary* and *extended* partitions. The extended partition can be given any number of sub-partitions, each with its own drive letter and a maximum capacity of 32M. Effectively, this allows the PC to have disks with no practical limit on size.

Finally, DOS 4 scrapped the 32M limit altogether, by allowing double-word sector numbers.

Because of these restrictions care should be taken if changing operating systems on a hard disk, particularly if restoring an earlier DOS version.

Some hard disks require the installation of a device driver, which oversees the operation of the hard disk.

### Soft format

The final stage is the *soft format*. This is similar to the floppy format except that no data is actually written to the cylinder. The routine simply blanks out the disk directory and file allocation table at the start of the partition. To the user, the disk is blank but any previous data still exists on the hard disk and can, theoretically at least, be recovered.

Note that partitioning and soft formatting are functions of DOS, and not usually allowed for in application programs. Therefore there are no interrupts to deal with them.

### Hard disk information

Several interrupts use a table of hard disk information. For the first hard disk, this table is pointed to by the vector for interrupt 41h. Any second physical hard disk has a table of information pointed to by interrupt 46h.

## Interleaving

On floppies, sectors are usually numbered consecutively on each track. On hard disks, a process called *interleaving* is often used.

The data from a complete sector is read into a buffer as the drive head passes over it. The data is then transferred into the PC's memory. This process takes a little time so that, by the time the buffer has been emptied into RAM, the heads have already moved on and are well into the next sector. If sectors are numbered sequentially, the drive has to wait for almost a complete revolution of the disk before the second sector can be read.

To overcome this problem, consecutive sectors can be written alternately on the track. Thus the sectors may appear in the order 1, 4, 2, 5, ... This gives time for the first sector to be transferred to RAM, while the head passes over the next sector. The head should be at the start of logical sector 2 (physically, the third sector) by the time the CPU is ready to receive the next block of data. This is 2:1 interleaving.

If the disk spins very fast, there may still be insufficient time, so sequentially-numbered sectors may be stored even further apart. For example, 3:1 interleaving would store sectors in the order 1, 4, 7, 2, 5, 8, ...

The interleave ratio is a measure of the efficiency of the drive; the aim is to get the access time as low as possible and have the heads reading or writing for as great a proportion of the time as possible. With a ratio of 2:1 the whole track is read in two revolutions; a ratio of 3:1 takes three revolutions.

Combined with the disk speed, the ratio gives you the access time for reading/writing a track. The time taken to read a complete track is given by:

*Access time* = *Interleave factor* x 60/*Disk speed (rpm)*

This assumes an efficient interleave ratio; if the ratio is too small, so that sectors are missed, access time increases dramatically.

## Reading and writing disk sectors

With disk operations, you are getting into the domain where DOS – the *Disk* Operating System – is master. DOS works with files, of course, and decides where on the disk each will be stored. Operating on sectors can be a little tricky since you can never be sure where a file physically resides (without considerable work). Even so, DOS does provide facilities for working directly with sectors.

Sector-based operations are useful for delicate disk surgery, particularly if you need to repair a damaged directory or recover a lost file.

The ROM BIOS interrupt 13h functions described below use the CL register for passing the number of the sector on the track. Where the number of sectors is greater than 256, the sector number is stored as a 10-bit value, with the top two bits being stored in bits 6 and 7 of CH, and the bottom eight bits in CL.

**Reading sectors**

The BIOS provides function 02h of interrupt 13h for reading one or more sectors.

You must specify the first sector and the number of sectors to be read. All sectors must be on the same drive, track and side. You also need to specify the location where the data is to be stored, with the start address pointed to by ES:BX.

---

*Interrupt:* 13h
*Function:* 02h
*Service:* Read sectors from disk
*Entry values:* AH=02h
AL=number of sectors to read
CH=track (and sector)
CL=sector
DH=head
DL=drive
ES:BX=start of data buffer
*Exit values:* AH=error code (if CF=1)
AL=number of sectors read (if CF=0)

---

Success or failure is indicated by the carry flag, with any error code returned in AH (see below). For hard disks with more than 256 cylinders, the top two bits of CL are combined with CH to get the cylinder number.

DOS has an entire interrupt devoted to the same function.

*Interrupt:* 25h
*DOS version:* 1
*Service:* Read sectors from disk
*Entry values:* AL=logical drive number (A=0)
CX= number of sectors to read
(standard disks)
-1 (large disks - DOS 4)
DX=first sector (DOS numbering)
(standard disks)
DS:BX=start of data buffer
*Exit values:* AH=DOS error code (if CF=1)
AL=BIOS error code (if CF=1)
Flags register on stack

---

The most important distinction to note is that this service uses the DOS sector numbering system, rather than the BIOS system.

**DOS 4 extensions**

Under DOS 4 you can access sectors on disks with capacities in excess of 32M using interrupt 25h. In this case, CX must be set to -1 (even if accessing a sector in the first 32M) and DS:BX points to a 10-byte buffer of information, as shown in Figure 11.7. If you do not set CX=-1, DOS 4 returns with AX=0207h.

**Large disk data buffer**

| Offset (hex) | Size (bytes) | Meaning |
|---|---|---|
| 00 | 4 | First sector |
| 04 | 2 | Number of sectors to read/write |
| 06 | 4 | Start of data buffer |

*Figure 11.7*

When reading or writing sectors on floppy disks (in DOS 4 onwards), you should always call interrupt 21h, function 47h (Check Current Directory – see Chapter 12) before calling interrupt 25h or 26h.

**Writing sectors**

A similar BIOS function is used to write data to one or more sectors.

---

| | |
|---|---|
| *Interrupt:* | 13h |
| *Function:* | 03h |
| *Service:* | Write sectors to disk |
| *Entry values:* | AH=03h |
| | AL=number of sectors to write |
| | CH=track (and sector) |
| | CL=sector |
| | DH=head |
| | DL=drive |
| | DS:BX=start of data buffer |
| *Exit values:* | AH=error code (if CF=1) |
| | AL=no. of sectors written (CF=0) |

---

DOS, with unusual extravagance, allocates another complete interrupt number to the task.

---

| | |
|---|---|
| *Interrupt:* | 26h |
| *DOS version:* | 1 |
| *Service:* | Write sectors to disk |
| *Entry values:* | AL=logical drive number (A=0) |
| | CX= number of sectors to write (standard disks) |
| | -1 (large disks - DOS 4) |
| | DX=first sector (DOS numbering) (standard disks) |
| | DS:BX=start of data buffer |
| *Exit values:* | AH=DOS error code (if CF=1) |
| | AL=BIOS error code (if CF=1) |
| | Flags register on stack |

---

When accessing large disks (above 32M) under DOS 4, the data buffer is the same as that shown in Figure 11.7 above.

**Verification of data**

You can check that data is not corrupt with the verification function.

---

| | |
|---|---|
| *Interrupt:* | 13h |
| *Function:* | 04h |

| | |
|---|---|
| *Service:* | Verify disk sectors |
| *Entry values:* | AH=04h |
| | AL=number of sectors to verify |
| | CH=track |
| | CL=sector |
| | DH=head |
| | DL=drive |
| *Exit values:* | AH=error code (if CF=1) |
| | AL=no. of sectors verified (CF=0) |

This service performs a CRC check on the data, returning an error code if any fault is detected. The service does not verify that the written data matches that in memory; to do that you must write a comparison routine. If data is not written correctly, it may result in a CRC error. However, such an error is more likely to be the result of a disk fault.

DOS has a different function, which turns the verification feature on or off. When verification is on, all data is checked after it has been read or written.

| | |
|---|---|
| *Interrupt:* | 21h |
| *Function:* | 2Eh |
| *DOS version:* | 1 |
| *Service:* | Disk write verification |
| *Entry values:* | AH=2Eh |
| | AL= 00h (verify off) |
| | 01h (verify on) |
| | DL=00h |
| *Exit values:* | None |

This is the basis of the VERIFY command. The main problem with this service is that it slows disk access quite considerably.

You can check whether DOS verification is on or off with function 54h.

| | |
|---|---|
| *Interrupt:* | 21h |
| *Function:* | 54h |
| *DOS version:* | 2 |
| *Service:* | Check verification status |
| *Entry values:* | AH=54h |
| *Exit values:* | AL= 00h (verify off) |
| | 01h (verify on) |

## Disk status

The BIOS functions that form interrupt 13h, described above, return a status code in AH. A code of 00h indicates that the operation was a success; otherwise some sort of error has occurred. The codes returned by these functions are listed in Figure 11.8. The status code can be checked at any time up to the next call to interrupt 13h with function 01h.

*Interrupt:* 13h
*Function:* 01h
*Service:* Check disk status
*Entry values:* AH=01h
*Exit values:* AH=status code

**BIOS disk status codes (AH)**

| Code (hex) | Meaning |
|---|---|
| 01 | Bad command |
| 02 | Missing address mark |
| 03 | Disk write-protected |
| 04 | Sector not found |
| 05 | Reset failure |
| 06 | Drive empty/drive door open |
| 07 | Hard disk parameter table invalid |
| 08 | DMA error |
| 09 | DMA boundary error |
| 0A | Bad hard disk sector mark |
| 10 | CRC error |
| 11 | Hard disk CSC error |
| 20 | Controller error |
| 40 | Seek failure |
| 80 | Time-out error |
| AA | Hard disk not ready |
| BB | General hard disk error |
| CC | Hard disk write error |
| E0 | Hard disk status error |

*Figure 11.8*

The value returned by this service after floppy disk access can also be inspected in memory location 0441h. The seven bytes that follow (0442h-0448h) store other floppy disk and hard disk parameters. The hard disk BIOS routines also use location 0474h; the Floppy Disk Controller uses ports 034Fh and 03F5h.

**DOS error codes**

The DOS disk functions return the same error codes in AH but also supply additional information in AL if the carry flag is set (see Figure 11.9).

After a disk error has occurred, the program should usually try the operation at least once more, particularly when accessing a floppy disk. When a drive is first accessed the speed may not be sufficient, the drive door may not be shut, and so on. In this case, another try is worthwhile before the user is notified of the error.

If an error is encountered, the action taken should depend on the user's response to the error message.

**DOS disk error codes (AL)**

| Code (hex) | Meaning |
|---|---|
| 00 | Disk write-protected |
| 01 | Bad drive number |
| 02 | Drive not ready |
| 04 | CRC error |
| 06 | Seek error |
| 07 | Unknown disk format |
| 08 | Sector not found |
| 0A | Write error |
| 0B | Read error |
| 0C | General error |

*Figure 11.9*

**AT-compatibles**

On AT-compatibles and PS/2s there is an extra BIOS function that returns disk information.

*Interrupt:* 13h
*Function:* 15h
*Service:* Check disk type
*Entry values:* AH=15h
DL=drive
*Exit values:* AH= 00h (drive does not exist)
01h (floppy drive, with no mechanism for detecting disk changes)
02h (floppy drive, able to detect disk changes)
03h (hard disk)
CX:DX=number of 512-byte sectors (if AH=03h)

---

Particularly useful is the fact that this function can tell you whether the disk drive is of a type that can detect when a floppy disk has been removed. In these cases, function 16h can be very useful within a program. This function tells you if the disk has been changed since the last disk access.

---

*Interrupt:* 13h
*Function:* 16h
*Service:* Check floppy disk change
*Entry values:* AH=16h
DL=drive
*Exit values:* AH= 00h (disk not changed)
01h (invalid call)
06h (disk has been changed)
80h (drive not ready)

---

Of course, even if the disk has been removed, the 'new' disk is not necessarily different. There are various ways of checking the disk; in particular, under DOS 4 and later versions you can check the disk's volume serial number.

When a disk change has been detected, a call to function 17h will update the disk table in RAM.

## Resetting the drive

After any disk error, the drive should be reset. This is done with function 00h of interrupt 13h.

| | |
|---|---|
| *Interrupt:* | 13h |
| *Function:* | 00h |
| *Service:* | Reset disk |
| *Entry values:* | AH=00h |
| *Exit values:* | None |

This function repositions the head over a particular track.

DOS provides a similar service.

| | |
|---|---|
| *Interrupt:* | 21h |
| *Function:* | 0Dh |
| *DOS version:* | 1 |
| *Service:* | Reset disk |
| *Entry values:* | AH=0Dh |
| *Exit values:* | None |

This function also writes away any unstored data in the RAM disk buffers. However, you should always close a file properly (see Chapter 13), since this function does not update the directory; as a result, any change in file length is not recorded.

## Disk compression

Standalone disk compression utilities have been available for a number of years. Now, however, disk compression has become a part of the operating system with the inclusion of DoubleSpace in DOS 6. The advantage of disk compression is that the amount of hard disk storage space that is required is dramatically reduced; the disadvantage is that the files become that much more inaccessible.

DoubleSpace uses several new functions of interrupt 1Ah, brief details of which are given here for information. These new functions are the Microsoft

Real-time Compression Interface (MRCI). However, it is strongly recommended that all compression activities be left to the operating system. Tampering with the built-in compression procedures can have unexpected results.

The first subfunction checks that DoubleSpace has been installed. Any values can be put in CX and DX. The interrupt will reverse these values. For example, if CX='AB' and DX='CD' before the interrupt is called, the exit values will be CX='DC' and DX='BA'. The calling routine should check that the correct values have been returned.

---

| | |
|---|---|
| *Interrupt:* | 1Ah |
| *Function:* | B001h |
| *DOS version:* | 6 |
| *Service:* | Check compression installation |
| *Entry values:* | AH=B001h |
| | CX=any |
| | DX=any |
| *Exit values:* | AX= 0 (success) |
| | 1 (failure) |
| | CX=DX reversed |
| | DX=CX reversed |
| | ES:DI=pointer to compression information buffer |

---

The information returned is shown in Figure 11.10.

**Compression information buffer**

| Offset | Bytes | Meaning |
|---|---|---|
| 00h | 4 | Vendor ID |
| 04h | 2 | Compression server version number |
| 06h | 2 | MRCI version number |
| 08h | 4 | Far pointer of server compression entry |
| 0Ch | 2 | Server capabilities (bit fields) |
| 0Eh | 2 | Hardware assistance (bit fields) |
| 10h | 2 | Maximum number of bytes for compression |

*Figure 11.10*

**Compression request buffer**

| Offset | Bytes | Meaning |
|---|---|---|
| 00h | 4 | Pointer to source |
| 04h | 2 | Size of source (bytes) |
| 06h | 2 | Offset where changed data starts (when updating) |
| 08h | 4 | Pointer to destination |
| 0Ch | 2 | Size of destination (bytes) |
| 0Eh | 2 | Minimum compress size |
| 10h | 4 | Incremental decompression state |

*Figure 11.11*

Four subfunctions are used for compressing data. Before calling the subfunctions a buffer of information must be set up (Figure 11.11).

*Interrupt:* 1Ah
*Function:* 0001h-0010h
*DOS version:* 6
*Service:* Compress data
*Entry values:* AX= 0001h (Standard)
0004h (Update)
0008h (Max)
0010h (Max update)
CX= 0 (Client is application)
1 (Client is operating system)
DS:SI=pointer to compression request buffer
ES:BX=pointer to compression information buffer
*Exit values:* AX=error code

The error codes are given in Figure 11.12.

Two subfunctions are used to decompress data.

*Interrupt:* 1Ah
*Function:* 0002h, 0020h
*DOS version:* 6
*Service:* Decompress data
*Entry values:* AX= 0002h (Standard)

| | |
|---|---|
| | 0020h (Incremental) |
| | CX= 0 (Client is application) |
| | 1 (Client is operating system) |
| | DS:SI=pointer to compression request buffer |
| | ES:BX=pointer to compression information buffer |
| *Exit values:* | AX=error code |

**Compression errors**

| Value | Meaning |
|---|---|
| 0 | Success |
| 1 | Unsupported function |
| 2 | Server busy |
| 3 | Destination buffer too small |
| 4 | Could not compress data (compress only) |
| 5 | Bad format for compressed data (decompress only) |

*Figure 11.12*

# 12 The Disk Directory and FAT

Once a disk has been formatted, data can be transferred between the disk and RAM sector by sector. It is feasible to carry out all operations at this level, keeping track of the position of data and by-passing DOS altogether; feasible but not very practical. As data grows or shrinks, its space requirements vary and the original data must either be split or moved elsewhere. Working out where everything is becomes almost impossible without some sort of rigid structure. This is the purpose of the disk directory and file allocation table (FAT).

You can do all this yourself, of course, but most programmers prefer to leave the tedium of looking after files to DOS, freeing the program to get on with the more important aspects of an application. Working via DOS also ensures compatibility between systems and makes data transfer between applications possible.

Although DOS is not part of the PC, it is supplied with every PC and compatible and, from the programmer's point of view, can be treated as a standard feature. These last three chapters concentrate on the main aspects of DOS, which are crucial to the design of all applications. The background operation of DOS is also described, in order to give an idea of how the operating system functions. Since these chapters relate to the way in which DOS stores data – which is software-based and independent of the hardware – the interrupts described are all part of DOS.

This chapter looks at the way DOS allocates space on the disk.

## The DOS FORMAT command

Control of the disk environment begins with the FORMAT command.

Taking up from where we left off in the last chapter, the FORMAT command performs the following tasks:

1. Each track is formatted, using BIOS interrupt 13h, function 05h.
2. A *boot record* is stored on the first sector of the disk. This record stores some basic disk information and, on a system disk, includes the routine to load the operating system.
3. Two copies of the *file allocation table* (FAT) are stored immediately after the boot record. These are used to record the location of files on the disk.
4. Immediately following on from this, a blank disk directory is stored. This will be used to list the files and their attributes.
5. If a system disk is being created (with the FORMAT /S option), the two hidden system files and COMMAND.COM are copied onto the disk. The directory and FAT are updated accordingly.
6. If required, a volume label is attached to the disk and stored in the directory.
7. From DOS 4 a volume serial number is stored on the disk. This serial number is derived from the current date and time, so the chances of having two disks with the same serial number are very remote. The serial number is used by some DOS utilities to guard against incorrect disk changes.

## The directory structure

The main directory, stored immediately after the FAT, is the *root directory*. This consists of a number of records, one for each file on the disk. There is also a record for each sub-directory and one for the volume label. Indeed, anything stored on the disk – apart from the boot sector, FAT and root directory, which occupy fixed positions – has an entry in the root directory or a sub-directory.

Each entry in the directory has a length of 32 bytes. The structure of the directory entries is shown in Figure 12.1.

**Contents of file directory entries**

| Bytes | Meaning |
|---|---|
| 0-7 | Filename |
| 8-10 | Extension |
| 11 | Attributes |
| 12-21 | Reserved (unused) |
| 22-23 | Time stamp |
| 24-25 | Date stamp |
| 26-27 | Start cluster |
| 28-31 | File size |

*Figure 12.1*

There is room for sixteen entries in each 512-byte sector. The number of sectors allocated to the root directory – and hence the number of entries it can store – depends on the disk format. The amount of space allocated to the FAT and root directory for the most common disk formats is shown in Figure 12.2.

**Space allocations for FAT & root directory**

| | | Size in sectors | | Entries | Cluster |
|---|---|---|---|---|---|
| | | FAT x2 | Root dir | in root directory | size (sectors) |
| 5¼" | SS DD | 2 | 4 | 64 | 1 |
| | DS DD | 4 | 7 | 112 | 2 |
| | HD | 14 | 14 | 224 | 1 |
| 3½" | DS DD | 6 | 7 | 112 | 2 |
| | HD | 18 | 14 | 224 | 1 |
| | ED | 18 | 15 | 240 | 2 |
| Hard disks | | ? | 32 | 512 | ? |

NB FAT and cluster size vary for hard disks

*Figure 12.2*

*Filename (bytes 0-7)*

Each file is given a name. This may be up to eight characters long, consisting of letters, numbers and some symbols. The range of permissible characters is shown in Figure 12.3. Note that DOS 2 introduced some extra restrictions, so take care if dealing with DOS 1 disks. (DOS 1 also allowed the use of <>|/ characters.)

Some filenames are *reserved*; these include the DOS internal command names (DIR, COPY, etc.) and the names of the standard devices (PRN, CON, etc. – see Chapter 14).

Although little-used, the extended ASCII characters can be used in a DOS filename. Such a name can be created on the DOS command line using the **Alt**-number pad procedure, though this is some-

**Valid filename characters**

| Character | Hex | Explanation |
|---|---|---|
| | 20 | Space (not for DOS commands) |
| ! | 21 | Exclamation |
| # | 23 | Hash |
| $ | 24 | Dollar |
| % | 25 | Percent |
| & | 26 | Ampersand |
| ' | 27 | Apostrophe |
| ( | 28 | Open bracket |
| ) | 29 | Close bracket |
| - | 2D | Minus |
| 0-9 | 30-39 | Decimal numbers |
| A-Z | 41-5A | Upper case letters |
| ^ | 5E | Carat |
| _ | 5F | Underscore |
| ` | 60 | Forward apostrophe |
| a-z | 61-6A* | Lower case letters |
| { | 7B | Open brace |
| } | 7D | Close brace |
| ~ | 7E | Tilde |
| | 80-FF | Extended ASCII characters |

* Lower case letters converted to upper case (41h - 5Ah)

*Figure 12.3*

what long-winded. The use of **Alt-255**, which displays as a blank, is particularly useful. For extended ASCII characters, code page 850 should be used. (Note that if a filename begins with σ (character E5h) the first filename byte actually holds 05h – see 'Deleting files' later.)

The filename slot may also be used for a subdirectory or volume name, or to indicate a deleted file (see below).

If the filename is less than eight characters long, the remaining bytes are filled with blanks (20h).

Spaces can also be used within a filename, with care. There is no problem for volume names that include spaces, but proper files that include blanks within the name will not be recognised by DOS commands such as COPY and DIR.

DOS 2.0 onwards indicates the end of a directory by putting 00h in the first character of the filename for the entry after the last valid file.

*Extension (bytes 8-10)*

The extension is used as further identification of the file, usually to specify the file type. Again, if it is less than three characters long it is padded with blanks.

Note that the full stop that is used to join the filename and extension in DOS commands is purely cosmetic; it is not actually stored in the directory.

The extensions COM, EXE, SYS and BAT are used by DOS for specific purposes. Most application programs have their own file-naming convention.

*Attribute (byte 11)*

This byte tells DOS what sort of file the entry is. Each bit has a specific meaning and the byte is created by combining them all. The meaning of the attribute byte is described later.

*Time stamp (bytes 22-23)*

This is the time at which the file was created or last updated. When a file is changed, the current time (as held by the system) is stored here; when a file is copied, the time is copied to the new directory entry, unchanged. Similarly, renaming a file has no effect on the time.

**Structure of time stamp word**

```
Bits
 15 14 13 12 11 10  9  8  7  6  5  4  3  2  1  0
 .  .  .  .  .  .  .  .  .  .  .  .  .  .  .  .
 |      Hour      |      Minutes     | Seconds / 2  |
 .  .  .  .  .  .  .  .  .  .  .  .  .  .  .  .
        Byte 23          |          Byte 22
```

Example time stamp

```
Entry in directory appears as D943
```

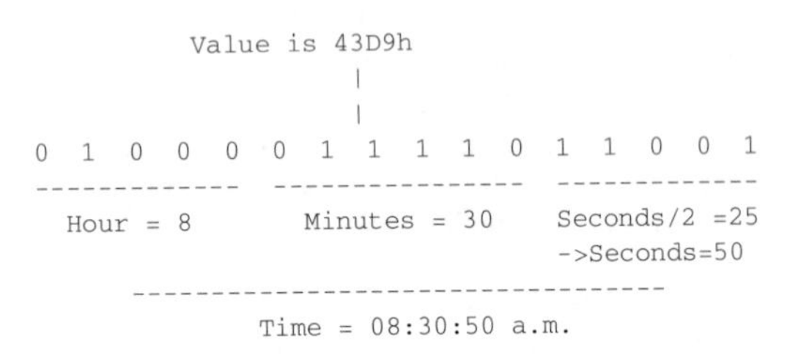


*Figure 12.4*

The time is held in a word, with the low byte first. The meaning of this word is illustrated in Figure 12.4.

Note that there is not enough room to store the seconds in full. Therefore, the time is only stored to the nearest 2 seconds. To get the actual number of seconds, you must multiply the value of the last five bits by 2. The seconds are not shown on the normal DOS directory but are shown in some other utility programs. The seconds part of the entry is generally of little purpose, especially if the internal time maintained by the system is not absolutely accurate.

The time is not validated at any stage. Therefore, any program that changes the time stamp must include a suitable validation routine to make sure that sensible values are being stored.

**Structure of date stamp word**

```
Bits
 15 14 13 12 11 10  9  8  7  6  5  4  3  2  1  0
 .  .  .  .  .  .  .  .  .  .  .  .  .  .  .  .  .
 |     Year - 1980      |   Month   |       Day      |
 .  .  .  .  .  .  .  .  .  .  .  .  .  .  .  .  .
        Byte 25            |         Byte 24
```

Example date stamp

```
Entry in directory appears as 1813
```

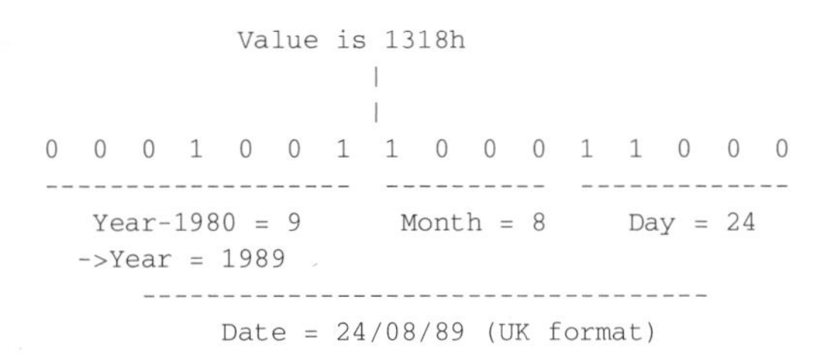


*Figure 12.4*

*Date stamp (byte 24-25)*
This is another word, with the low byte stored first, showing the date of creation or last change to the file. The structure of the date stamp is shown in Figure 12.5 The comments relating to the time stamp also apply here.

*Start cluster (bytes 26-27)*
The *start cluster* is the number of the first cluster used for storing the file. The location of the rest of the file is identified by the FAT.

*File size (bytes 28-31)*
The *file size* is the actual size in bytes. The space on disk is always allocated in complete clusters (for example, two sectors or 1024 bytes on a floppy disk). However, files do not usually fill a cluster complete-

ly. To calculate the disk usage in clusters, divide the file size by the cluster size (in bytes) and round up. To calculate disk usage in bytes, multiply the result by the number of bytes per cluster. For example, if a file is stored on floppy disk and is 1220 bytes long, the disk usage will be:

$$\textit{Clusters used} = \mathrm{INT}\left(\frac{1220-1}{1024}\right) + 1 = 2$$

$$\textit{Bytes used} = 2 \times 1024 = 2048$$

The general formula is:

$$\textit{Bytes used} = \left(\mathrm{INT}\left(\frac{\textit{File siz}-1}{\textit{Clustr siz}}\right) + 1\right) \times \textit{Cluster size}$$

The file size is stored as a double word, with the low word first, and the low byte first for each word (i.e. the bytes are in reverse order).

Some applications always store data in convenient blocks: for example, 128 or 256 bytes. In these cases, the file size is always shown in multiples of these blocks, even though the actual end-of-file marker might come sooner. Remember, DOS calculates the size from the parameters given when the file is saved, so will use whatever values are supplied by the application.

## The file attributes

The use of the attribute byte is shown in Figure 12.6. The meaning of each bit is as follows:

- Read-only. If this bit is set, the file cannot be changed, though its contents can still be read.
- Hidden. Hidden files are not shown in the directory listings and are ignored by commands such as COPY, TYPE, REN and DEL.
- System. The system files are usually IBMBIO.COM and IBMDOS.COM, or MSDOS.SYS and IO.SYS. System files are usually also hidden.
- Volume label. If this bit is set, the entry is a volume label. No corresponding data exists elsewhere on the disk and the other bits in the attribute byte should be clear. There should be

**File attribute byte**

| Bit | Meaning (if set) |
|---|---|
| 0 | Read-only file |
| 1 | Hidden file |
| 2 | System file |
| 3 | Volume label |
| 4 | Sub-directory |
| 5 | Archive |
| 6-7 | Not used |

NB Under DOS 1 only bits 1 and 2 were used

*Figure 12.6*

only one volume label in the root directory and none in the sub-directories.

- Sub-directory. This bit indicates that this 'file' has the same structure of the root directory and is used for storing sub-directory entries. The other bits in the attribute byte should be clear.
- Archive. This bit, if set, indicates that the file has been changed or is a new file. The bit is automatically set by DOS when writing updated files (as long as you go through the DOS interrupts). The XCOPY and BACKUP commands will copy only files with the archive bit set if the /M parameter is used. Other parameters are used to clear the archive bit. With care, you can make use of the archive bit in an application.

More information on the volume label and sub-directory is given later.

In the normal course of events, only certain combinations of attributes are meaningful, as illustrated in Figure 12.7. It is unwise to tamper with this system, since files that have unconventional attributes may cause problems with other applications. However, sub-directories may also be given read-only and system attributes if required.

**Practical attribute values**

| Code (hex) | R-O | Hidden | Sys | Vol | Subd | Arch |
|---|---|---|---|---|---|---|
| 00 | | | | | | |
| 01 | X | | | | | |
| 02 | | X | | | | |
| 03 | X | X | | | | |
| 04 | | | X | | | |
| 05 | X | | X | | | |
| 06 | | X | X | | | |
| 07 | X | X | X | | | |
| 08 | | | | X | | |
| 10 | | | | | X | |
| 12 | | X | | | | X |
| 20 | | | | | | X |
| 21 | X | | | | | X |
| 22 | | X | | | | X |
| 23 | X | X | | | | X |
| 24 | | | X | | | X |
| 25 | X | | X | | | X |
| 26 | | X | X | | | X |
| 27 | X | X | X | | | X |

*Figure 12.7*

### Attribute interrupts

You can check the attribute byte for a file with interrupt 21h, function 43h, subfunction 00h.

| | |
|---|---|
| *Interrupt:* | 21h |
| *Function:* | 43,00h |
| *DOS version:* | 2 |
| *Service:* | Get attributes of file |
| *Entry values:* | AH=43h |
| | AL=00h |
| | DS:DX=address of ASCIIZ file specification |
| *Exit values:* | AX=error code (if CF=1) |
| | DX:AX=attribute byte |

The filename must be stored as an ASCIIZ string, pointed to by DS:DX. The attribute is returned in CL; CH is always 0.

You can change the attribute for a file with subfunction 01h. The new attribute should be placed in CL, CH being cleared. The filename is pointed to by DS:DX, as above.

| | |
|---|---|
| *Interrupt:* | 21h |
| *Function:* | 43,01h |
| *DOS version:* | 2 |
| *Service:* | Set attributes of file |
| *Entry values:* | AH=43h |
| | AL=01h |
| | CX=new attribute byte |
| | DS:DX=address of ASCIIZ file specification |
| *Exit values:* | AX=error code (if CF=1) |

These functions are used by utilities such as ATTRIB.

## Volume labels

When formatting a disk with DOS, you are given an opportunity to store a volume label. At any time, you can change or add a label (if there is not one there) with the LABEL command. The label can be displayed with the VOL command. The volume label can be up to eleven characters long.

The label is treated as a file, so you can get or change it with the standard interrupts. This is demonstrated in Figure 12.8, using the interrupts described in the next chapter.

```
FINDVOL:        ;Displays a disk's volume label

      ;This is a totally self-contained
      ;program which could be converted
      ;into a routine

      ;Entry values: None
      ;Exit values:  AX, BX, CX, DX changed

      jmp volst

fname           db '*.*',00h
```

```
volst:
        mov cx,08h                  ;CX=Volume attribute
        lea dx,fname                ;Point to filename
        mov ah,4eh
        int 21h                     ;Find first matching
                                    ;file
        lea dx,9eh                  ;Point to filename
        mov bx,9eh
        mov byte ptr [bx+08h],'$' ;Add a $
        mov ah,09h
        int 21h                     ;Display volume name
        lea dx,0a7h
        mov byte ptr [bx+0ch],'$'
        int 21h
        int 20h
```

*Figure 12.8*

Although there is nothing to stop you putting more than one volume label in the root directory, or a volume label in other directories, the additional labels are ignored by DOS commands.

## Sub-directories

The root directory is soon filled up, especially on low-capacity floppies. Under DOS 1, there is nothing you can do about this situation. Once the directory is full, no more data can be stored on the disk, regardless of the amount of free space remaining.

DOS 2 introduced the principle of sub-directories. As described above, the root directory is a series of fixed-length records, each giving information about a file, sub-directory or volume name. A sub-directory is simply a random access file which mimics this record structure. Because it is a file, it can be of any length and may be stored anywhere on the disk. Therefore, there is no limit to the number of entries it may hold, or to the number of sub-directories there may be. Any sub-directory may have further sub-directories as entries, and there can be any practical number of directory levels.

By inspecting the directories, you can produce a tree of directory entries. This procedure is used by programs such as TREE.

The root directory is the *parent directory* of any sub-directories it contains. These in turn, are the parent directories of any further sub-directories that they hold.

The only difference between the sub-directory file and any other file is that the sub-directory bit is set in the attribute byte. (It is therefore feasible to create a directory in an application, using the structure described above, and then convert it to a sub-directory by updating the attribute byte.)

**Special directory entries**

The root directory contains the names of files, possibly a volume label and the names of any sub-directories. The first two entries in every sub-directory are reserved for a specific use and are given particular 'filenames':

| | |
|---|---|
| . | Sub-directory |
| .. | Parent directory |

The full stop (2Eh) is an entry for the sub-directory itself. This entry duplicates the entry in the parent directory. Any reference in a DOS command to this 'file' will be taken as a reference to the directory itself.

The double full stop (2E2Eh) holds the details of the parent directory. This entry provides a vital link to allow movement up and down the chain of directories. The start cluster for this entry points to the start of the first cluster of the parent directory. There is also a special case; a start cluster of 0000h indicates that the parent is the root directory.

## The current drive

The interrupts described in the next chapter provide various options for manipulating files. In each case, a filename is required. This may take the form of either a full file specification, including drive and path from root directory, or just a part of the specification, where either the drive or the path are assumed.

Unless specified otherwise, DOS assumes that a reference is being made to the *current drive*. This is the drive that is used by DOS if no particular drive is specified. Initially it is the drive containing the system disk but it can be changed from the DOS command line. This is done by entering the drive letter followed by a colon. Within the DOS interrupts, however, the drive is generally referred to by a number. 0 represents drive A, 1 is drive B, and so on.

You can check the current directory with function 19h of interrupt 21h.

---

| | |
|---|---|
| *Interrupt:* | 21h |
| *Function:* | 19h |
| *DOS version:* | 1 |
| *Service:* | Get current drive |
| *Entry values:* | AH=19h |
| *Exit values:* | AL=default drive (0=A, 1=B, etc.) |

---

The number of the current drive is also held in memory at 03F2h.

The current drive is changed with function 0Eh.

---

| | |
|---|---|
| *Interrupt:* | 21h |
| *Function:* | 0Eh |
| *DOS version:* | 1 |
| *Service:* | Change current drive |
| *Entry values:* | AH=0Eh |
| | DL=drive number (0=A, 1=B, etc.) |
| *Exit values:* | AL=drive count |

---

This function also returns the number of *logical drives* available, including:

- Physical drives (both floppy and hard)
- A logical drive B for single floppy systems
- The additional logical drives on the hard disk partitions
- Any RAM disk

To find the number of drives, without changing the current drive, use function 19h to get the current drive in AL, then transfer this value to DL before calling function 0Eh.

**Boot drive**

DOS 4 provides a subfunction of function 33h that returns the drive that was used to boot the system.

| | |
|---|---|
| *Interrupt:* | 21h |
| *Function:* | 33,05h |
| *DOS version:* | 4 |
| *Service:* | Get boot drive |
| *Entry values:* | AH=33h |
| | AL=05h |
| *Exit values:* | DL=boot drive (1=A, 3=C) |

There are only two possible return values.

## The current directory

In the same way as for the drives, DOS maintains a *current directory* for each drive. This is the directory in which all work will be done if no particular directory is specified. Initially, the current directory is the root directory of each drive. You can check the current directory with DOS function 47h. You must specify the drive and a location for DOS to store the path to the current directory.

| | |
|---|---|
| *Interrupt:* | 21h |
| *Function:* | 47h |
| *DOS version:* | 2 |
| *Service:* | Check current directory |
| *Entry values:* | AH=47h |
| | DL=drive (0=default) |
| | DS:SI=address for pathname |
| *Exit values:* | AX=error code (if CF=1) |
| | DS:SI=address of pathname |

After the interrupt has finished, DS:SI will point to an ASCIIZ string consisting of the path from the root, excluding the drive specifier and initial backslash. For example, if the current drive on the hard disk is C:\UTILS, then specifying drive 2 for the function returns 'UTILS', followed by a null byte. If the current directory is the root, the ASCIIZ string consists of the null character alone.

Any error is indicated by the carry flag being set (CF=1), with an error code stored in AX. The meaning of this code is the same as that for the interrupts in the previous chapter (see Figures 11.6 and 11.7).

You can change the current directory with function 3Bh. This function is similar to function 47h above but this time the path to the current directory (excluding the drive specifier and backslash) must be put in a buffer pointed to by DS:DX.

| | |
|---|---|
| *Interrupt:* | 21h |
| *Function:* | 3Bh |
| *DOS version:* | 2 |
| *Service:* | Change directory |
| *Entry values:* | AH=3B |
| | DS:DX=address of ASCIIZ directory name |
| *Exit values:* | AX=error code (if CF=1) |

These functions are used by the DOS CD (CHDIR) command.

## Manipulating sub-directories

Versions of DOS from 2.0 onwards provide functions to create and delete sub-directories. These form the basis of the MD (MKDIR) and RD (RMDIR) commands. There is no interrupt (or DOS command) to rename a sub-directory, although this is easy to achieve.

### Creating a sub-directory

A new sub-directory is created with DOS function 39h. You can give either the full path to the directory or just a part of it. If no drive is specified, DOS assumes the new directory is to be on the current drive. If the first directory in the path does not start with a backslash, DOS assumes that the path is from the current directory, rather than the root. Therefore, this function works in the same way as the MD command. (To be more precise, the DOS command automatically follows the rules set by this function.)

| | |
|---|---|
| *Interrupt:* | 21h |
| *Function:* | 39h |
| *DOS version:* | 2 |
| *Service:* | Make directory |
| *Entry values:* | AH=39 |
| | DS:DX=address of ASCIIZ directory name |
| *Exit values:* | AX=error code (if CF=1) |

The new sub-directory name is added to the relevant directory, one cluster is allocated to the sub-directory and the first two entries – '.' and '..' – are stored in the sub-directory. Extra clusters will be added as the directory expands.

**Deleting a sub-directory**

Function 3Ah works in a similar way to function 39h described above. The sub-directory must be empty and must not be the current directory.

| | |
|---|---|
| *Interrupt:* | 21h |
| *Function:* | 3Ah |
| *DOS version:* | 2 |
| *Service:* | Remove directory |
| *Entry values:* | AH=3Ah |
| | DS:DX=address of ASCIIZ directory name |
| *Exit values:* | AX=error code (if CF=1) |

The sub-directory is deleted in the same way as a normal file. That is, the first character is changed to E5h, as described below. The directory can be recovered by changing the first character back again.

You can overcome the limitation on emptiness very easily, by making the program delete all existing files first.

**Renaming a sub-directory**
From the DOS prompt, the only way to rename a sub-directory is by creating a new directory, copying all the files to it and then deleting the original files and directory. It is strange that no DOS command exists to perform what should be a very simple process.

## The file allocation table (FAT)

On a new disk, DOS stores the files sequentially. When a file is deleted, a gap is created. The next time a file is created or extended, DOS uses this gap before any later spaces. There is no clever routine to find the biggest gap; DOS uses the sledgehammer approach, which requires the minimum effort. DOS always starts searching at the beginning of the disk and uses the gaps as it finds them. If a file does not fit entirely in a gap, DOS stores as much of the file as possible there and moves on to the next gap. Files that are split in this way are said to be *fragmented*. DOS makes no attempt to avoid fragmentation, even if there is plenty of free space at the end of the disk.

Obviously, some careful work needs to be done to keep track of where files are stored. This information is recorded in the *file allocation table* (FAT). DOS always works in terms of clusters, each of which is made up of one or more sectors, depending on the disk format (as shown in Figure 12.2). The FAT is a table of values, one for each cluster on the disk. The clusters are numbered sequentially from the start of the disk, in a similar way to the DOS sector numbering system.

The first few clusters are reserved for the boot sector, two copies of the FAT and the root directory. The remainder of the disk is used for file storage.

DOS uses the entries in the FAT to create a chain of information for each file. The file's directory entry points to the first cluster used for the data. The entry for this cluster in the FAT points to the next cluster that is used, and so on down the chain. Therefore, you can work forwards from the directory entry to find all the clusters used for a file. The last cluster used by a file contains the value FFFh or FFFFh.

This method of chaining clusters together is used for all files, regardless of whether or not they are fragmented. A string of such clusters is called a *chain*.

**Lost and cross-linked clusters**

Generally, there will be one chain for each file. However, if the disk is corrupted in any way, there may be 'lost' clusters that no longer belong to a file. These lost clusters in turn form chains: hence CHKDSK's attempt to 'Convert lost chains to files?' This utility simply adds a directory entry pointing to the first cluster in the chain. The file thus created (FILE*nnnn*.CHK) may or may not be usable.

Another favourite message of the CHKDSK program is 'Files cross-linked at cluster *nnn*.' This indicates that two apparently valid entries in the FAT point to the same cluster; in other words, there is a chain that seems to belong to the end of two separate files. There is no way of knowing which is the correct one. The best solution is to make a copy of the disk and then try amending the FAT so that the two possibilities can be tried, to find out which is the correct one.

## Fragmentation

Fragmentation eventually causes disk operations to slow down, especially on hard disks, since the heads must be physically moved to several different parts of the disk in order to read a single file. The movement of heads is the slowest part of the process. Various utilities exist that will tidy up a disk by rewriting it, with the files stored in consecutive clusters. However, this process is potentially very destructive and, if interrupted before complete, can wreck an entire disk. Therefore, you should always take back-ups of all files before starting on this procedure.

## FAT structure

DOS keeps two identical copies of the FAT; quite why this is so is a bit of a mystery, since they are stored side by side and any corruption of the first track is likely to damage both copies of the FAT. Anyway, DOS never uses the second copy.

The size of the FAT entry for each cluster depends on the disk format:

- Floppy disks and hard disks with capacity less than 20M have 12-bit entries (1½ bytes).
- Hard disks of 20M or more have 16-bit entries (2 bytes).

20M disks have more clusters than the maximum 4096 value which can be stored in a 12-bit entry. Therefore, a 2-byte entry is needed to hold the larger cluster numbers.

The first two entries in the FAT (which can be considered as relating to clusters 0 and 1) are reserved. The first byte in the FAT is an indication of the disk format, as shown in Figure 12.9; this value is not tremendously helpful. The disk type code is copied from the boot record (see Figure 3.3).

The other bytes in the first two entries – either two or three bytes – are filled with the value FFh.

To tie in with this usage, the first data cluster after the root directory is numbered 2. The clusters holding the boot sector, FAT and root directory do not need FAT entries, of course.

Note that a copy of the FAT and the current directory is also held in memory and regularly updated. However, you should not rely on this, as an unnoticed disk swap may result in directories being corrupted. (WordStar is one program which uses the directory in memory; swapping floppy disks without telling WordStar that you have done so can result in the entire disk being corrupted.)

**Disk type, as indicated by first byte of FAT**

| | Disk type | | 1st byte (hex) |
|---|---|---|---|
| 8" | | | FD/FE |
| 5.25" | 8 sector | SS DD* | FE |
| | | DS DD* | FF |
| | 9 sector | SS DD* | FC |
| | | DS DD | FD |
| | 15 sector | HD | F9 |
| 3.5" | 8 sector | SS* | FA |
| | | DS* | FB |
| | 9 sector | SS* | F9 |
| | | DS | F9 |
| | 18 sector | HD | F0 |
| | 36 sector | ED | F0 |
| | Hard disks | | F8 |

| 1st byte (Hex) | Disk type |
|---|---|
| F0 | 3½" HD, ED |
| F8 | Hard disk |
| F9 | 3½" DD; 5¼" HD |
| FA | 3½" SS DD (8)* |
| FB | 3½" DS DD (8)* |
| FC | 5¼" SS DD (9)* |
| FD | 5¼" DS DD (9); 8"* |
| FE | 5¼" SS DD (8); 8"* |
| FF | 5¼" DS DD (8)* |

* Now obsolete

*Figure 12.9*

**16-bit FAT entries**

Making sense of the FAT entries is reasonably straightforward for the 2-bit entries used on most hard disks. The entry for cluster *n* is in bytes (*n* x 2) and (*n* x 2) + 1. This entry is a word pointing to the next cluster, with the low byte stored first.

**12-bit FAT entries**

The reason for using 12-bit entries is also a bit of a mystery. Presumably it is to save space but, in fact, the savings are minimal. The use of 12-bit entries provides immense complications to the decoding of the information stored in the FAT.

Each group of three bytes holds two entries. The first entry is stored as the low byte followed by the high four bits. The second entry is stored as the bottom 4 bits followed by the high 8 bits. Therefore, the middle byte of the group has four bits from each of the entries and, to extend this absurd system further, these two 4-bit values are stored in reverse order. For example, if two FAT entries are 0123h and 0456h, they are stored in three bytes as:

```
23 61 45
```

**Decoding the 12-bit entries**

The entry for cluster $n$ can be found in the bytes:

$$\mathrm{INT}\left(\frac{nx3}{2}\right) \text{ and } \mathrm{INT}\left(\frac{nx3}{2}+1\right)$$

'INT' represents the integer part of the result.

These two bytes must be treated as being in reverse order, so the second byte should be put first to form a single word. The rule is: if $n$ is even, ignore the top four bits; if $n$ is odd, ignore the last four bits.

Some FAT values have special meanings; the effect of FAT values is shown in Figure 12.10.

**Meaning of FAT entries**

| 12-bit Value | 16-bit Values | Meaning |
|---|---|---|
| 000h | 0000h | Cluster not used |
| 001h | 0001h | Impossible value |
| 002h-FEFh | 0002h-FFEFh | Pointer to next cluster |
| FF0h-FF6h | FFF0h-FFF6h | Reserved cluster |
| FF7h | FFF7h | Cluster contains bad sector |
| FF8h-FFFh | FFF8h-FFFFh | End of file |

*Figure 12.10*

## Recovering FAT information

Unfortunately there is no simple interrupt to get the FAT data; you must use the procedures described above. However, you can get general FAT information with function 1Bh.

---

*Interrupt:* 21h
*Function:* 1Bh
*DOS version:* 1
*Service:* Get FAT information for current drive
*Entry values:* AH=1Bh
*Exit values:* AL=sectors per cluster
CX=bytes per sector
DX=clusters
DS:BX=address of ID byte

---

For the disk in the current drive, this gives the number of sectors per cluster, the number of bytes per sector and the number of clusters on the disk. It also gives the address of the FAT in memory; you can get the disk code from there but should not use it for anything else. You can also calculate the disk capacity:

*Disk capacity* = *total clusters* x *sectors per cluster* x *bytes per sector*

Similarly, function 1Ch allows you to get the same information for any drive.

---

*Interrupt:* 21h
*Function:* 1Ch
*DOS version:* 1
*Service:* Get FAT information for any drive
*Entry values:* AH=1Ch
DL=drive (0=default, 1=A, 2=B, etc.)
*Exit values:* AL=sectors per cluster
CX=bytes per sector
DX=clusters
DS:BX=address of ID byte

---

In this case, you must specify DL=0 to get information for the current drive (after which the function is identical to 1Bh). For any other drive, DL must hold the drive number but the usual number must be incremented by 1: drive A is numbered 1, B is 2 and so on. This inconsistency between DOS functions is rather frustrating.

Finally, DOS provides function 36h to give some additional information.

---

| | |
|---|---|
| *Interrupt:* | 21h |
| *Function:* | 36h |
| *DOS version:* | 1 |
| *Service:* | Get free clusters |
| *Entry values:* | AH=36h |
| | DL=drive (0=default, 1=A, 2=B, etc.) |
| *Exit values:* | AX= sectors per cluster |
| | FFFFh (invalid drive) |
| | BX=number of free clusters |
| | CX=bytes per sector |
| | DX=total clusters on disk |

---

This function is similar to those above but includes the number of free clusters. You can calculate the amount of free space on the disk by:

*Free bytes* = *free clusters* x *sectors per cluster* x *bytes per sector*

Remember that, as on a directory listing, the total number of bytes in each file plus the total free bytes will not equal the total disk space, since the directory records the actual size of the files but space is allocated in whole clusters.

DOS automatically updates the directory and both copies of the FAT when it performs any file operation. Therefore, if you make any manual adjustments, make sure the process is seen right through to the end.

## Deleting files

When a file is deleted, DOS simply changes the first character of the filename in the directory to σ (E5h) and erases the entry in the FAT. (Note that, in some circumstances, DOS 1 also uses E5h to indicate an unused entry.) No other change is made. The directory entry remains intact and the file itself is not altered. The next time a file is created or changed, it will use the first available space, and almost certainly overwrite a deleted file. At that stage, the file becomes irrevocably damaged.

If no files are created or changed, you can recover a deleted file by replacing the first character with any suitable letter or number and reassembling the FAT entry. If part of a file has been overwritten, it may be possible to recover some of the file by locating the remaining chains and then converting them to files.

## Disk access

Before accessing any disk, DOS issues a Command 1 (Media Check) to the disk device driver (see Chapter 14). The purpose is to check whether the disk has been replaced since the last access. If the result is that there has been no change, DOS assumes that the FAT and directory in memory are still accurate and works with these. If the disk has been changed, DOS re-reads the FAT and directory. If the answer is 'Don't know', DOS checks the file buffers. If they are empty, DOS assumes the disk has been changed and re-reads the FAT and directory, then issues a Command 2 (Build BPB) to the device driver. If the buffers contain unwritten data, DOS writes the data away to disk, assuming no change has taken place. If the disk has in fact been changed, the new disk will be corrupted.

# 13 Files

This chapter looks at the DOS file-handling facilities. Although these are not related to the PC hardware in any way, they are central to almost all PC applications.

## Data transfer areas

Much of the information that is passed to and from DOS is transferred via the Data Transfer Area (DTA). This is an area of memory used for temporary data storage. The default DTA is 128 bytes long and is stored in the PSP (see Chapter 3). You can change the default DTA with interrupt 21h, function 1Ah. All you need to do is point to the new transfer area.

| | |
|---|---|
| *Interrupt:* | 21h |
| *Function:* | 1Ah |
| *DOS version:* | 1 |
| *Service:* | Set disk transfer area address |
| *Entry values:* | AH=1Ah |
| | DS:DX=new address of DTA |
| *Exit values:* | None |

You can identify the location of the DTA with function 2Fh.

| | |
|---|---|
| *Interrupt:* | 21h |
| *Function:* | 2Fh |
| *DOS version:* | 2 |
| *Service:* | Get address of DTA |
| *Entry values:* | AH=2Fh |
| *Exit values:* | AX=error code |
| | ES:BX=address of DTA |

This is much simpler than trying to calculate the location as an offset in the PSP.

## Disk buffers

When a file has been opened, DOS sets aside a disk buffer in memory for data being transferred to and from a file. This is to improve program efficiency; disk access is comparatively slow, so needs to be kept to a minimum. Any instruction to write data to a file actually results in the data being written to the buffer. Only when the buffer is full does DOS write the entire buffer to disk, and then clear the buffer ready for new data. Similarly, when reading data, DOS always reads a complete buffer of data at a time, regardless of how much data is requested. Before reading the data in, DOS checks to see if the data that is required is already held in the buffer; new data is only read if the data does not already exist in the buffer. When a file is closed, the entire contents of the buffer are written away.

This has the advantage of speeding up access. The disadvantage is that if you leave a program without closing a file, any data not written away will be lost. For this reason, the user should always follow the correct exit procedure for any program. If a programmer wants to be sure that all data is safe, any file should be closed after an instruction to write data to it, and then re-opened.

The file buffer size defaults to two sectors but can be changed with the BUFFERS directive in CONFIG.SYS. The figure given in the `BUFFERS = n` instruction should be the number of sectors required. Different applications may require different buffer sizes, in which case you must find a suitable balance. Too small a buffer results in the program being slowed down, because of the large number of disk accesses that are required; too large a buffer means that a greater proportion of memory is taken up and on the infrequent occasions when disk access is required, this takes much longer.

In memory, the buffer physically exists as a 528-byte block; each sector is preceded by a 16-byte header.

## File specifications

Most of the interrupts described in this chapter require a file specification to be supplied. This specification consists of up to four parts:

- The drive, consisting of a letter and colon
- The directory path, consisting of a string of sub-directory names, separated by a backslash
- The filename, up to eight characters long
- The extension, separated from the filename by a full stop

The only part of the specification that is obligatory is the filename.

- If there is no drive letter, the current drive is assumed.
- If there is no directory path, the current directory is assumed.
- If the path begins with a backslash, it is assumed to start in the root directory.
- If there is no backslash, the path is taken from the current directory.

In other words, the entry must be given in precisely the same way as that required by the DOS commands.

Physically, the file specification must be stored in memory as an ASCIIZ string: that is, a plain string of text, terminated by the null (00h) character.

If the path includes the special '.' or '..' entries, indicating the current or parent directory, then DOS treats these as any other directory entry. Since both entries physically exist in each sub-directory, they are found automatically and the entry points to the required place on disk. Therefore, no special programming is needed to cater for these two cases.

### Networks

A drive, file or device is on a network (a *resource*) is referred to by the *network name*, which takes the following form:

*\\computer\share\path*

The *computer* name identifies the network server that 'owns' the resource; the *share* name identifies the resource (drive or other device); the *path* is a standard DOS path, consisting of directories and a filename (but with no drive letter). The path is optional.

## Ambiguous file specifications

In some cases, you can specify an *ambiguous* file specification, which includes the ? and * wildcards. Any character or string of characters in the filename or extension (or both) can be replaced by these characters, following the standard DOS conventions. There are DOS interrupts to find the first and subsequent matching files. Therefore, again, DOS incorporates some useful routines, obviating the need for writing your own complex routines.

### Finding matching files

If you want to identify a group of files that match an ambiguous file specification – for example, to copy, delete or list them – DOS provides two interrupts to do this.

The ambiguous specification must be indicated by DS:DX, and then function 4Eh of interrupt 21h can be called.

| | |
|---|---|
| *Interrupt:* | 21h |
| *Function:* | 4Eh |
| *DOS version:* | 2 |
| *Service:* | Find first matching file |
| *Entry values:* | AH=4Eh |
| | CX=file attribute |
| | DS:DX=address of ASCIIZ file specification |
| *Exit values:* | AX=error code (if CF=1) |

**DTA after file found**

| Offset (hex) | Bytes (hex) | Use |
|---|---|---|
| 0 | 15 | 'Next file' information |
| 15 | 1 | File attribute |
| 16 | 2 | Time stamp |
| 18 | 2 | Date stamp |
| 1A | 4 | File size |
| 1E | 0D | Filename, period, extension (ASCIIZ) |

*Figure 13.1*

DOS returns the first matching file, putting the name in the DTA. The layout of the DTA after this interrupt has finished is shown in Figure 13.1.

If CF=1, either a disk error has occurred or no matching file was found. The error code is returned in AX.

You can also specify attributes to be matched, to further refine the search. Permissible attributes are hidden, system or sub-directory. If you specify the volume attribute, the file specification is ignored.

Having located the first matching file, you can go on to find subsequent matches with function 4Fh.

| | |
|---|---|
| *Interrupt:* | 21h |
| *Function:* | 4Fh |
| *DOS version:* | 2 |
| *Service:* | Find next matching file |
| *Entry values:* | AH=4Fh |
| | DS:DX=address of information from previous search |
| *Exit values:* | AX=error code (if CF=1) |

The interrupt returns the next matching file in the DTA. DOS keeps track of where it has got to, so each call to this routine will produce a new file. When the end of the list is reached, the carry flag is set. Figure 13.2 provides a program to list all files that match a given specification.

```
SEARCH:         ;Searches for all files that match
                ;a given specification and prints
                ;them in a list (Demonstration
                ;Prog)

      jmp searchst

fnamea          db '\*.*',00h ;Put file
                              ;specification here,
                              ;or get by parsing
                              ;the command line

searchst:
      push ax
      push bx
      push cx
      push dx
      push di
      mov cx,16h
      lea dx,fnamea           ;Point to file
                              ;specification
      mov ah,4eh
      int 21h                 ;Find first match
      jc quit                 ;Exit if not found

show:
      lea dx,9eh
      mov bx,9eh
      mov byte ptr [bx+0ch],'$'
                            ;Add $ to name in PSP
      mov ah,09h
      int 21h                 ;Print name
      call blank              ;Blank name in PSP
      lea dx,fnamea
      mov ah,4fh
      int 21h                 ;Get mext match
      jnc show                ;Repeat if found

quit:
      pop di
      pop dx
      pop cx
      pop bx
      pop ax
      int 20h                 ;To make into
                              ;routine put RET here

blank:                        ;Fill area to be
                              ;used by filename
                              ;with blanks
      push cx
```

```
        mov cx,0ch              ;Repeat 12 times
        xor di,di
put:
        mov byte ptr [bx+di],20h  ;Store space
        inc di
        loop put
        pop cx
        ret
```

*Figure 13.2*

## DOS error codes

For the interrupt 21h functions from 38h onwards, DOS uses a set of standard error codes. Usually the error is indicated by the carry flag being set (CF=1) and an error code is returned in AH. Sometimes, however, the carry flag is not set, so you should always check AH anyway. If AH=0, no error has occurred. These standard error codes and their meanings are listed in Figure 13.3.

For the DOS 3 functions, all routines return extra error information. You can only access this by a call to function 59h.

---

*Interrupt:* 21h
*Function:* 59h
*DOS version:* 3
*Service:* Get error codes
*Entry values:* AH=59h
BX=0000h
*Exit values:* AX=extended error code
BH=type of error
BL=possible action
CH=location of error

---

Function 59h gives the extended error code in AX. The routine also returns the type of error, the possible action that may be taken and the location of the error. All this information is tabulated in Figure 13.4.

**DOS 2 error codes**

| Code (hex) | Error |
|---|---|
| 01 | Bad function number |
| 02 | File not found |
| 03 | Path not found |
| 04 | All handles in use |
| 05 | Access denied |
| 06 | Invalid handle number |
| 07 | Memory blocks corrupt |
| 08 | Insufficient memory |
| 09 | Address for memory block invalid |
| 0A | Invalid environment |
| 0B | Bad format |
| 0C | Access code invalid |
| 0D | Data error |
| 0E | Not used |
| 0F | Drive specification invalid |
| 10 | Cannot delete current directory |
| 11 | Wrong device |
| 12 | No more matching files |

*Figure 13.3*

**DOS 3 error codes (AX)**

| Code (hex) | Error |
|---|---|
| 01 | Function number invalid |
| 02 | File not found |
| 03 | Path not found |
| 04 | All file handles in use |
| 05 | Access denied |
| 06 | File handle invalid |
| 07 | Memory blocks invalid |
| 08 | Insufficient memory |
| 09 | Memory address invalid |
| 0A | Environment command invalid |
| 0B | Format invalid |
| 0C | File use code invalid |
| 0D | Data invalid |
| 0E | Not used |
| 0F | Drive specifier invalid |

| Code (hex) | Error |
|---|---|
| 10 | Cannot remove current directory |
| 11 | Different device |
| 12 | No more matching files |
| 13 | Disk write-protected |
| 14 | Disk identifier invalid |
| 15 | Drive not ready |
| 16 | Bad command |
| 17 | Data error on disk |
| 18 | Request header invalid |
| 19 | Seek error |
| 1A | Bad media |
| 1B | Sector not found |
| 1C | Out of paper (printer) |
| 1D | Write error |
| 1E | Read error |
| 1F | General failure |
| 20 | File sharing error |
| 21 | File locking error |
| 22 | Disk change error |
| 23 | No free FCBs |
| 24 | Sharing buffer exceeded |
| 25 | Code page mismatch |
| 26 | Handle EOF |
| 27 | Handle disk full |
| 28-31 | Not used |
| 32 | Not supported |
| 33 | Not list |
| 34 | Duplicate name |
| 35 | Bad network patch |
| 36 | Network busy |
| 37 | Device does not exist |
| 38 | Too many commands |
| 39 | Hardware error |
| 3A | Bad network response |
| 3B | Unexpected network error |
| 3C | Hardware fault |
| 3D | Print queue full |
| 3E | No spool space |
| 3F | Print Cancelled |
| 40 | Network name deleted |
| 41 | Network access denied |
| 42 | Bad device type |
| 43 | Bad network name |

| Code (hex) | Error |
|---|---|
| 44 | Too many names |
| 45 | Too many sessions |
| 46 | Sharing paused |
| 48 | Redirection paused |
| 49-4F | Not used |
| 50 | File exists |
| 51 | Duplicate FCB |
| 52 | Unable to create directory |
| 53 | Critical error |
| 54 | Out of structures |
| 55 | Already assigned |
| 56 | Invalid password |
| 57 | Invalid parameter |
| 58 | Network write default |
| 5A | Not loaded |

**Type of error (BH)**

| Code (hex) | Meaning |
|---|---|
| 01 | Lack of resources |
| 02 | Temporary problem |
| 03 | Unauthorised access |
| 04 | Internal DOS error |
| 05 | Hardware fault |
| 06 | DOS software error |
| 07 | Application software error |
| 08 | Not found |
| 09 | Bad format |
| 0A | Locked |
| 0B | Media error |
| 0C | Exists already |
| 0D | General |

**Possible action (BL)**

| Code | Meaning |
|---|---|
| 01 | Try again |
| 02 | Try again later |
| 03 | User can solve problem |
| 04 | Close files, end program |
| 05 | End program immediately |
| 06 | Ignore error |
| 07 | User action, then retry |

**Location of error (CH)**

| Code | Meaning |
|---|---|
| 01 | Unknown |
| 02 | Disk drive |
| 03 | Not used |
| 04 | Serial device |
| 05 | Memory |

*Figure 13.4*

A great deal of information is available but most of the time it can be ignored; only substantial programs need be concerned with using these additional codes.

DOS makes this information available in the following circumstances:

- On the return from a critical error handler
- After a file or disk operation has concluded with the carry flag set
- After a file operation using FCBs returns with AH=FFh

DOS 4 allows you to set the error codes, which will be returned by the next call to function 59h.

*Interrupt:* 21h
*Function:* 5D,0Ah
*DOS version:* 4
*Service:* Set error codes
*Entry values:* AH=5Dh
AL=0Ah
DS:SI=pointer to error codes
*Exit values:* None

The error codes are stored in memory in the 44 bytes pointed to be DS:SI. The registers for function 59h are in the order AX, BX, CX, DX, SI, DI, DS, ES. These are followed by four zero bytes and the two words containing the computer ID and program ID respectively. (The computer ID is 0 for the local computer; the program ID is 0 for the local program.)

## File handles and FCBs

DOS provides two distinct ways of dealing with files. Chronologically, the first method involved File Control Blocks (FCBs). These were the only file-handling method available under DOS 1. The procedure is that a block of information must be set up before calling any interrupt relating to a file. This is a rather arduous task. It also has the disadvantage that it does not allow for the use of sub-directories, always working with the current directory only.

DOS 2 introduced the concept of file handles. This is a much simpler method, which is also able to deal with paths to sub-directories automatically. Since most computers now have DOS 2 at the very least, it is not unreasonable to ignore FCBs altogether. However, the FCB services are listed later for reference.

## Operations with file handles

To use any file, the file must first be *opened*. This simply involves telling DOS the specification of the file to be used: the drive, path and name. DOS assumes defaults for the drive and path if not specified. The operating system then allocates a unique number to the file. This is the *file handle*. In all future operations, it is the file handle that is used, rather than the filename. When the file is later *closed*, the file handle is freed for use by another file.

The allocation of file handles is made by DOS automatically; you should not assume that if you reopen the file it will necessarily have the same handle. The handle numbers associated with files are only temporary.

When you open a file, DOS tells you the number that has been allocated; it is up to you to store it

**Default DOS file handles**

| Handle | Device Name | Device |
|---|---|---|
| 0 | CON: | Keyboard |
| 1 | CON: | Screen |
| 2 | CON: | Screen error |
| 3 | AUX: | First connected serial device |
| 4 | PRN: | First connected parallel device |

*Figure 13.5*

away for future use. You should not attempt to interfere with the file numbering system.

The first five file handles are reserved for specific devices (see Figure 13.5).

The numbers that follow are allocated in sequence. Under DOS 2, there is a maximum of 20 file handles available at any one time. This should be sufficient for most purposes but, if not, DOS 3 allows you to increase the number of file handles with the FILES directive in CONFIG.SYS. Increasing this value allows more files to be open at any one time but produces a slightly increased overhead in memory usage.

Under DOS 3.3 you can change the number of file handles from within a program, using function 67h.

| | |
|---|---|
| *Interrupt:* | 21h |
| *Function:* | 67h |
| *DOS version:* | 3.3 |
| *Service:* | Set number of file handles |
| *Entry values:* | AH=67h |
| | BX=number of handles |
| *Exit values:* | AX=error code (if CF=1) |

## Creating and opening files

Before using a file – either to read data or write to it – the file must be created if it does not exist, or reopened if it does. DOS provides four interrupts to do this. In each case, you must put the ASCIIZ file specification in memory, pointed to by DS:DX. If no error occurs during the process, the carry flag will be clear (CF=0) and the file handle will be returned in AX; if there is an error, the carry flag is set (CF=1) and the standard error code is returned in AH. In each case, if the procedure is a success, space for the file buffer is allocated in memory.

**Creating a new file in DOS 2**

For DOS 2, there is only one way to create a new file.

---

| | |
|---|---|
| *Interrupt:* | 21h |
| *Function:* | 3Ch |
| *DOS version:* | 2 |
| *Service:* | Create a file |
| *Entry values:* | AH=3Ch |
| | CX=file attribute |
| | DS:DX=address of ASCIIZ file specification |
| *Exit values:* | AX= file handle (CF=0) |
| | error code (CF=1) |

---

If there is an existing file with the name given, it is overwritten by the new file. Even if you do not subsequently write any data to the file, all existing data in the file is lost. An error code will be returned if the disk is full or the file already exists; in this last case, an 'Access denied' error is returned.

You can check whether the file exists with function 4Eh (above).This check should be carried out as a matter of course, unless the file is a temporary one which can be overwritten quite safely.

Figure 13.6 gives an example of how the function may be used.

```
RECREATE:       ;Recreate file & write data to it

      ;This file creates a new file even if
      ;a file of that name already exists

      ;Calls PARSE, NEXTPARM (both Fig 2.19)

      jmp recst

messagez      db 'Cannot open file$'
handlez       dw ?
handle2z      db '$'
filedata      db 'Sample text'

recst:
      call parse                ;Parse command line
      call nextparm             ;Identify PARAMETER
                                ;(i.e. filename)
      jc endcreate              ;End if no name
      xor cx,cx
      lea dx,parameter          ;Point to filename
      mov ah,3ch
      int 21h                   ;Create file
      jnc ok4
      lea dx,messagez           ;Error message
      mov ah,09h
      int 21h
      jmp endcreate
ok4:
      mov [handlez],ax
      mov bx,[handlez]
      lea dx,filedata           ;Point to data
      mov cx,0Bh                ;Data is 11
                                ;characters long
      mov ah,40h
      int 21h                   ;Write data
      mov ah,3eh
      int 21h                   ;Close file

endcreate:
      int 20h
```

*Figure 13.6*

**Creating a new file in DOS 3**

In DOS 3, to create a new file which does not already exist, use function 5Bh.

| | |
|---|---|
| *Interrupt:* | 21h |
| *Function:* | 5Bh |
| *DOS version:* | 3 |
| *Service:* | Create a new file |
| *Entry values:* | AH=5Bh |
| | CX=file attribute |
| | DS:DX=address of ASCIIZ pathname |
| *Exit values:* | AX= file handle (CF=0) |
| | error code (CF=1) |

This is the best function if the user is supplying the name, since it will fail if the file already exists. Therefore, you cannot overwrite an existing file accidentally.

This function is illustrated in Figure 13.7.

```
CREATE:         ;Creates a file

      ;Gives error message if file already
      ;exists

      ;Calls PARSE, NEXTPARM (both Fig 2.19)

      jmp createst

message         db 'File exists or bad filename$'
handlec         dw ?

createst:
      call parse                ;Parse the command
                                ;line
      call nextparm             ;Identify the
                                ;PARAMETER (i.e.
                                ;filename)
      jc endcreate              ;End if no name
      xor cx,cx
      lea dx,parameter          ;Point to filename
      mov ah,5bh
      int 21h                   ;Create file
      jnc ok                    ;Jump if no error
      lea dx,message            ;Otherwise, display
                                ;message
      mov ah,09h
      int 21h
      jmp endcreate

ok:
      mov [handlec],ax          ;If created, save
                                ;handle
```

```
      mov bx,handlec
      mov ah,3eh
      int 21h
endcreate:
      int 20h
```

*Figure 13.7*

Note that a file that is created with a read-only attribute can be written until it is first closed.

If you are prepared to let DOS decide the filename, use function 5AH.

| | |
|---|---|
| *Interrupt:* | 21h |
| *Function:* | 5Ah |
| *DOS version:* | 3 |
| *Service:* | Create a temporary file |
| *Entry values:* | AH=5Ah |
| | CX=file attribute |
| | DS:DX=address of ASCIIZ pathname |
| *Exit values:* | AX=error code (if CF=1) |
| | DS:DX=address of ASCIIZ file specification (if CF=0) |

This is sometimes useful for creating temporary files, though generally function 3Ch (above) is better. You must supply the file specification in the usual way, but with twelve spaces where the filename and extension would usually be. You can include the drive and directory if these are not the defaults. DOS will fill the gaps with a name of its own, based on the current date and time. This function is used by utilities such as MORE. However, it is up to the user – or program – to delete the file when it is no longer needed.

**Opening an existing file**

When a file already exists, it can be opened with function 3Dh.

| | |
|---|---|
| *Interrupt:* | 21h |
| *Function:* | 3Dh |
| *DOS version:* | 2 |
| *Service:* | Open a file |

| | |
|---|---|
| *Entry values:* | AH=3Dh |
| | AL=file use code |
| | DS:DX=address of ASCIIZ file specification |
| *Exit values:* | AX= file handle (CF=0) |
| | error code (CF=1) |

The main complication here is the *file use code* which must be specified in AL. The meaning of the code is shown in Figure 13.8.

The bottom three bits indicate whether the file is to be opened for reading, writing or both. For DOS 2, the remaining bits must be cleared.

For DOS 3 and above, the top four bits are used to indicate how DOS should cope with any attempt to open the file by another program. Bits 4 to 6 indicate the message that should be passed to the other

**File use codes**

| Bit | Meaning | |
|---|---|---|
| 7 | Set if file cannot be used by subprogram | |
| 6 | ) | |
| 5 | ) Disk share mode (see below) | |
| 4 | ) | |
| 3 | Reserved | |
| 2 | ) | (000 Read only |
| 1 | ) Access type | (001 Write only |
| 0 | ) | (010 Read/write |

N.B. Only bits 0,1,2 are available for DOS 2

**Disk share modes (bits 0,1,2)**

| Bit 2 1 0 | Meaning |
|---|---|
| 0 0 0 | Compatible mode |
| 0 0 1 | No read/write |
| 0 1 0 | No write |
| 0 1 1 | No read |
| 1 0 0 | Not available to sub-program |

*Figure 13.8*

```
REOPEN:         ;Reopens an existing file

      ;Gives error message if file
      ;does not exist

      ;Calls PARSE, NEXTPARM (both Fig 2.19)

      jmp reopenst

message         db 'Cannot open file$'
handle          dw ?            ;File handle
handle2         db '$'
filedata        db 'Filler'

reopenst:
      call parse                ;Parse the command
                                ;line
      call nextparm             ;Identify the
                                ;PARAMETER (i.e.
                                ;filename)
      jc endopen                ;End if no name
      xor cx,cx
      lea dx,parameter          ;Point to file
      mov al,02h
      mov ah,3dh
      int 21h                   ;Open file
      jnc ok2                   ;Jump if alright
      lea dx,message            ;Otherwise display
                                ;error message
      mov ah,09h
      int 21h
      jmp endopen

ok2:
      mov [handle],ax           ;Save file handle
      mov bx,[handle]
      lea dx,filedata           ;Point to data
      mov cx,06h
      mov ah,40h
      int 21h                   ;Write to file
      mov ah,3eh                ;Close file
      int 21h

endopen:
      int 20h
```

*Figure 13.9*

program; bit 7 decides whether the open file is to be made available to a sub-program of the current program. These bits are only of any real interest in a network environment.

Figure 13.9 includes a program to re-open an existing file.

**Creating and opening files in DOS 4**

DOS 4 combines all the options above into a single function.

| | | |
|---|---|---|
| *Interrupt:* | 21h | |
| *Function:* | 6Ch | |
| *DOS version:* | 4 | |
| *Service:* | Create/open a file | |
| *Entry values:* | AH=6Ch | |
| | AL=00H | |
| | BH=error/save code | |
| | BL=file use code | |
| | CX=file attribute | |
| | DH=00h | |
| | DL=opening method | |
| *Exit values:* | AX= | file handle (if CF=0) |
| | | error code (if CF=1) |
| | CL= | 01h (file exists and opened) |
| | | 02h (new file created) |
| | | 03h (existing file overwritten) |

BH should be 00h for normal critical-error handling or 20h to ignore interrupt 24h. Add 40h if you want the file automatically saved to disk whenever data is written (as for function 67h).

The opening method in DL determines how to handle existing files: 00h (abandon if file exists), 01h (open file) or 02h (overwrite). In these cases the function will fail if the file does not exist. To create a new file if it does not yet exist, add 10h to the method code.

## File types

Files generally fall into two distinct categories:

- *Sequential files* consist of a continuous string of data, with no recognisable structure. These are created by programs such as word processors.
- *Random access files* are divided into fixed-length *records*, each of which holds a single set of data. The records are usually sub-divided into fields, each of which holds one item of data. These files are created by programs such as databases.

The file-handle functions make no distinction between sequential and random access files.

Any record-based random access file can be considered as a sequential file; the start of any record can be found by a simple calculation. A sequential file can be treated as a random access file with a record length of 1. Either way, it makes no real difference. However, for ease of use, it is normal to create a distinction between the two file types.

For data that is structured, access is faster if records are of fixed length because you can jump to the required position instantly. For unstructured files – such as text files – it is easier to treat the file as sequential. With this type of file you will need to read and write the entire file when it is amended, unless changes are only made at the end of the file.

## The file pointer

Whichever type of file you are using, DOS keeps track of the current position in the file with a *file pointer*. When a file is opened, the pointer is set at the end of the file. When a new file is created, obviously the pointer is set to the start (even if you are overwriting an existing file). When data is read or written, the pointer is always updated to point to the next byte.

To read or write data, you must first move the file pointer to the required position with function 42h.

| | |
|---|---|
| *Interrupt:* | 21h |
| *Function:* | 42h |
| *DOS version:* | 2 |
| *Service:* | Move file pointer |
| *Entry values:* | AH=42h |
| | AL=offset code |
| | BX=file handle |
| | CX:DX=number of bytes to move pointer |
| *Exit values:* | AX=error code (if CF=1) |
| | DX:AX=new pointer offset (if CF=0) |

Before calling this service, you must specify the file handle and an offset for the file pointer. The offset is used as follows:

- If AL=0, the value in CX:DX is the offset from the beginning of the file (and is always positive).
- If AL=1, the value in CX:DX is the offset from the current pointer position (and may be either positive or negative).
- If AL=2, the file pointer is moved to the end of the file (CX and DX must be zero).

For a sequential file, you can use this function as follows:

- Set AL=0 to read or write from the start of the file. To start a little way into the file, set a positive offset (this is not usually practical with sequential files, since you will have to shunt everything along the file if the amended portion is of a different length). Usually, you will read to the end of the file and then rewrite the entire file.
- When only some of the file is to be read, set AL=1 with an offset of 0. You can then continue reading from the current pointer position.
- Set AL=2 to append new data to the end of the file. The function always returns the current file size in this case (in terms of the actual bytes used, not as a multiple of the cluster size).

For random access files:

- To read or write a particular record, set AL=0 with the offset calculated from:

*offset* = (*record number* - 1) x *record length*

- To read the next record, set AL=1 and the offset to be 0. To read or write other records, set the offset to be either positive or negative in multiples of the record length.
- To add new records, set AL=2. The total number of records in the file is the offset that is returned divided by the record length.

## Reading and writing data

There are only two functions for reading and writing data. Remember that in both of these cases, data is not necessarily read from or written to the disk itself. All operations are carried out with the file buffer. If the data to be read is not in the buffer, the buffer is refreshed; if the data that is written fills the buffer, the buffer is stored away.

DOS has its own internal mechanism for keeping track of the start of the buffer relative to the position of the corresponding data in the file.

**Reading data**

The location where the data is to be stored must be pointed to by DS:DX. The number of bytes to be read must be given. For random access records, the number of bytes is the number of records multiplied by the record length. The data is read with function 3Fh.

| | |
|---|---|
| *Interrupt:* | 21h |
| *Function:* | 3Fh |
| *DOS version:* | 2 |
| *Service:* | Read from a file |
| *Entry values:* | AH=3Fh |
| | BX=file handle |
| | CX=number of bytes to be read |
| | DS:DX=address of DTA |
| *Exit values:* | AX= number of bytes read (CF=0) |
| | return code (CF=1) |

The data is read from the current pointer position (which can be changed with the function 42h, described above). The pointer is set to the byte after the last one read. Always check the carry flag and error codes after reading data.

**Writing data**

Data is written in a similar way to the above, using function 40h.

---

| | |
|---|---|
| *Interrupt:* | 21h |
| *Function:* | 40h |
| *DOS version:* | 2 |
| *Service:* | Write to a file |
| *Entry values:* | AH=40h |
| | BX=file handle |
| | CX= number of bytes to be written |
| | 00h (to truncate file at pointer) |
| | DS:DX=address of DTA |
| *Exit values:* | AX= number of bytes written (CF=0) |
| | error code (CF=1) |

---

Although the carry flag is set for most errors, this is not necessarily the case. For example, if the disk is full, the flag is not set. In this case, data *has* been written, but not enough of it. You should always check that everything is all right by comparing the number of bytes written with the number of bytes originally specified.

There is a special case, where CX is set to 0000h. Here the function sets a new end-of-file marker at the current pointer position. For example, for a sequential file, you can rewrite the file up to a particular position. If you want to lose all the data that follows, follow on with a second call to the function with CX set to 0.

## Closing files

When you have finished with a file, you *must* close it. Remember that the buffer may still contain data that has yet to be written to the file. A file is closed with function 3EH.

| | |
|---|---|
| *Interrupt:* | 21h |
| *Function:* | 3Eh |
| *DOS version:* | 2 |
| *Service:* | Close a file |
| *Entry values:* | AH=3Eh |
| | BX=file handle |
| *Exit values:* | AX=error code (if CF=1) |

Any data left in the buffer is written away, and the memory occupied by the buffer is freed for other uses. The file handle is also freed for the next file to be opened.

You should always close files as soon as possible. There are only a limited number of handles, so in complex programs you do not want these to be tied up unnecessarily with files that are no longer being used.

**Data security**

To ensure data security, and be certain that any changes are always written away immediately, you can close the file after any data has been written and then reopen it. This makes disk accesses slightly longer but in some circumstances the extra time can be justified.

Alternatively, duplicate the file handle (function 45h, below) and then close the duplicate file.

DOS 3.3 offers a more satisfactory method, with function 68h.

| | |
|---|---|
| *Interrupt:* | 21h |
| *Function:* | 68h |
| *DOS version:* | 3.3 |
| *Service:* | Save buffer contents |
| *Entry values:* | AH=68h |
| | BX=file handle |
| *Exit values:* | AX=error code (if CF=1) |

This function saves and clears the file buffer, and updates the directory – in the same way as for function 3Eh – but does not close the file.

## Duplicating file handles

It is sometimes useful to be able to refer to two parts of the same file: for example, to move data from one record to another in a random access file. Instead of moving the file pointer to and fro, it is easier to open the file twice and therefore have two file pointers. Each pointer is automatically updated as the data is read from one place and written to another.

To open a file for a second time, use function 45h.

---

| | |
|---|---|
| *Interrupt:* | 21h |
| *Function:* | 45h |
| *DOS version:* | 2 |
| *Service:* | Duplicate a file handle |
| *Entry values:* | AH=45h |
| | BX=first file handle |
| *Exit values:* | AX= new file handle (CF=0) |
| | return code (CF=1) |

---

DOS returns a second file handle in AX. From this point on, DOS treats the data as if DOS is in two separate files. Each of the 'files' has its own file buffer in memory and each must be closed separately.

As an alternative, you can use function 46h.

---

| | |
|---|---|
| *Interrupt:* | 21h |
| *Function:* | 46h |
| *DOS version:* | 2 |
| *Service:* | Force duplication of handle |
| *Entry values:* | AH=46h |
| | BX=file handle to copy |
| | CX=second file handle |
| *Exit values:* | AX=error code (if CF=1) |
| | CX=second file handle |

---

Here, DOS uses an existing file handle, closing the corresponding file first.

## End-of-file markers

DOS does not automatically add an end-of-file marker to any file. If you tell it to create a file that is ten characters long it will do just that; there is no extra character put at the end to indicate that the file has finished. DOS will know where the file ends by the file size stored in the directory.

It is usual, however, to denote the end of the file by some special character, particularly for sequential files. The preferred convention is to end such files with the Ctrl-Z (ASCII 26 or 1Ah) character. Although there is no reason why you should stick to this convention it is a useful one to adopt, particularly for text files. This character is recognised by many programs. For example, the DOS TYPE command will read and display any file until it encounters a Ctrl-Z character.

Another frequently-used convention is to denote the end of a file by the null character (00h).

## ASCII files

For many purposes, a file must be specified as an *ASCII file*. In such a file, the only characters allowed are the standard ASCII characters (in the range 20h to 7Fh), plus certain control characters: carriage return (0Dh), line feed (0Ah) and end-of-file (1Ah). These denote the end of paragraph, end of line and end of file respectively. The tab (09h) and form feed (0Ch) characters may also be encountered. Extended ASCII characters should not normally occur in such a file.

Any file that contains just these characters can be redirected to a printer without amendment and will print as expected.

## Comma-delimited files

Many programs, particularly database and spreadsheet applications, produce *comma-delimited files*.

These are standard ASCII files but with a few extra conditions. Each paragraph, ending with a carriage return/line feed sequence, consists of a group of individual items, separated by commas. Any text should be enclosed in double quotes (22h). Many programs are able to read these files and then allocate the data to a more formal structure. This type of sequential file is often used to transfer data from one spreadsheet or database program to another.

## Files in networks

Using a DOS file on a network is not as complex as it may appear. The file needs to be on a drive that is accessible to all terminals. You must then make sure that only one machine can update the file at a time. 'Read access' by several machines at once is permissible but 'Write access' must be restricted to a single machine. To allow only one program access to a file, you must set the appropriate file-use code when the file is opened.

**Locking files**

Even if you allow sharing of data, you can *lock* part of a file so that other users cannot change its contents. This is done with function 5Ch, subfunction 00h. Before calling the service, you must specify the file handle, the offset (from the start of the file) of the area to lock, and the amount of data to be locked.

| | |
|---|---|
| *Interrupt:* | 21h |
| *Function:* | 5C,00h |
| *DOS version:* | 3.1 |
| *Service:* | Lock file |
| *Entry values:* | AH=5Ch |
| | AL=00h |
| | BX=file handle |
| | CX:DX=offset |
| | SI:DI=locked data length |
| *Exit values:* | AX=error code (if CF=1) |

The program that has locked the file can then write to that section of it, but any other program that attempts to access this part of the file will get the 'Access denied' error.

Subfunction 01h of the same service is used to unlock the file.

---

| | |
|---|---|
| *Interrupt:* | 21h |
| *Function:* | 5C,01h |
| *DOS version:* | 3.1 |
| *Service:* | Unlock file |
| *Entry values:* | AH=5Ch |
| | AL=01h |
| | BX=file handle |
| | CX:DX=offset |
| | SI:DI=locked data length |
| *Exit values:* | AX=error code (if CF=1) |

---

Files should always be locked for as short a time as possible. The file should be locked (AL=00h) just before the data is written and unlocked (AL=01h) immediately afterwards. Of course, any such program should also incorporate a number of checks to make sure that another user hasn't changed the file between the initial read of the data and the lock; that two users are not trying to access the same file at the same time; and so on.

Note that the function to close a file does not unlock the file. This must be done explicitly with the interrupt above.

**Network functions**

DOS keeps a list of networked devices; each of these has a number, a network name and a local name. The local name is a drive letter or a device name (such as PRN for the parallel printer). The names are stored as ASCIIZ strings in RAM buffers. The numbers are allocated in strict sequence by DOS.

There are two DOS functions that provide a collection of facilities for programs intended to run on a network.

---

| | |
|---|---|
| *Interrupt:* | 21h |
| *Function:* | 5Fh |

| | |
|---|---|
| *DOS version:* | 3.1 |
| *Service:* | Network device functions |
| *Entry values:* | AH=5Fh |
| | AL= 02h (Get network device details)<br>03h (Assign network device)<br>04h (Remove device from network) |
| | BX=network device number (AH=02h) |
| | BL=device (03 printer, 04 disk drive) (AH=03h) |
| | CX=user-defined parameter (if AH=03h) |
| | DS:SI points to 16-byte buffer for local name |
| | ES:DI points to 128-byte buffer for network name and password |
| *Exit values:* | AX=error code (if CF=1) |
| | DS:SI points to local name |
| | ES:DI points to network name |

---

| | |
|---|---|
| *Interrupt:* | 21h |
| *Function:* | 5Eh |
| *DOS version:* | 3.1 |
| *Service:* | Network computer/printer functions |
| *Entry values:* | AH=5Eh |
| | AL= 00h (Get computer's network name)<br>02h (Set printer init. codes)<br>03h (Get printer init. codes) |
| | BX=network device number (if AL=02h or 03h) |
| | CX=length of printer code (if AL=02h) |
| | DS:DX points to 16-byte buffer (if AL=01h) |
| | DS:SI points to printer string (if AL=02h) |
| | ES:DI points to printer data buffer (if AL=03h) |
| *Exit values:* | CX=length of printer code (if AL=03h) |
| | CH>00h (if AL=01h and name is valid) |
| | CL=network device number (if AL=01h) |
| | DS:DX points to computer name (if AL=01h) |
| | ES:DI points to printer code (if AL=03h) |

## Renaming files

A file can be renamed with function 56h. The old file specification must be pointed to by DS:DX; the new file specification is pointed to by ES:DI.

| | |
|---|---|
| *Interrupt:* | 21h |
| *Function:* | 56h |
| *DOS version:* | 2 |
| *Service:* | Rename a file |
| *Entry values:* | AH=56h |
| | DS:DX=address of old name (ASCIIZ) |
| | ES:DI=address of new name (ASCIIZ) |
| *Exit values:* | AX=error code (if CF=1) |

The new specification does not have to be in the same directory. DOS will move an entry from one directory to another if necessary. However, the new file must be on the same drive. Although DOS effectively moves a file as well as renaming it, actually it is only the directory entry that changes; the file itself is not affected.

For a method of renaming a group of files, see the section on renaming files using FCBs, below.

## Deleting files

To delete a single file, use DOS function 41h.

| | |
|---|---|
| *Interrupt:* | 21h |
| *Function:* | 41h |
| *DOS version:* | 2 |
| *Service:* | Delete a file |
| *Entry values:* | AH=41h |
| | DS:DX=address of ASCIIZ file specification |
| *Exit values:* | AX=error code (if CF=1) |

The file must have the read/write attribute; it must not be read-only.

The FCB version is performed by function 13h, described later, which allows you to delete a group of files.

This interrupt changes the first character of the filename to σ (E5h) and rewrites the FAT. The file itself is unaffected, so it can be recovered, assuming the data has not been overwritten.

## Date and time stamps

If you are using file handles, you can get or set the date and time stamp for an open file with function 57h. Subfunction 00h retrieves the current stamp.

| | |
|---|---|
| *Interrupt:* | 21h |
| *Function:* | 57,00h |
| *DOS version:* | 2 |
| *Service:* | Get date and time stamp |
| *Entry values:* | AH=57h |
| | AL=00h |
| | BX=file handle |
| *Exit values:* | AX=error code (if CF=1) |
| | CX=time |
| | DX=date |

The date and time are returned or set using the same format as for the stamp stored in the directory (as described in Chapter 12).

Subfunction 01h sets a new stamp.

| | |
|---|---|
| *Interrupt:* | 21h |
| *Function:* | 57,01h |
| *DOS version:* | 2 |
| *Service:* | Set date and time stamp |
| *Entry values:* | AH=57h |
| | AL=01h |
| | BX=file handle |
| | CX=time |
| | DX=date |
| *Exit values:* | AX=error code (if CF=1) |

If the date and time are changed, this function only takes effect when the file is closed.

## File Control Blocks (FCBs)

Under DOS 1, all file operations have to be carried out using File Control Blocks (FCBs). Rather than allocating a file handle, each open file is controlled by a block of data in memory. The structure of this block is shown in Figure 13.10.

Before invoking any file-based interrupt, you must put the relevant data in this block and the location of the FCB must be pointed to by DS:DX.

The essential information is the drive, filename and extension. DOS will fill in the rest, but you may want to change the block number, record size and current record. DOS always works in terms of blocks, one block filling the DTA and consisting of a number of whole records. The record size defaults to 80h.

The main disadvantage of using FCBs is that programming is more complex and many more instructions are required to keep track of the current

**File Control Block (FCB)**

| Offset (hex) | Bytes (hex) | Use |
|---|---|---|
| 00 | 01 | Drive |
| 01 | 08 | Filename |
| 09 | 03 | Extension |
| 0C | 02 | Current block number |
| 0E | 02 | Record size |
| 10 | 04 | File size |
| 14 | 02 | Date created |
| 16 | 0A | Reserved |
| 20 | 01 | Current record number |
| 21 | 01 | Relative record number |

N.B. The block starting at 16h stores the new filename and extension during renaming.

*Figure 13.10*

situation. Also, you cannot use sub-directories implicitly; all the functions assume that you are working with the default directory so this must be set before calling the function.

The FCB functions treat sequential and random access files differently.

## Finding files

You can locate individual files, in a similar manner to the functions that use file handles, with function 11h.

| | |
|---|---|
| *Interrupt:* | 21h |
| *Function:* | 11h |
| *DOS version:* | 1 |
| *Service:* | Find first matching file |
| *Entry values:* | AH=11h |
| | DS:DX=address of FCB |
| *Exit values:* | AL= 00h (file found) |
| | FFh (file not found) |

This service finds the first file that matches the ambiguous specification stored in the FCB. The ambiguous specification is replaced with the name of the first file. A copy of the FCB is stored in the DTA. You can also restrict the search by specifying attributes, as before. Note that although volume labels were not used in DOS 1, you can specify them with this function.

Subsequent matching files are found with function 12h.

| | |
|---|---|
| *Interrupt:* | 21h |
| *Function:* | 12h |
| *DOS version:* | 1 |
| *Service:* | Find next matching file |
| *Entry values:* | AH=12h |
| | DS:DX=address of FCB |
| *Exit values:* | AL= 00h (file found) |
| | FFh (file not found) |

## Parsing the command line

If using FCBs, there is a function to automatically parse the command line. Before calling the function, you must specify the addresses of the FCB and the command line.

| | |
|---|---|
| *Interrupt:* | 21h |
| *Function:* | 29h |
| *DOS version:* | 1 |
| *Service:* | Parse filename |
| *Entry values:* | AH=29h<br>AL=parsing code<br>DS:SI=address of command line<br>ES:DI=address of FCB |
| *Exit values:* | AL= 00h (success)<br>01h (wildcards found)<br>FFh (invalid drive)<br>DS:SI=address of next character in command line<br>ES:DI=address of FCB |

The service returns the location of the filename in the command line. If there is an ambiguous

**Parsing codes (Interrupt 21h, function 29h)**

| Bit | Meaning if clear | Meaning if set |
|---|---|---|
| 7-4 | Always 0 | |
| 3 | Do not change extension | Change extension in FCB to extension in command line |
| 2 | Do not change filename | Change filename in FCB to extension in command line |
| 1 | Do not change drive specifier | Change drive specifier in FCB to extension in command line |
| 0 | File specification starts at first byte | Skip blanks and other separators to find file specification |

*Figure 13.11*

filename containing asterisks, these are converted to question marks. You must put a code in AL to specify the way in which the interrupt is to operate (see Figure 13.11).

## File size

You can check the size of any file with function 23h.

| | |
|---|---|
| *Interrupt:* | 21h |
| *Function:* | 23h |
| *DOS version:* | 1 |
| *Service:* | Get size of file |
| *Entry values:* | AH=23h |
| | DS:DX=address of FCB |
| *Exit values:* | AL= 00h (success) |
| | 01h (file not found) |

This gives the number of records in the file. To get the size of the file in bytes, set the record length in the FCB to 1.

## Creating and opening files

The same method is used to create and open files with FCBs, regardless of the file type. Files are created with function 16h.

| | |
|---|---|
| *Interrupt:* | 21h |
| *Function:* | 16h |
| *DOS version:* | 1 |
| *Service:* | Create a file |
| *Entry values:* | AH=16h |
| | DS:DX=address of FCB |
| *Exit values:* | AL= 00h (success) |
| | FFh (directory full) |

If the file already exists, its present contents are lost.

An existing file is opened with function 0Fh.

*Interrupt:* 21h
*Function:* 0Fh
*DOS version:* 1
*Service:* Open a file
*Entry values:* AH=0Fh
DS:DX=address of FCB
*Exit values:* AL= 00h (success)
FFh (failure)

Note that for sequential files, the record size should be set to 1. The record number then becomes equal to the byte number in the file.

## Reading and writing sequential files

Data can be read from a sequential file with function 14h. You must specify in the FCB the blocks to be read.

*Interrupt:* 21h
*Function:* 14h
*DOS version:* 1
*Service:* Read sequential record
*Entry values:* AH=14
DS:DX=address of FCB
*Exit values:* AL= 00h (success)
01h (end of file; no data read)
02h (DTA too small)
03h (end of file; some data read)

This service automatically updates the FCB after the data has been read. The data is stored in the DTA. It is extracted from the file buffer, if it is already there; otherwise, it is read into the buffer from disk.

Sequential file data is written with function 15h.

*Interrupt:* 21h
*Function:* 15h
*DOS version:* 1
*Service:* Write sequential record
*Entry values:* AH=15h

| | |
|---|---|
| | DS:DX=address of FCB |
| *Exit values:* | AL= 00h (success)<br>01h (disk full; nothing written)<br>02h (DTA too small) |

This service transfers data from the DTA to the buffer. If the buffer is full, the entire buffer is written to disk. The block and record numbers are updated accordingly.

## Reading and writing random access files

Before carrying out any activity with a random access file, you must set the position of the data to be read or written. The block and record number must be stored in the FCB. The position is then set with function 24h.

| | |
|---|---|
| *Interrupt:* | 21h |
| *Function:* | 24h |
| *DOS version:* | 1 |
| *Service:* | Prepare field for random record |
| *Entry values:* | AH=24h<br>DS:DX=address of FCB |
| *Exit values:* | AL= 00h (success)<br>FFh (failure) |

A single record can be read with function 21h.

| | |
|---|---|
| *Interrupt:* | 21h |
| *Function:* | 21h |
| *DOS version:* | 1 |
| *Service:* | Read random record |
| *Entry values:* | AH=21h<br>AS:DX=address of FCB |
| *Exit values:* | AL= 00h (success)<br>01h (end of file; no data read)<br>02h (DTA too small)<br>03h (end of file; some data read) |

Several records can be read with function 27h.

| | |
|---|---|
| *Interrupt:* | 21h |
| *Function:* | 27h |
| *DOS version:* | 1 |
| *Service:* | Read random records |
| *Entry values:* | AH=27h |
| | CX=number of records to read |
| | DS:DX=address of FCB |
| *Exit values:* | AL= 00h (success) |
| | 01h (end of file; no data read) |
| | 02h (DTA too small) |
| | 03h (end of file; some data read) |
| | CX=number of records read |

All data that is read is stored in the DTA, so this must be large enough for the number of records specified. The block and record numbers are automatically updated.

Similarly, a single record can be written with function 22h.

| | |
|---|---|
| *Interrupt:* | 21h |
| *Function:* | 22h |
| *DOS version:* | 1 |
| *Service:* | Write random record |
| *Entry values:* | AH=22h |
| | DS:DX=address of FCB |
| *Exit values:* | AL= 00h (success) |
| | 01h (disk full; nothing written) |
| | 02h (DTA too small) |

In this case, the position in the file is not updated.

Several records can be written with function 28h. All the records must be in the DTA before the function is called.

| | |
|---|---|
| *Interrupt:* | 21h |
| *Function:* | 28h |
| *DOS version:* | 1 |
| *Service:* | Write random records |
| *Entry values:* | AH=28h |
| | CX=number of records to write |
| | DS:DX=address of FCB |

| | |
|---|---|
| *Exit values:* | AL= 00h (success)<br>01h (disk full; nothing written)<br>02h (DTA too small)<br>CX=number of records written |

This service updates the current position in the file.

There is a special case when the number of records is 0. The service then truncates the file after writing the single record specified.

## Closing FCB files

A file that has been opened with FCBs is closed with function 10h.

| | |
|---|---|
| *Interrupt:* | 21h |
| *Function:* | 10h |
| *DOS version:* | 1 |
| *Service:* | Close a file |
| *Entry values:* | AH=10h<br>DS:DX=address of FCB |
| *Exit values:* | AL= 00h (success)<br>FFh (failure) |

First of all, DOS compares the directory entry with the FCB to make sure the disk has not been swapped. If the disk has been swapped or any other problem arises, an error message is returned.

Note that the DOS functions do not generally check to see that the same disk is in a floppy drive. It is up to individual programs to guard against this: for example, by always writing new data away, or by reading the directory and checking the date and time stamps, etc.

## Renaming and deleting files with FCBs

### Renaming files

DOS 1 uses function 17h to rename a file. In this case, the file must be in the current directory.

| | |
|---|---|
| *Interrupt:* | 21h |
| *Function:* | 17h |
| *DOS version:* | 1 |
| *Service:* | Rename a file |
| *Entry values:* | AH=17h |
| | DS:DX=address of FCB |
| *Exit values:* | AL= 00h (success) |
| | 01h (file not found) |

This service has the advantage that it can rename files using an ambiguous specification. The asterisks in the old and new names are expanded to question marks; any character in the new name where there is a question mark stays the same as the original.

### Deleting files

To delete a file using FCBs, use function 13h.

| | |
|---|---|
| *Interrupt:* | 21h |
| *Function:* | 13h |
| *DOS version:* | 1 |
| *Service:* | Delete a file |
| *Entry values:* | AH=13h |
| | DS:DX=address of FCB |
| *Exit values:* | AL= 00h (success) |
| | FFh (file not found) |

In this case, of course, there is no path but you can specify a group of files with an ambiguous specification. Note that the 'Are you sure?' message that appears when using the 'DEL *.*' command is not part of this function; it is part of the DOS DEL routine.

The only effect of this function is to change the first character of the filename in the directory to σ (E5h) and update the FAT.

## Redirection, pipes and filters

Three special types of file operation are provided directly at the DOS command line.

**Redirection**

Output from a program can be redirected to other than the normal destination. The new destination can be a file, the screen, a printer or another device. The DOS redirection operator is '>'. For example, to print the contents of the ASCII file TEST.TXT enter:

```
TYPE TEST.TXT > PRN
```

A second option is to use the '>>' operator, which appends the data to an existing file rather than creating a new one. Alternatively, you can get input from a source other than the normal one with '<'.

**Pipes**

A *pipe* takes the output from one program and uses it as the input for another: for example, SORT and MORE. The DOS pipe is represented by the '|' symbol. You can display a file in sections with:

```
TYPE TEST.TXT | MORE
```

The output from the TYPE command becomes the input for MORE, which displays the data it receives one page at a time.

**Filters**

A *filter* is a program which takes data in one form and converts it to another form: for example, SORT takes an ASCII file and sorts it into alphabetical order. Another example is the FIND utility, which creates a file that includes specific text only. Other filter programs can be devised to convert WordStar to ASCII, for example.

These various DOS options can be combined into single commands at the DOS prompt. For example:

```
DIR | SORT > PRN
```

This command takes the output from the DIR command to become the input for SORT; the sorted output is redirected to the printer.

# 14 Device Drivers

From the moment power is supplied, the CPU starts processing. Having completed the initial programs in ROM, the CPU starts going round in circles, checking the ports for data, issuing interrupts and going round to start again. You can only achieve something useful if the CPU is connected to the real world via some form of device.

Each device is a separate entity, with its own controlling software. The device may be either an integral part of the computer or a totally separate unit, connected only via a serial or parallel cable. In any event, the CPU must know how to communicate with the device. This is the task of the *device driver*.

A device driver is a piece of software that is dedicated to communications between the CPU and a particular device. It takes output from the CPU and converts it into meaningful data for the device; and it takes any response from the device and converts it to instructions the CPU can understand.

Device drivers are a feature of DOS. The variety and operation of device drivers is so great that it would be sufficient to fill a whole book; therefore, only brief coverage is given here.

The main need for device drivers is when trying to communicate with different printers, for which there are very many different types. Further information on device drivers, with particular reference to printers, can be found in the *Newnes PC Printers Pocket Book*.

## Standard device drivers

There are two basic types of device driver. The first group are the *standard device drivers*. These form part of the DOS BIOS and are used for communications between the CPU and the keyboard, screen, disk drives, serial ports and parallel ports.

The standard device drivers are loaded into memory when the system is booted and there they remain until the machine is switched off or rebooted. Every device driver is dependent on the physical characteristics of the device. Therefore, the internal devices for different PCs will have different characteristics and hence different device drivers. Thus the DOS BIOS (IBMBIO.COM or IO.SYS) will be different from one PC to another.

All drivers accept the same commands and are able to handle the same sort of input in the same way. Therefore, they output data in a standard form.

When any instruction is given via an interrupt to perform some activity, it is passed to the device driver.

**Standard device names**

Each of the standard devices is given a name or drive letter:

- NUL, the null device
- CON, the console, which includes both the keyboard and screen
- COM1 or AUX, the first serial port
- COM2 and COM3, additional serial ports
- LPT1 or PRN, the first parallel port
- LPT2 and LPT3, additional parallel ports
- CLOCK$, the real-time clock
- A and B, the floppy disk drives
- C, D etc., the hard disk drives

**Standard devices**

| Device | Type | Device Name |
|---|---|---|
| Null device | Character | NUL: |
| Console (keyboard & screen) | Character | CON: |
| First serial port | Character | COM1: or AUX: |
| Second serial port | Character | COM2: |
| First parallel port | Character | LPT1: or PRN: |
| Second parallel port | Character | LPT2: |
| Real Time Clock | Character | CLOCK$ |
| Floppy disk drive | Block | Usually A: and B: |
| Hard disk drive | Block | Usually C: etc. |

*Figure 14.1*

The *null device* is used when you want to ignore output. For example, screen messages from DOS commands can be omitted by redirecting them to NUL.

The *console* is a rather peculiar combination. All input is assumed to be from the keyboard while output is sent to the screen. The standard devices are listed in Figure 14.1.

## Installable device drivers

Additional device drivers can be installed to replace existing drivers. Device drivers may be hardware-orientated, such as MOUSE.SYS, which controls the operation of the mouse; or they can be theoretical devices, such as RAMDRIVE.SYS, which partitions off a part of memory to act like a disk.

Alternatively, a device driver can amend the operation of an existing device. For instance, ANSI.SYS amends the way in which the screen and keyboard are used.

Installable drivers are loaded into memory when the PC is booted. They cannot be added later. These device drivers must be specified in CONFIG.SYS by an instruction in the form:

```
device = spec
```

The file specification, *spec*, must include the full drive and path if the driver is not in the root directory of the boot drive.

Note that installable drivers are not allowed under DOS 1.

## Device types

Devices fall into two distinct categories: character devices and block devices.

### Character devices

Most drivers are for character devices. These send and receive data character by character. They include the console, serial and parallel ports, and (for want of somewhere better to put it) the null device. Each character device driver controls a single device at a time.

Each of these devices is given a *device name*. This name can be up to eight characters long and ends with a colon. The standard device names were listed in Figure 14.1.

The colon in the name is superfluous when used in a DOS command. For example, `COPY CON PRN` copies anything typed at the keyboard to the printer; `COPY AUX CON` copies anything received at the serial port to the screen.

You can also redirect more permanently with the MODE or CTTY commands.

Whenever any command is given that relates to a file, DOS searches the list of devices before checking the directory. If the name given is a device name, DOS uses the device for the operation rather than a file. For example, if you copy a file to 'PRN', DOS will direct the output to the printer rather than creating a new file with that name. It is unlikely that there will be any confusion, since the standard device names are reserved and DOS will not allow you to create files with those names.

The device names are stored in a hidden DEV directory; this is another reserved name.

**Block devices**

All other devices are *block devices*. These send and receive data a block at a time, a block usually being 512 bytes. The block device drivers handle large amounts of data and include disk drives and other storage devices.

Block devices do not have names; instead they have *drive identifiers*. A drive identifier consists of a single letter and a colon (here the colon is important). The identifier is not fixed for any particular device but is allocated when the device is installed.

Block device drivers can control more than one device: for example, a floppy disk driver can control two floppy drives, if these are of the same type. If two floppy drives use a different type of disk, then the second drive must have its own installable device driver. Note that two drive identifiers are allocated to the floppy drive even if there is only one physical floppy device; the second relates to logical drive B.

Hard disk drives are allocated the letters C onwards, any RAM drives follow on from the hard drives, and network drives follow on from these.

## Structure of device drivers

The device drivers are loaded into memory in strict order. The null device always comes first. This is followed by the installable drivers. Finally, the standard device drivers are loaded. All devices are loaded one after another, with no gaps.

Each device driver consists of three parts, stored consecutively in memory:

- The *device header* holds basic information about the device.
- The *strategy routine* stores the current contents of the registers when the device driver is called.
- The *interrupt routine* holds the main program which processes any requests to the driver.

**Structure of MS-DOS device drivers**

| Start Byte (hex) | No. Bytes | Purpose |
|---|---|---|
| 0 | 4 | Pointer to next device |
| 4 | 2 | Attributes |
| 6 | 2 | Pointer to strategy routine |
| 8 | 2 | Pointer to interrupt routine |
| 0A | 8 | Device name |
| 12 | *n1* | Strategy routine |
| 12+*n1* | *n2* | Interrupt routine |

*n1* = Length of strategy routine
*n2* = Length of interrupt routine

*Figure 14.2*

**The device header**

The device header stores five important pieces of information (see Figure 14.2).

*Pointer to next device*

This is the segment and offset address of the next device driver in memory. DOS uses these pointers to move through the chain of device drivers until it finds the one it wants. In the physical file on disk (for installable drivers), the pointer exists as FFFF:FFFF. During installation DOS replaces this with the actual address in memory. The last device driver in the chain keeps the dummy value.

*Device attributes*

This two-byte word gives a variety of information about the device and how it can respond to certain requests (see Figure 14.3).

**Device attribute word**

| Bit | Character/ Block/Both | Meaning if set (=1) | Meaning if clear (=0) |
|---|---|---|---|
| 15 | Both | Character device | Block device |
| 14 | Both | IOCTL commands supported | IOCTL not supported |
| 13 | Block | IBM format | Non-IBM format |
| 12 | Character | Output until busy supported | Not supported |
| 11 | Both | Device Open/Close and Removable Media commands supported | Not supported |
| 10 | Not used | | |
| 9 | Not used | | |
| 8 | Not used | | |
| 7 | Not used | | |
| 6 | Both | Get/Set Logical Device commands supported | Not supported |
| 5 | Not used | | |
| 4 | Character | Int 29H for fast console I/O implemented | Not implemented |
| 3 | Character | Current clock device | Not current clock |
| 2 | Character | Null device | Not null device |
| 1 | Character | Standard output device | Not std output device |
| 0 | Character | Standard input device | Not std input device |

*Figure 14.3*

*Pointer to strategy routine*
This is the offset of the start of the strategy routine (see below) from the start of the device header.

*Pointer to interrupt routine*
This is the offset of the start of the interrupt routine (see below) from the start of the device header.

*Device name/number of devices*
For character devices, the name can be up to eight characters long, excluding the colon. For block devices, this section holds the number of devices controlled by the driver; reducing the number effectively makes a drive inaccessible.

**The strategy routine**

The only purpose of the strategy routine is to store the segment and offset address of the request header (see below).

**Interrupt routine**

The interrupt routine saves the current register values and then inspects the request header to see what action is required. The corresponding subroutine is then called. On completion of the subroutine, the interrupt routine updates the status word and puts any required parameters in the data area. The registers are restored, and the routine then exits back to DOS.

The actual routines that do the work are, of necessity, limited in the facilities they can call upon. They can use the BIOS interrupts, memory locations and internal ports. Using the BIOS interrupts results in calls to the standard device drivers. In general, however, the interrupt routine cannot call the DOS interrupts, since these may result in calls to the installable device drivers, resulting in a loop. The only exception is the subroutine to handle command 00h (Initialisation), which may use certain DOS functions.

The rules for device drivers are very rigidly defined. There are only twenty possible commands for them to process, and each of these has its own strict limits. There must be a subroutine for each of the commands, even if it says 'Do nothing'. The commands are numbered 0 to 19.

## The request header

When DOS needs to issue a command to the device driver, it first builds a *request header* in memory. This header is used by DOS to pass information to the device driver, and by the device driver to pass responses back. The format of the request header is shown in Figure 14.4.

**The request header**

| Offset | Bytes | Meaning | Set by |
|---|---|---|---|
| 0 | 1 | Length of header | MS-DOS |
| 1 | 1 | Unit code | MS-DOS |
| 2 | 1 | Command code | MS-DOS |
| 3 | 2 | Status | Driver |
| 5 | 8 | Reserved | |
| 13 | *n* | (Variable) | MS-DOS |

*Figure 14.4*

*Length of header*

The length of the data area, at the end of the request header, depends on the routine that is being called. The total length of the request header, including this data area, is stored in the first byte.

*Unit code*

The unit code, for block devices only, is the number of the unit to be accessed.

*Command code*

This is the command to be processed, in the range 0-19.

*Status*

The two-byte status word is set by the device driver. It is used to tell DOS how the command has been handled (Figure 14.5). The high-order byte indicates the success or otherwise of the operation. If there was an error, a suitable code is placed in the low-order byte. Again, all of this is rigidly defined. DOS expects to get certain codes back, so any device driver must fit in with this scheme.

*Data area*
DOS defines the length of the data area and the information it expects to receive; the device driver supplies the required data on its return.

**Device status word**

**High order byte**

| Value | Meaning |
|---|---|
| 00 | Device driver still processing request. |
| 01 | Processing completed without error. |
| 02 | Device is busy. (Response to command 6 only) |
| 80 | Error encountered. (Low order byte indicates nature of error) |

**Low order byte**

| Value | Meaning |
|---|---|
| 00 | Write-protect violation |
| 01 | Unknown unit |
| 02 | Device not ready |
| 03 | Unknown command |
| 04 | CRC error |
| 05 | Bad drive request structure length |
| 06 | Seek error |
| 07 | Unknown media |
| 08 | Sector not found |
| 09 | Printer out of paper |
| 0A | Write fault |
| 0B | Read fault |
| 0C | General fault |
| 0D | Not used |
| 0E | Not used |
| 0F | Invalid disk change (DOS 3 only) |

*Figure 14.5*

## Device driver procedures

When a device operation is required, the sequence of events (over which we have very little control) is as follows:

1 The application program issues a call to a DOS function.

2 If action by a device is necessary, DOS checks the name in each device header in turn, until it finds the required driver.

3 DOS creates a request header. The register pair ES:BX is set to point to the segment and offset of the request header.

4 DOS issues a call to the driver's strategy routine, thus initialising the device driver.

5 The strategy routine saves the request header's segment and offset address, then returns control to DOS.

6 DOS calls the device driver's interrupt routine.

7 The interrupt routine acts upon the command, rewrites the request header, and returns control to DOS.

8 DOS acts upon the response, then passes control back to the application program.

9 The application program responds according to the DOS code that is returned.

## The BIOS Parameter Block (BPB)

Each block device controls one or more units, and for each unit there must be a BIOS Parameter Block (BPB) in memory. This is simply a record of information for the unit. The structure of the BPB is shown in Figure 14.6 (with offsets given from the start of the boot sector – see Figure 3.3). Similar information is given in the Disk Parameter Block (Figure 11.6).

**BIOS Parameter Block (BPB)**

| Offset | Bytes | Meaning |
|---|---|---|
| 0Bh | 2 | Number of bytes per sector |
| 0Dh | 1 | Number of sectors per allocation unit |
| 0Eh | 2 | Number of reserved sectors |
| 10h | 1 | Number of FATs |
| 11h | 2 | Number of entries in root directory |
| 13h | 2 | Total number of sectors on the media |
| 15h | 1 | Type of media |
| 16h | 2 | Size of FAT in sectors |
| 18h | 2 | Number of sectors per track |
| 1Ah | 2 | Number of heads |
| 1Ch | 4 | Number of hidden sectors (2 bytes for DOS 1-3) |
| 20h | 4 | Number of sectors (if value at 13h = 0) – DOS 4 onwards |

*Figure 14.6*

The locations of the BPBs for each device is stored in a BPB table.

The BPB originates in the boot sector of the disk or other device. The device driver reads in the BPB when it is initialised and re-reads it whenever the media has been changed (or may have been changed). For floppy disks, the system always assumes that there may have been a disk swap whenever the disk is accessed, since there is no way of knowing whether or not this is the case.

Therefore, immediately after any access, the BPB will be the same as that on the storage media but at other times it is not safe to assume that this is true. The BPB should always be accurate for fixed media, such as hard disks.

## IOCTL (Input/Output Control)

Under DOS 1, communications with devices were very straightforward. It was simply a matter of either reading or writing a character or block at a time. DOS 2 introduced a more complex but potentially more powerful option, that of the IOCTL (Input/Output Control) functions.

A buffer is set up in memory and all communications between the application program and device driver are handled by passing data through this buffer. The driver must be specially written to allow this kind of data transfer; if a driver supports the IOCTL functions, bit 14 of the attribute field in the device header should be set. All actions are then channelled through a single interrupt: function 44h of interrupt 21h.

| | |
|---|---|
| *Interrupt:* | 21h |
| *Function:* | 44h |
| *DOS version:* | 2 |
| *Service:* | IOCTL functions |
| *Entry values:* | AH=44h |
| | AL=subfunction |
| *Exit values:* | (Various) |

The contents of the registers vary, depending on the particular IOCTL function required.

## Device commands

There are only twenty possible commands that can be issued to a device driver, and each of these has a predefined purpose.

In some cases, the command is only relevant to block devices. Although the situation should not arise, character devices should none the less indicate that the function has been dealt with, by setting the status in the request header to 10h. Commands relating only to character devices should be dealt with in a similar way by block devices.

## ANSI.SYS

ANSI.SYS is a device driver that enhances the keyboard and screen routines. This driver works only with the DOS interrupts; it has no effect on opera-

**ANSI command set**

| Code | Effect |
|---|---|
| `Esc[HEsc[J` | Clears screen |
| `Esc[K` | Clears to end of line |
| `Esc[2J` | Clears to bottom of screen |
| `Esc[y;xH` | Moves cursor to (*x*,*y*) (col,row) |
| `Esc[nA` | Moves cursor up *n* rows |
| `Esc[nB` | Moves cursor down *n* rows |
| `Esc[nC` | Moves cursor right *n* columns |
| `Esc[nD` | Moves cursor left *n* columns |
| `Esc[s` | Save cursor position |
| `Esc[u` | Restore cursor position |
| `Esc[n;nR` | Get cursor position |
| `Esc[6n` | Get device status |
| `Esc[a;6p` | Redefine ASCII character *a* by ASCII 6 |
| `Esc[0;f;"s";13p` | Redefine function key *f* by string *s* where F1 = 59, F2 = 60, ..., F10 = 68 |

*Figure 14.7*

tions carried out with the BIOS interrupts or those that work directly with the hardware. The aim of the ANSI device driver is to fill some of the gaps in DOS: for example, the lack of any ability to move the cursor or change display mode.

These various device options, combined with the interrupts described throughout this book, provide the programmer with the opportunity to develop powerful and effective applications.

# Appendix
# Interrupt Summary

This appendix lists the BIOS and DOS interrupts. For each service the interrupt number, function and (where applicable) DOS version number are given. The page number where the interrupt is described is also given.

| Int | Fn | Ver | Service/Values | Page |
|---|---|---|---|---|
| 06h | | | Mouse interrupt | 191 |
| | | *Entry:* | BX=button status | |
| | | | CX=X co-ordinate | |
| | | | DX=Y co-ordinate | |
| | | *Exit:* | (Defined by programmer) | |
| 10h | 00h | | Set video mode | 223 |
| | | *Entry:* | AH=00h | |
| | | | AL=new video mode | |
| | | *Exit:* | None | |
| 10h | 01h | | Set cursor size | 238 |
| | | *Entry:* | AH=01h | |
| | | | CH=first raster line (20h no cursor) | |
| | | | CL=last raster line | |
| | | *Exit:* | None | |
| 10h | 02h | | Set cursor position | 240 |
| | | *Entry:* | AH=02h | |
| | | | BH=page (0 for graphics modes) | |
| | | | DH=row | |
| | | | DL=column | |
| | | *Exit:* | None | |
| 10h | 03h | | Get cursor information | 240 |
| | | *Entry:* | AH=03h | |
| | | | BH=page | |
| | | *Exit:* | CH=first raster line | |
| | | | CL=last raster line | |
| | | | DH=row | |
| | | | DL=column | |
| 10h | 04h | | Get light pen information | 192 |
| | | *Entry:* | AH=04h | |
| | | *Exit:* | AH=01h (Switch set) | |
| | | | 00h (Switch clear) | |
| | | | DH=character row | |
| | | | DL=character code | |
| | | | CX=pixel row (EGA/Hercules) | |
| | | | CH=pixel row (CGA) | |
| | | | DX=pixel column | |
| 10h | 05h | | Select active display page | 226 |
| | | *Entry:* | AH=05h | |

| | | | | |
|---|---|---|---|---|
| | | | AL=page | |
| | | *Exit:* | None | |
| 10h | 06h | | Scroll window up | 228 |
| | | *Entry:* | AH=06h<br>AL=number of lines to scroll<br>BH=attribute for new line<br>CH=top row<br>CL=left column<br>DH=bottom row<br>DL=right column | |
| | | *Exit:* | None | |
| 10h | 07h | | Scroll window down | 228 |
| | | *Entry:* | AH=07h<br>AL=number of lines to scroll<br>BH=for new line filler attribute<br>CH=top row<br>CL=left column<br>DH=bottom row<br>DL=right column | |
| | | *Exit:* | None | |
| 10h | 08h | | Read character | 236 |
| | | *Entry:* | AH=08h<br>BH=page | |
| | | *Exit:* | AH=attribute<br>AL=character | |
| 10h | 09h | | Display character | 230 |
| | | *Entry:* | AH=09<br>AL=character<br>BH=page<br>BL=attribute (text modes)<br>CX=repeat count (0 for continuous repeat) | |
| | | *Exit:* | None | |
| 10h | 0Ah | | Display character | 229 |
| | | *Entry:* | AH=0Ah<br>AL=character<br>BH=page (text modes)<br>BL=colour (graphics modes)<br>CX=repeat count (0 for continuous repeat) | |
| | | *Exit:* | None | |
| 10h | 0Bh | | Select colour palette | 218 |
| | | *Entry:* | AH=0Bh<br>BH=palette<br>BL=colour | |
| | | *Exit:* | None | |
| 10h | 0Ch | | Display pixel | 215 |
| | | *Entry:* | AH=0Ch<br>AL=colour (add 80h for XOR)<br>CX=pixel column<br>DL=pixel row | |
| | | *Exit:* | None | |

| | | | | |
|---|---|---|---|---|
| 10h | 0Dh | | Read pixel colour | 216 |
| | | *Entry:* | AH=0Dh<br>CX=pixel column<br>DL=pixel row | |
| | | *Exit:* | AL=colour | |
| 10h | 0Eh | | Display teletype character | 230 |
| | | *Entry:* | AH=0E<br>AL=character<br>BH=page<br>BL=colour (graphics modes) | |
| | | *Exit:* | None | |
| 10h | 0Fh | | Get video mode | 225 |
| | | *Entry:* | AH=0Fh | |
| | | *Exit:* | AH=width (characters)<br>AL=video mode<br>BH=page | |
| 10h | 10h, 00h | | Set EGA/VGA palette colour | 219 |
| | | *Entry:* | AH=10h<br>AL=00h<br>BH=physical colour value<br>BL=logical colour number | |
| | | *Exit:* | None | |
| 10h | 10h, 01h | | Set EGA/VGA border colour | 220 |
| | | *Entry:* | AH=10h<br>AL=01h<br>BH=border colour value | |
| | | *Exit:* | None | |
| 10h | 10h, 02h | | Set whole EGA/VGA palette | 219 |
| | | *Entry:* | AH=10h<br>AL=02h<br>ES:DX points to 17-byte table of colour values plus border colour | |
| | | *Exit:* | None | |
| 10h | 10h, 03h | | Select intensity/blink for attribute bit 7 (EGA/VGA) | 220 |
| | | *Entry:* | AH=10h<br>AL=01h<br>BL= 00h (intense background)<br>01h (blink) | |
| | | *Exit:* | None | |
| 10h | 10h, 07h | | Get VGA palette colour | 220 |
| | | *Entry:* | AH=10h<br>AL=07h<br>BL=logical colour number | |
| | | *Exit:* | BH=physical colour value | |
| 10h | 10h, 08h | | Get VGA border colour | 221 |
| | | *Entry:* | AH=10h<br>AL=08h | |
| | | *Exit:* | BH=border colour value | |

| | | | |
|---|---|---|---|
| 10h | 10h, 09h | Get whole VGA palette | 220 |
| | *Entry:* | AH=10h<br>AL=09h<br>ES:DX points to 17-byte table of colour values plus border colour | |
| | *Exit:* | None (table updated) | |
| 10h | 10h, 10h | Set DAC register | 221 |
| | *Entry:* | AH=10h<br>AL=10h<br>BX=register number<br>CH=green component (00h-3Fh)<br>CL=blue component<br>DH=red component | |
| | *Exit:* | None | |
| 10h | 10h, 12h | Set block of DAC registers | 222 |
| | *Entry:* | AH=10h<br>AL=12h<br>BX=first register number<br>CX=number of registers<br>ES:DX points to table of RGB values (3 bytes each) | |
| | *Exit:* | None | |
| 10h | 10h, 13h | Set VGA DAC page | 222 |
| | *Entry:* | AH=10h<br>AL=13h<br>BH= 00h (4 pages, if BL=00h)<br>01h (16 pages, if BL=00h)<br>page number (if BL=01h)<br>BL= 00h (select number of pages)<br>01h (select page number) | |
| | *Exit:* | None | |
| 10h | 10h, 15h | Get DAC register | 221 |
| | *Entry:* | AH=10h<br>AL=15h<br>BX=register number | |
| | *Exit:* | BX=register number<br>CH=green component (00h-3Fh)<br>CL=blue component<br>DH=red component | |
| 10h | 10,17h | Get block of DAC registers | 222 |
| | *Entry:* | AH=10h<br>AL=17h<br>BX=first register number<br>CX=number of registers<br>ES:DX points to table of RGB values (3 bytes each) | |
| | *Exit:* | None (table updated) | |
| 10h | 10h, 1Ah | Get VGA DAC page | 223 |
| | *Entry:* | AH=10h<br>AL=1Ah | |
| | *Exit:* | BH=page number<br>BL= 00h (4 pages) | |

01h (16 pages)

---

| | | | |
|---|---|---|---|
| 10h | 10h, 1Bh | Convert DAC to greys | 223 |
| | *Entry:* | AH=10h<br>AL=1Bh<br>BX=first register number<br>CX=number of registers | |
| | *Exit:* | None | |

---

| | | | |
|---|---|---|---|
| 10h | 11h [txt] | Load/select character table | 206 |
| | *Entry:* | AH=11h<br>AL= 00h (Load user-defined chars)<br>01h (Load ROM 8x14 characters) (not MCGA)<br>02h (Load ROM 8x8 characters)<br>03h (Select character table)<br>04h (Load ROM 8x16 characters) (not EGA)<br>10h (User-defined, adjust height)<br>11h (ROM 8x14, adjust height) (not MCGA)<br>12h (ROM 8x8, adjust height) (not MCGA)<br>14h (ROM 8x16, adjust height) (VGA)<br>BL=table number<br>BH=bytes per character (AL=00h, 10h)<br>CX=number of characters (AL=00h, 10h)<br>DX=start character (AL=00h, 10h)<br>ES:BP points to character table (AL=00h, 10h) | |
| | *Exit:* | None | |

---

| | | | |
|---|---|---|---|
| 10h | 11h [gr] | Load/select character table | 207 |
| | *Entry:* | AH=11h<br>AL= 20h (Load extended ASCII 8x8 characters)<br>21h (Load user-defined chars)<br>22h (Load ROM 8x14 characters) (not MCGA)<br>23h (Load ROM 8x8 characters)<br>24h (Load ROM 8x16 characters) (not EGA)<br>BL= 00h (Variable number of rows)<br>01h (14 rows)<br>02h (25 rows)<br>03h (43 rows)<br>(Not used for AL=20h)<br>CX=bytes per character (if AL=21h)<br>DL=number of rows (if BL=00h, AL>20h)<br>ES:BP points to character table (if AL=20h or 21h) | |
| | *Exit:* | None | |

---

| | | | |
|---|---|---|---|
| 10h | 11h, 30h | Get character table information | 207 |
| | *Entry:* | AH=11h<br>AL=30h<br>BH=00h (Interrupt 1Fh table)<br>01h (Interrupt 43h table)<br>02h (ROM 8x14 table)<br>03h (ROM 8x8 table, upper half) | |

| Int | Function | | Description | Page |
|---|---|---|---|---|
| | | | 04h (ROM 8x8 table, lower half) | |
| | | | 05h (ROM 9x14 table) | |
| | | | 06h (ROM 8x16 table) | |
| | | | 07h (ROM 9x16 table) | |
| | | *Exit:* | CX=character height | |
| | | | DL=number of rows -1 | |
| | | | ES:BP points to character table | |
| 10h | 12h | | Multi-line print-screen (not CGA) | 259 |
| | | *Entry:* | AH=12h | |
| | | | BL=20h | |
| | | *Exit:* | None | |
| 10h | 13h | | Display EGA string (EGA etc., not early PCs) | 235 |
| | | *Entry:* | AH=13h | |
| | | | AL= 00h (attribute fixed, do not move cursor) | |
| | | | 01h (attribute fixed, move cursor) | |
| | | | 02h (attribute not fixed, do not move cursor) | |
| | | | 03h (attribute not fixed, move cursor) | |
| | | | BL=attribute (if AL=00h or 01h) | |
| | | | BH=page | |
| | | | CX=string length | |
| | | | DX=cursor position | |
| | | | ES:BP points to text string | |
| | | *Exit:* | None | |
| 11h | | | Get configuration list | 23 |
| | | *Entry:* | None | |
| | | *Exit:* | AX=configuration list code | |
| 12h | | | Get user RAM | 27 |
| | | *Entry:* | None | |
| | | *Exit:* | AX=user RAM | |
| 13h | 00h | | Reset disk | 283 |
| | | *Entry:* | AH=00h | |
| | | *Exit:* | None | |
| 13h | 01h | | Check disk status | 280 |
| | | *Entry:* | AH=01h | |
| | | *Exit:* | AH=status code | |
| 13h | 02h | | Read sectors from disk | 276 |
| | | *Entry:* | AH=02h | |
| | | | AL=number of sectors to read | |
| | | | CH=track | |
| | | | CL=sector | |
| | | | DH=head | |
| | | | DL=drive | |
| | | | ES:BX=start of data buffer | |
| | | *Exit:* | AH=error code (if CF=1) | |
| | | | AL=number of sectors read (if CF=0) | |
| 13h | 03h | | Write sectors to disk | 278 |
| | | *Entry:* | AH=03h | |
| | | | AL=number of sectors to write | |
| | | | CH=track | |
| | | | CL=sector | |

| | | | | |
|---|---|---|---|---|
| | | | DH=head<br>DL=drive<br>DS:BX=start of data buffer | |
| | | *Exit:* | AH=error code (if CF=1)<br>AL=no. of sectors written (CF=0) | |
| 13h | 04h | | Verify disk sectors | 278 |
| | | *Entry:* | AH=04h<br>AL=number of sectors to verify<br>CH=track<br>CL=sector<br>DH=head<br>DL=drive | |
| | | *Exit:* | AH=error code (if CF=1)<br>AL=no. of sectors verified (CF=0) | |
| 13h | 05h | | Format disk track | 268 |
| | | *Entry:* | AH=05h<br>CH=track<br>DH=head<br>DL=drive<br>ES:BX=location of list of address marks | |
| | | *Exit:* | AH=error code (if CF=1) | |
| 13h | 15h | | Check disk type | 282 |
| | | *Entry:* | AH=15h<br>DL=drive | |
| | | *Exit:* | AH=00h (drive does not exist)<br>01h (floppy drive, with no mechanism for detecting disk changes)<br>02h (floppy drive, able to detect disk changes)<br>03h (hard disk)<br>CX:DX=number of 512-byte sectors (if AH=03h) | |
| 13h | 16h | | Check floppy disk change | 282 |
| | | *Entry:* | AH=16h<br>DL=drive | |
| | | *Exit:* | AH=00h (disk not changed)<br>01h (invalid call)<br>06h (disk has been changed)<br>80h (drive not ready) | |
| 13h | 17h | | Set floppy disk type | 268 |
| | | *Entry:* | AH=17h<br>AL= 01h (5¼" double-density drive)<br>02h (5¼" high density drive, DD disk)<br>03h (5¼" high density drive and disk)<br>04h (3½" drive) | |
| | | *Exit:* | AH=error code (if CF=1) | |
| 13h | 18h | | Set disk parameters | 268 |
| | | *Entry:* | AH=18h<br>CH=number of tracks<br>CL=sectors per track<br>DL=drive | |
| | | *Exit:* | AH=error code (if CF=1)<br>ES:DI points to disk parameter table | |

| Int | Function | | Description | Page |
|---|---|---|---|---|
| 14h | 00h | | Initialise serial port | 249 |
| | | *Entry:* | AH=00h<br>AL=protocol code<br>DX=port number | |
| | | *Exit:* | AH=main status code<br>AL=modem status code | |
| 14h | 01h | | Send character to serial port | 252 |
| | | *Entry:* | AH=01h<br>AL=character to send<br>DX=port number | |
| | | *Exit:* | AH=main status code | |
| 14h | 02h | | Get character from serial port | 252 |
| | | *Entry:* | AH=02h<br>DX=port number | |
| | | *Exit:* | AH=main status code<br>AL=character received | |
| 14h | 03h | | Check serial port status | 253 |
| | | *Entry:* | AH=03h | |
| | | *Exit:* | AH=main status code<br>AL=modem status code | |
| 15h | 83h | | Interval timer (AT only) | 138 |
| | | *Entry:* | AH=00h (start timer)<br>01h (stop timer)<br>CX:DX=interval (microseconds)<br>ES:BX=address of status byte | |
| | | *Exit:* | CF=0 (success)<br>1 (failure) | |
| 15h | 84h | | Get joystick information (not PCs) | 194 |
| | | *Entry:* | AH=84h<br>DX= 00h (digital data)<br>01h (analogue values) | |
| | | *Exit:* | AL=digital settings (bits 4 to 7)<br>AX, BX, CX, DX = analogue values | |
| 15h | 86h | | Wait for interval (AT only) | 139 |
| | | *Entry:* | AH=86h<br>CX:DX=interval (microseconds) | |
| | | *Exit:* | CF=0 (success)<br>1 (failure) | |
| 15h | 88h | | Get extended memory size (not PCs) | 28 |
| | | *Entry:* | AH=88h | |
| | | *Exit:* | AX=extended memory (K) | |
| 16h | 00h | | Read character from keyboard | 170 |
| | | *Entry:* | AH=00h | |
| | | *Exit:* | AH=scan code<br>AL=ASCII code | |
| 16h | 01h | | Read character if available | 174 |
| | | *Entry:* | AH=01h | |
| | | *Exit:* | AH=scan code | |

| | | | | |
|---|---|---|---|---|
| | | | AL=ASCII code<br>ZF= 0 (character available)<br>1 (buffer empty) | |
| 16h | 02h | | Get keyboard status | 154 |
| | | *Entry:* | AH=02h | |
| | | *Exit:* | AL=keyboard status byte | |
| 16h | 03h | | Set key repeat values (AT, PS/2) | 169 |
| | | *Entry:* | AH=03h<br>AL=05h<br>BH=delay time<br>BL=repeat rate | |
| | | *Exit:* | None | |
| 16h | 05h | | Put keypress in buffer (not early PCs) | 166 |
| | | *Entry:* | AH=05h<br>CH=Scan code<br>CL=ASCII code | |
| | | *Exit:* | AL=00h (success)<br>01h (failure) | |
| 16h | 10h | | Read character from full-sized keyboard | 171 |
| | | *Entry:* | AH=10h | |
| | | *Exit:* | AH=scan code<br>AL=ASCII code | |
| 16h | 11h | | Read character from full-sized keyboard | 174 |
| | | *Entry:* | AH=11h | |
| | | *Exit:* | AH=scan code<br>AL=ASCII code<br>ZF= 0 (character available)<br>1 (buffer empty) | |
| 16h | 12h | | Get full-sized keyboard status | 156 |
| | | *Entry:* | AH=12h | |
| | | *Exit:* | AH=Second keyboard status byte<br>AL=First keyboard status byte | |
| 17h | 00h | | Send character to parallel port | 255 |
| | | *Entry:* | AH=00h<br>AL=character<br>DX=port number | |
| | | *Exit:* | AH=status code | |
| 17h | 01h | | Initialise parallel port | 254 |
| | | *Entry:* | AH=01h<br>DX=port number | |
| | | *Exit:* | AH=status code | |
| 17h | 02h | | Check parallel port status | 256 |
| | | *Entry:* | AH=02h<br>DX=port number | |
| | | *Exit:* | AH=status code | |
| 19h | | | Restart system | 123 |
| | | *Entry:* | None | |
| | | *Exit:* | None | |

| Interrupt | Function | | Description | Page |
|---|---|---|---|---|
| 1Ah | 00h | | Get clock count | 136 |
| | | *Entry:* | AH=00h | |
| | | *Exit:* | AL=00h (not yet midnight) | |
| | | | 01h (past midnight) | |
| | | | CX=clock count (high order word) | |
| | | | DX=clock count (low order word) | |
| 1Ah | 01h | | Set clock count | 136 |
| | | *Entry:* | AH=01h | |
| | | | CX=clock count (high order word) | |
| | | | DX=clock count (low order word) | |
| | | *Exit:* | None | |
| 1Ah | 0001h+ 6 | | Compress data | 285 |
| | | *Entry:* | AX=0001h (Standard) | |
| | | | 0004h (Update) | |
| | | | 0008h (Max) | |
| | | | 0010h (Max update) | |
| | | | CX= 0 (Client is application) | |
| | | | 1 (Client is operating system) | |
| | | | DS:SI=pointer to compression request buffer | |
| | | | ES:BX=pointer to compression information buffer | |
| | | *Exit:* | AX=error code | |
| 1Ah | 0002h+ 6 | | Decompress data | 285 |
| | | *Entry:* | AX=0002h (Standard) | |
| | | | 0020h (Incremental) | |
| | | | CX= 0 (Client is application) | |
| | | | 1 (Client is operating system) | |
| | | | DS:SI=pointer to compression request buffer | |
| | | | ES:BX=pointer to compression information buffer | |
| | | *Exit:* | AX=error code | |
| 1Ah | 02h | | Get RTC time (AT-compatibles) | 147 |
| | | *Entry:* | AH=02h | |
| | | | CH=hours (BCD) | |
| | | | CL=minutes (BCD) | |
| | | | DH=seconds (BCD) | |
| | | *Exit:* | CF=0 (RTC functioning) | |
| | | | 1 (RTC not functioning) | |
| | | | Other flags changed | |
| 1Ah | 03h | | Set RTC time (AT-compatibles) | 147 |
| | | *Entry:* | AH=03h | |
| | | | CH=hours (BCD) | |
| | | | CL=minutes (BCD) | |
| | | | DH=seconds (BCD) | |
| | | | DL= 0 (GMT only) | |
| | | | 1 (GMT and BST) | |
| | | *Exit:* | CF=0 (RTC functioning) | |
| | | | 1 (RTC not functioning) | |
| | | | Other flags changed | |
| 1Ah | 04h | | Get RTC date (AT-compatibles) | 144 |
| | | *Entry:* | AH=04h | |

| | | | | | |
|---|---|---|---|---|---|
| | | | | CH=century (BCD) | |
| | | | | CL=year (BCD) | |
| | | | | DH=month (BCD) | |
| | | | | DL=day (BCD) | |
| | | | *Exit:* | CF=0 (RTC functioning) | |
| | | | | 1 (RTC not functioning) | |
| | | | | Other flags changed | |
| 1Ah | 05h | | | Set RTC date | 145 |
| | | | *Entry:* | AH=05h (AT-compatibles) | |
| | | | | CH=century (BCD) (19 or 20) | |
| | | | | CL=year (BCD) | |
| | | | | DH=month (BCD) | |
| | | | | DL=day (BCD) | |
| | | | *Exit:* | CF=0 (RTC functioning) | |
| | | | | 1 (RTC not functioning) | |
| | | | | Other flags changed | |
| 1Ah | 06h | | | Set RTC alarm (AT-compatibles) | 150 |
| | | | *Entry:* | AH=06h | |
| | | | | CH=hours (BCD) | |
| | | | | CL=minutes (BCD) | |
| | | | | DH=seconds (BCD) | |
| | | | *Exit:* | CF=0 (alarm now set) | |
| | | | | 1 (alarm was already set) | |
| 1Ah | 07h | | | Clear RTC alarm | 150 |
| | | | *Entry:* | AH=07h | |
| | | | *Exit:* | None | |
| 1Ah | B001h | 6 | | Check compression installation | 284 |
| | | | *Entry:* | AH=B001h | |
| | | | | CX=any | |
| | | | | DX=any | |
| | | | *Exit:* | AX=0 (success) | |
| | | | | 1 (failure) | |
| | | | | CX=DX reversed | |
| | | | | DX=CX reversed | |
| | | | | ES:DI=pointer to compression information buffer | |
| 20h | | 1 | | Terminate program | 84 |
| | | | *Entry:* | CS=PSP address | |
| | | | *Exit:* | None | |
| 21h | 00h | 1 | | Terminate program | 84 |
| | | | *Entry:* | AH=00h | |
| | | | | CS=PSP address | |
| | | | *Exit:* | None | |
| 21h | 01h | 1 | | Keyboard input with echo (with Break) | 172 |
| | | | *Entry:* | AH=01h | |
| | | | *Exit:* | AL=character | |
| 21h | 02h | 1 | | Display character | 232 |
| | | | *Entry:* | AH=02h | |
| | | | | DL=character | |
| | | | *Exit:* | None | |

| | | | | |
|---|---|---|---|---|
| 21h | 03h | 1 | Get character from serial port | 253 |
| | | *Entry:* | AH=03h | |
| | | *Exit:* | AL=character | |
| 21h | 04h | 1 | Send character to serial port | 252 |
| | | *Entry:* | AH=04h | |
| | | | DL=character to send | |
| | | *Exit:* | None | |
| 21h | 05h | 1 | Send character to parallel port | 255 |
| | | *Entry:* | AH=05h | |
| | | | DL=character | |
| | | *Exit:* | None | |
| 21h | 06h | 1 | Display character (see also Chap 6) | 232 |
| | | *Entry:* | AH=06h | |
| | | | DL=character other than FFh | |
| | | *Exit:* | None | |
| 21h | 06h | 1 | Keyboard input (see also Chapter 8) | 175 |
| | | *Entry:* | AH=06h | |
| | | | DL=FFh | |
| | | *Exit:* | AL=input character | |
| | | | ZF= 0 (character available) | |
| | | | 1 (buffer empty) | |
| 21h | 07h | 1 | Keyboard input without echo (no Break) | 171 |
| | | *Entry:* | AH=07h | |
| | | *Exit:* | AL=character | |
| 21h | 08h | 1 | Keyboard input without echo (with Break) | 172 |
| | | *Entry:* | AH=08h | |
| | | *Exit:* | AL=character | |
| 21h | 09h | 1 | Display string | 233 |
| | | *Entry:* | AH=09h | |
| | | | DS:DX=start of string | |
| | | *Exit:* | None | |
| 21h | 0Ah | | Keyboard string input | 177 |
| | | *Entry:* | AH=0Ah | |
| | | | DS:DX=start of input buffer | |
| | | *Exit:* | None | |
| 21h | 0Bh | 1 | Check keyboard buffer | 175 |
| | | *Entry:* | AH=0Bh | |
| | | *Exit:* | AL=00h (buffer empty) | |
| | | | FFh (character available) | |
| 21h | 0Ch | 1 | Clear keyboard buffer, call int 21h | 176 |
| | | *Entry:* | AH=0Ch | |
| | | | AL=function (01, 06, 07, 08, 0A) | |
| | | *Exit:* | (Various - as for selected function) | |
| 21h | 0Dh | 1 | Reset disk | 283 |
| | | *Entry:* | AH=0Dh | |
| | | *Exit:* | None | |

| | | | | |
|---|---|---|---|---|
| 21h | 0Eh | 1 | Change current drive | 300 |
| | | *Entry:* | AH=0Eh<br>DL=drive number (0=A, 1=B, etc.) | |
| | | *Exit:* | AL=drive count | |
| 21h | 0Fh | 1 | Open a file | 349 |
| | | *Entry:* | AH=0Fh<br>DS:DX=address of FCB | |
| | | *Exit:* | AL=00h (success)<br>FFh (failure) | |
| 21h | 10h | 1 | Close a file | 352 |
| | | *Entry:* | AH=10h<br>DS:DX=address of FCB | |
| | | *Exit:* | AL=00h (success)<br>FFh (failure) | |
| 21h | 11h | 1 | Find first matching file | 346 |
| | | *Entry:* | AH=11h<br>DS:DX=address of FCB | |
| | | *Exit:* | AL=00h (file found)<br>FFh (file not found) | |
| 21h | 12h | 1 | Find next matching file | 346 |
| | | *Entry:* | AH=12h<br>DS:DX=address of FCB | |
| | | *Exit:* | AL=00h (file found)<br>FFh (file not found) | |
| 21h | 13h | 1 | Delete a file | 353 |
| | | *Entry:* | AH=13h<br>DS:DX=address of FCB | |
| | | *Exit:* | AL=00h (success)<br>FFh (file not found) | |
| 21h | 14h | 1 | Read sequential record | 349 |
| | | *Entry:* | AH=14<br>DS:DX=address of FCB | |
| | | *Exit:* | AL=00h (success)<br>01h (end of file; no data read)<br>02h (DTA too small)<br>03h (end of file; some data read) | |
| 21h | 15h | 1 | Write sequential record | 349 |
| | | *Entry:* | AH=15h<br>DS:DX=address of FCB | |
| | | *Exit:* | AL=00h (success)<br>01h (disk full; nothing written)<br>02h (DTA too small) | |
| 21h | 16h | 1 | Create a file | 348 |
| | | *Entry:* | AH=16h<br>DS:DX=address of FCB | |
| | | *Exit:* | AL=00h (success)<br>FFh (directory full) | |

| | | | | |
|---|---|---|---|---|
| 21h | 17h | 1 | Rename a file | 353 |
| | | *Entry:* | AH=17h<br>DS:DX=address of FCB | |
| | | *Exit:* | AL=00h (success)<br>01h (file not found) | |
| 21h | 19h | 1 | Get current drive | 300 |
| | | *Entry:* | AH=19h | |
| | | *Exit:* | AL=default drive (0=A, 1=B, etc.) | |
| 21h | 1Ah | 1 | Set disk transfer area address | 313 |
| | | *Entry:* | AH=1Ah<br>DS:DX=new address of DTA | |
| | | *Exit:* | None | |
| 21h | 1Bh | 1 | Get FAT information for current drive | 309 |
| | | *Entry:* | AH=1Bh | |
| | | *Exit:* | AL=sectors per cluster<br>CX=bytes per sector<br>DX=clusters<br>DS:BX=address of ID byte | |
| 21h | 1Ch | 1 | Get FAT information for any drive | 309 |
| | | *Entry:* | AH=1Ch<br>DL=drive (0=default, 1=A, 2=B, etc.) | |
| | | *Exit:* | AL=sectors per cluster<br>CX=bytes per sector<br>DX=clusters<br>DS:BX=address of ID byte | |
| 21h | 1Fh | 5 | Get current DPB | 272 |
| | | *Entry:* | AH=1Fh | |
| | | *Exit:* | AL=00h (Success)<br>FFh (Failure)<br>DS:BX=address of DPB | |
| 21h | 21h | 1 | Read random record | 351 |
| | | *Entry:* | AH=21h<br>AS:DX=address of FCB | |
| | | *Exit:* | AL=00h (success)<br>01h (end of file; no data read)<br>02h (DTA too small)<br>03h (end of file; some data read) | |
| 21h | 22h | 1 | Write random record | 351 |
| | | *Entry:* | AH=22h<br>DS:DX=address of FCB | |
| | | *Exit:* | AL=00h (success)<br>01h (disk full; nothing written)<br>02h (DTA too small) | |
| 21h | 23h | 1 | Get size of file | 348 |
| | | *Entry:* | AH=23h<br>DS:DX=address of FCB | |
| | | *Exit:* | AL=00h (success)<br>01h (file not found) | |

| | | | | |
|---|---|---|---|---|
| 21h | 24h | 1 | Prepare field for random record | 350 |
| | | *Entry:* | AH=24h<br>DS:DX=address of FCB | |
| | | *Exit:* | AL=00h (success)<br>FFh (failure) | |
| 21h | 25h | | Set interrupt vector | 133 |
| | | *Entry:* | AH=25h<br>AL=interrupt number<br>DS:DX=pointer to interrupt handler | |
| | | *Exit:* | None | |
| 21h | 26h | 1 | Create PSP | 83 |
| | | *Entry:* | AH=26h<br>DX=segment address | |
| | | *Exit:* | None | |
| 21h | 27h | 1 | Read random records | 351 |
| | | *Entry:* | AH=27h<br>CX=number of records to read<br>DS:DX=address of FCB | |
| | | *Exit:* | AL=00h (success)<br>01h (end of file; no data read)<br>02h (DTA too small)<br>03h (end of file; some data read)<br>CX=number of records read | |
| 21h | 28h | 1 | Write random records | 351 |
| | | *Entry:* | AH=28h<br>CX=number of records to write<br>DS:DX=address of FCB | |
| | | *Exit:* | AL=00h (success)<br>01h (disk full; nothing written)<br>02h (DTA too small)<br>CX=number of records written | |
| 21h | 29h | 1 | Parse filename | 347 |
| | | *Entry:* | AH=29h<br>AL=parsing code<br>DS:SI=address of command line<br>ES:DI=address of FCB | |
| | | *Exit:* | AL=00h (success)<br>01h (wildcards found)<br>FFh (invalid drive)<br>DS:SI=address of next character in command line<br>ES:DI=address of FCB | |
| 21h | 2Ah | 1 | Get date | 141 |
| | | *Entry:* | AH=2Ah | |
| | | *Exit:* | AL=day of week (0=Sunday)<br>CX=year (1980-2099)<br>DH=month (1=January)<br>DL=day | |
| 21h | 2Bh | 1 | Set date | 141 |
| | | *Entry:* | AH=2Bh<br>CX=year (1980-2099) | |

| Interrupt | Function | Version | Description | Page |
|---|---|---|---|---|
| | | | DH=month (1=January) | |
| | | | DL=day | |
| | | *Exit:* | AL=00h (date valid) | |
| | | | FFh (date invalid) | |
| 21h | 2Ch | 1 | Get time | 146 |
| | | *Entry:* | AH=2C | |
| | | *Exit:* | CH=hours | |
| | | | CL=minutes | |
| | | | DH=seconds | |
| | | | DL=hundredths of seconds | |
| 21h | 2Dh | 1 | Set time | 146 |
| | | *Entry:* | AH=2Dh | |
| | | | CH=hours | |
| | | | CL=minutes | |
| | | | DH=seconds | |
| | | | DL=hundredths of seconds | |
| | | *Exit:* | AL=00h (time valid) | |
| | | | FFh (time invalid) | |
| 21h | 2Eh | 1 | Disk write verification | 279 |
| | | *Entry:* | AH=2Eh | |
| | | | AL= 00h (verify off) | |
| | | | 01h (verify on) | |
| | | | DL=00h | |
| | | *Exit:* | None | |
| 21h | 2Fh | 2 | Get address of DTA | 313 |
| | | *Entry:* | AH=2Fh | |
| | | *Exit:* | AX=error code | |
| | | | ES:BX=address of DTA | |
| 21h | 30h | 2 | Check DOS version number | 102 |
| | | *Entry:* | AH=30h | |
| | | *Exit:* | AH=minor version number | |
| | | | AL=major version number | |
| | | | BX,CX changed | |
| 21h | 31h | | Terminate and stay resident | 98 |
| | | *Entry:* | AH=31h | |
| | | | AL=termination code | |
| | | | DX=no. paragraphs to keep | |
| | | *Exit:* | AX=error code | |
| 21h | 32h | 5 | Get DPB | 272 |
| | | *Entry:* | AH=32h | |
| | | | DL=drive (0=current, 1=A, etc.) | |
| | | *Exit:* | AL=00h (Success) | |
| | | | FFh (Failure) | |
| | | | DS:BX=address of DPB | |
| 21h | 33h,00h | | Get Ctrl-Break status | 159 |
| | | *Entry:* | AH=33h | |
| | | | AL=00h | |
| | | *Exit:* | AL=FFh (if entry code is invalid) | |
| | | | DL= 00h (Ctrl-Break is off) | |
| | | | 01h (Ctrl-Break is on) | |

| Int | Function | No. | Description | Page |
|---|---|---|---|---|
| 21h | 33h,01h | | Set or clear Ctrl-Break operation | 159 |
| | | *Entry:* | AH=33h | |
| | | | AL=01h | |
| | | | DL= 00h (Turn Ctrl-Break off) | |
| | | | 01h (Turn Ctrl-Break on) | |
| | | *Exit:* | AL=FFh (if entry code is invalid) | |
| 05h | | | Print screen | 159 |
| 21h | 33,05h | 4 | Get boot drive | 301 |
| | | *Entry:* | AH=33h | |
| | | | AL=05h | |
| | | *Exit:* | DL=boot drive (1=A, 3=C) | |
| 21h | 33,06h | 5 | Get DOS version details | 102 |
| | | *Entry:* | AH=33h | |
| | | | AL=06h | |
| | | *Exit:* | BH=minor version number | |
| | | | BL=major version number | |
| | | | DH= 00h (DOS is in conventional memory) | |
| | | | 08h (DOS is in ROM) | |
| | | | 10h (DOS is in HMA) | |
| | | | DL=revision number (bits 0-2) | |
| 21h | 35h | | Get interrupt vector | 133 |
| | | *Entry:* | AH=35h | |
| | | | AL=interrupt number | |
| | | *Exit:* | ES:BX=interrupt vector | |
| 21h | 36h | 1 | Get free clusters | 310 |
| | | *Entry:* | AH=36h | |
| | | | DL=drive (0=default, 1=A, 2=B, etc.) | |
| | | *Exit:* | AX=sectors per cluster | |
| | | | FFFFh (invalid drive) | |
| | | | BX=number of free clusters | |
| | | | CX=bytes per sector | |
| | | | DX=total clusters on disk | |
| 21h | 38h [v2] | 2 | Get or set country-dependent information | 113 |
| | | *Entry:* | AH=38h | |
| | | | AL=country code (0-2) | |
| | | | DS:DX=address of 32 byte buffer | |
| | | *Exit:* | AX=error code (if CF=1) | |
| | | | BX=country code | |
| | | | DS:DX=address of information | |
| 21h | 38h [v3] | 3 | Get or set country-dependent information | 114 |
| | | *Entry:* | AH=38h | |
| | | | AL= 00h (current country) | |
| | | | 01h - FEh (country code) | |
| | | | FFh (code>=255) | |
| | | | BX=country code (if AL=FFh) | |
| | | | DS:DX=address of 32 byte buffer | |
| | | *Exit:* | AX=error code (if CF=1) | |
| | | | BX=country code | |
| | | | DS:DX=address of information | |

| | | | | |
|---|---|---|---|---|
| 21h | 39h | 2 | Make directory | 303 |
| | | *Entry:* | AH=39<br>DS:DX=address of ASCIIZ directory name | |
| | | *Exit:* | AX=error code (if CF=1) | |
| 21h | 3Ah | 2 | Remove directory | 303 |
| | | *Entry:* | AH=3Ah<br>DS:DX=address of ASCIIZ directory name | |
| | | *Exit:* | AX=error code (if CF=1) | |
| 21h | 3Bh | 2 | Change directory | 302 |
| | | *Entry:* | AH=3B<br>DS:DX=address of ASCIIZ directory name | |
| | | *Exit:* | AX=error code (if CF=1) | |
| 21h | 3Ch | 2 | Create a file | 326 |
| | | *Entry:* | AH=3Ch<br>CX=file attribute<br>DS:DX=address of ASCIIZ file specification | |
| | | *Exit:* | AX=file handle (CF=0)<br>error code (CF=1) | |
| 21h | 3Dh | 2 | Open a file | 329 |
| | | *Entry:* | AH=3Dh<br>AL=file use code<br>DS:DX=address of ASCIIZ file specification | |
| | | *Exit:* | AX=file handle (CF=0)<br>error code (CF=1) | |
| 21h | 3Eh | 2 | Close a file | 337 |
| | | *Entry:* | AH=3Eh<br>BX=file handle | |
| | | *Exit:* | AX=error code (if CF=1) | |
| 21h | 3Fh | 2 | Read from a file | 335 |
| | | *Entry:* | AH=3Fh<br>BX=file handle<br>CX=number of bytes to be read<br>DS:DX=address of DTA | |
| | | *Exit:* | AX=number of bytes read (CF=0)<br>return code (CF=1) | |
| 21h | 40h | 2 | Write to a file | 336 |
| | | *Entry:* | AH=40h<br>BX=file handle<br>CX= number of bytes to be written<br>00h (to truncate file at pointer)<br>DS:DX=address of DTA | |
| | | *Exit:* | AX=number of bytes written (CF=0)<br>error code (CF=1) | |
| 21h | 41h | 2 | Delete a file | 343 |
| | | *Entry:* | AH=41h<br>DS:DX=address of ASCIIZ file specification | |
| | | *Exit:* | AX=error code (if CF=1) | |

| | | | | |
|---|---|---|---|---|
| 21h | 42h | 2 | Move file pointer | 334 |
| | | *Entry:* | AH=42h<br>AL=offset code<br>BX=file handle<br>CX:DX=number of bytes to move pointer | |
| | | *Exit:* | AX=error code (if CF=1)<br>DX:AX=new pointer offset (if CF=0) | |
| 21h | 43,00h | 2 | Get attributes of file | 296 |
| | | *Entry:* | AH=43h<br>AL=00h<br>DS:DX=address of ASCIIZ file specification | |
| | | *Exit:* | AX=error code (if CF=1)<br>DX:AX=attribute byte | |
| 21h | 43,01h | 2 | Set attributes of file | 297 |
| | | *Entry:* | AH=43h<br>AL=01h<br>CX=new attribute byte<br>DS:DX=address of ASCIIZ file specification | |
| | | *Exit:* | AX=error code (if CF=1) | |
| 21h | 44h | 2 | IOCTL functions | 366 |
| | | *Entry:* | AH=44h<br>AL=subfunction | |
| | | *Exit:* | (Various) | |
| 21h | 45h | 2 | Duplicate a file handle | 338 |
| | | *Entry:* | AH=45h<br>BX=first file handle | |
| | | *Exit:* | AX=new file handle (CF=0)<br>return code (CF=1) | |
| 21h | 46h | 2 | Force duplication of handle | 338 |
| | | *Entry:* | AH=46h<br>BX=file handle to copy<br>CX=second file handle | |
| | | *Exit:* | AX=error code (if CF=1)<br>CX=second file handle | |
| 21h | 47h | 2 | Check current directory | 301 |
| | | *Entry:* | AH=47h<br>DL=drive (0=default)<br>DS:SI=address for pathname | |
| | | *Exit:* | AX=error code (if CF=1)<br>DS:SI=address of pathname | |
| 21h | 48h | 2 | Allocate memory | 87 |
| | | *Entry:* | AH=48h<br>BX=memory (in paragraphs) | |
| | | *Exit:* | AX=seg address of allocated mem<br>error code (if CF=1)<br>BX=largest memory size<br>(if allocation failed) | |
| 21h | 49h | 2 | Free memory | 88 |
| | | *Entry:* | AH=49h | |

| | | | | |
|---|---|---|---|---|
| | | | ES=segment of block to return | |
| | | *Exit:* | AX=error code (if CF=1) | |
| 21h | 4Ah | 2 | Modify allocated memory | 88 |
| | | *Entry:* | AH=4Ah<br>BX=memory (paragraphs)<br>ES=segment of block | |
| | | *Exit:* | AX=error code (if CF=1)<br>BX=largest memory size<br>(if allocation failed) | |
| 21h | 4Bh | 2 | Load/execute program | 86 |
| | | *Entry:* | AH=4Bh<br>AL= 00h (Load and run)<br>01h (Load but do not run)<br>03h (Load overlay)<br>05h (Set execution state – DOS 5)<br>DS:DX=address of ASCIIZ file specification<br>ES:BX=address of control block | |
| | | *Exit:* | AX=return code | |
| 21h | 4Ch | 2 | Terminate sub-program | 91 |
| | | *Entry:* | AH=4Ch | |
| | | *Exit:* | AL=error code | |
| 21h | 4Dh | 2 | Get return code of sub-program | 91 |
| | | *Entry:* | AH=4Dh | |
| | | *Exit:* | AL=return code | |
| 21h | 4Eh | 2 | Find first matching file | 316 |
| | | *Entry:* | AH=4Eh<br>CX=file attribute<br>DS:DX=address of ASCIIZ file specification | |
| | | *Exit:* | AX=error code (if CF=1) | |
| 21h | 4Fh | 2 | Find next matching file | 317 |
| | | *Entry:* | AH=4Fh<br>DS:DX=address of information from previous search | |
| | | *Exit:* | AX=error code (if CF=1) | |
| 21h | 51h | 2 | Get PSP segment address | 79 |
| | | *Entry:* | AH=51h | |
| | | *Exit:* | BX=segment address of PSP | |
| 21h | 50h | 2 | Set PSP address | 80 |
| | | *Entry:* | AH=50h<br>BX=segment address of PSP | |
| | | *Exit:* | None | |
| 21h | 54h | 2 | Check verification status | 279 |
| | | *Entry:* | AH=54h | |
| | | *Exit:* | AL=00h (verify off)<br>01h (verify on) | |
| 21h | 56h | 2 | Rename a file | 343 |
| | | *Entry:* | AH=56h<br>DS:DX=address of old name (ASCIIZ) | |

| | | | | |
|---|---|---|---|---|
| | | | ES:DI=address of new name (ASCIIZ) | |
| | | *Exit:* | AX=error code (if CF=1) | |
| 21h | 57,00h | 2 | Get date and time stamp | 344 |
| | | *Entry:* | AH=57h | |
| | | | AL=00h | |
| | | | BX=file handle | |
| | | *Exit:* | AX=error code (if CF=1) | |
| | | | CX=time | |
| | | | DX=date | |
| 21h | 57,01h | 2 | Set date and time stamp | 344 |
| | | *Entry:* | AH=57h | |
| | | | AL=01h | |
| | | | BX=file handle | |
| | | | CX=time | |
| | | | DX=date | |
| | | *Exit:* | AX=error code (if CF=1) | |
| 21h | 58,00h | 3 | Get allocation strategy | 88 |
| | | *Entry:* | AH=58h | |
| | | | AL=00h | |
| | | *Exit:* | AX=allocation strategy | |
| 21h | 58,01 | 3 | Set allocation strategy | 89 |
| | | *Entry:* | AH=58h | |
| | | | AL=01h | |
| | | | BX=allocation strategy | |
| | | *Exit:* | CF=0 (success) | |
| | | | 1 (failure) | |
| 21h | 58,02h | 5 | Get upper memory link | 90 |
| | | *Entry:* | AH=58h | |
| | | | AL=02h | |
| | | *Exit:* | AL=0 (not linked) | |
| | | | 1 (linked) | |
| 21h | 58,03h | 5 | Set upper memory link | 90 |
| | | *Entry:* | AH=58h | |
| | | | AL=03h | |
| | | | BH=00h | |
| | | | BL= 0 (link) | |
| | | | 1 (unlink) | |
| | | *Exit:* | CF=0 (success) | |
| | | | 1 (failure) | |
| 21h | 59h | 3 | Get error codes | 319 |
| | | *Entry:* | AH=59h | |
| | | | BX=0000h | |
| | | *Exit:* | AX=extended error code | |
| | | | BH=type of error | |
| | | | BL=possible action | |
| | | | CH=location of error | |
| 21h | 5Ah | 3 | Create a temporary file | 329 |
| | | *Entry:* | AH=5Ah | |
| | | | CX=file attribute | |
| | | | DS:DX=address of ASCIIZ pathname | |
| | | *Exit:* | AX=error code (if CF=1) | |

| | | | | |
|---|---|---|---|---|
| | | | DS:DX=address of ASCIIZ file specification (if CF=0) | |
| 21h | 5Bh | 3 | Create a new file | 328 |
| | | *Entry:* | AH=5Bh<br>CX=file attribute<br>DS:DX=address of ASCIIZ pathname | |
| | | *Exit:* | AX=file handle (CF=0)<br>error code (CF=1) | |
| 21h | 5C,00h | 3.1 | Lock file | 340 |
| | | *Entry:* | AH=5Ch<br>AL=00h<br>BX=file handle<br>CX:DX=offset<br>SI:DI=locked data length | |
| | | *Exit:* | AX=error code (if CF=1) | |
| 21h | 5C,01h | 3.1 | Unlock file | 341 |
| | | *Entry:* | AH=5Ch<br>AL=01h<br>BX=file handle<br>CX:DX=offset<br>SI:DI=locked data length | |
| | | *Exit:* | AX=error code (if CF=1) | |
| 21h | 5D,0Ah | 4 | Set error codes | 323 |
| | | *Entry:* | AH=5Dh<br>AL=0Ah<br>DS:SI=pointer to error codes | |
| | | *Exit:* | None | |
| 21h | 5Eh | 3.1 | Network computer/printer functions | 341 |
| | | *Entry:* | AH=5Eh<br>AL= 00h (Get computer's network name)<br>02h (Set printer init. codes)<br>03h (Get printer init. codes)<br>BX=network device number<br>(if AL=02h or 03h)<br>CX=length of printer code (if AL=02h)<br>DS:DX points to 16-byte buffer<br>(if AL=01h)<br>DS:SI points to printer string<br>(if AL=02h)<br>ES:DI points to printer data buffer (if AL=03h) | |
| | | *Exit:* | CX=length of printer code (if AL=03h)<br>CH>00h (if AL=01h and name is valid)<br>CL=network device number<br>(if AL=01h)<br>DS:DX points to computer name<br>(if AL=01h)<br>ES:DI points to printer code<br>(if AL=03h) | |
| 21h | 5Fh | 3.1 | Network device functions | 341 |
| | | *Entry:* | AH=5Fh<br>AL= 02h (Get network device details)<br>03h (Assign network device) | |

| | | | | |
|---|---|---|---|---|
| | | | 04h (Remove device from network) | |
| | | | BX=network device number (AH=02h) | |
| | | | BL=device (03 printer, 04 disk drive) (AH=03h) | |
| | | | CX=user-defined parameter (if AH=03h) | |
| | | | DS:SI points to 16-byte buffer for local name | |
| | | | ES:DI points to 128-byte buffer for network name and password | |
| | | *Exit:* | AX=error code (if CF=1) | |
| | | | DS:SI points to local name | |
| | | | ES:DI points to network name | |
| 21h | 62h | 3 | Get PSP segment address | 79 |
| | | *Entry:* | AH=62h | |
| | | *Exit:* | BX=segment address of PSP | |
| 21h | 65h | 3.3 | Extended country information | 117 |
| | | *Entry:* | AH=65h | |
| | | | AL= 01h (Get country information) | |
| | | | 02h (Get character trans table) | |
| | | | 04h (Get filename trans table) | |
| | | | 05h (Get filename char table) | |
| | | | 06h (Get collating sequence table) | |
| | | | 07h (Get double-byte character table) (DOS4) | |
| | | | 20h (Convert character) | |
| | | | 20h (Convert string) | |
| | | | 20h (Convert ASCIIZ string) | |
| | | | BX=code page (-1 for active code page) | |
| | | | CX=buffer size (29h if AL=01h, otherwise 05h) | |
| | | | DX=country code (-1 for default) | |
| | | | ES:DI points to buffer | |
| | | *Exit:* | AX=error code (if CF=1) | |
| | | | ES:DI points to data buffer | |
| 21h | 66h | 3.3 | Code page switching | 118 |
| | | *Entry:* | AH=66h | |
| | | | AL= 01h (Get current code page) | |
| | | | 02h (Set code page) | |
| | | | BX=code page (if AL=02h) | |
| | | *Exit:* | AX=error code (if CF=1) | |
| | | | BX=code page (if AL=01h) | |
| | | | DX=default code page (if AL=01h) | |
| 21h | 67h | 3.3 | Set number of file handles | 325 |
| | | *Entry:* | AH=67h | |
| | | | BX=number of handles | |
| | | *Exit:* | AX=error code (if CF=1) | |
| 21h | 68h | 3.3 | Save buffer contents | 337 |
| | | *Entry:* | AH=68h | |
| | | | BX=file handle | |
| | | *Exit:* | AX=error code (if CF=1) | |
| 21h | 6Ch | 4 | Create/open a file | 332 |
| | | *Entry:* | AH=6Ch | |
| | | | AL=00H | |

| Interrupt | Function | Version | Description | Page |
|---|---|---|---|---|
| | | | BH=error/save code<br>BL=file use code<br>CX=file attribute<br>DH=00h<br>DL=opening method | |
| | | *Exit:* | AX=file handle (if CF=0)<br>error code (if CF=1)<br>CL= 01h (file exists and opened)<br>02h (new file created)<br>03h (existing file overwritten) | |
| 22h | | | Termination address | 85 |
| 23h | | | Ctrl-Break handler address | 85 |
| 24h | | | Critical error handler address | 85 |
| 25h | | 1 | Read sectors from disk | 277 |
| | | *Entry:* | AL=logical drive number (A=0)<br>CX= number of sectors to read (standard disks)<br>-1 (large disks - DOS 4)<br>DX=first sector (DOS numbering) (standard disks)<br>DS:BX=start of data buffer | |
| | | *Exit:* | AH=DOS error code (if CF=1)<br>AL=BIOS error code (if CF=1)<br>Flags register on stack | |
| 26h | | 1 | Write sectors to disk | 278 |
| | | *Entry:* | AL=logical drive number (A=0)<br>CX= number of sectors to write (standard disks)<br>-1 (large disks - DOS 4)<br>DX=first sector (DOS numbering) (standard disks)<br>DS:BX=start of data buffer | |
| | | *Exit:* | AH=DOS error code (if CF=1)<br>AL=BIOS error code (if CF=1)<br>Flags register on stack | |
| 27h | | | Terminate and stay resident | 98 |
| | | *Entry:* | DX=no. paragraphs to keep | |
| | | *Exit:* | None | |
| 28h | | | MS-DOS idle handler | 95 |
| 2Fh | | 3 | Access background program | 95 |
| | | *Entry:* | AH=multiplex number<br>AL=function code | |
| | | *Exit:* | Various (depending on program) | |
| 33h | 00h | | Initialise mouse | 181 |
| | | *Entry:* | AX=0000h | |
| | | *Exit:* | AL=FFh (mouse installed)<br>00h (no mouse found)<br>BL=number of buttons | |

| | | | | |
|---|---|---|---|---|
| 33h | 01h | | Show mouse cursor | 188 |
| | | *Entry:* | AX=0001h | |
| | | *Exit:* | None | |
| 33h | 02h | | Hide mouse cursor | 188 |
| | | *Entry:* | AX=0002h | |
| | | *Exit:* | None | |
| 33h | 03h | | Get mouse information | 191 |
| | | *Entry:* | AX=0003h | |
| | | *Exit:* | BX=button status | |
| | | | CX=X co-ordinate | |
| | | | DX=Y co-ordinate | |
| 33h | 04h | | Set mouse cursor | 183 |
| | | *Entry:* | AX=0004h | |
| | | | CX=X co-ordinate | |
| | | | DX=Y co-ordinate | |
| | | *Exit:* | None | |
| 33h | 05h | | Get mouse button press | 190 |
| | | *Entry:* | AX=0005h | |
| | | | BL= 00h (left button) | |
| | | | 01h (right button) | |
| | | *Exit:* | AX=00h (button not pressed) | |
| | | | 01h (button pressed) | |
| | | | BX=number of presses since last call | |
| | | | CX=X co-ordinate at last press | |
| | | | DX=Y co-ordinate at last press | |
| 33h | 06h | | Get mouse button release | 190 |
| | | *Entry:* | AX=0006h | |
| | | | BL= 00h (left button) | |
| | | | 01h (right button) | |
| | | *Exit:* | AX=00h (button not pressed) | |
| | | | 01h (button pressed) | |
| | | | BX=number of presses since last call | |
| | | | CX=X co-ordinate at last release | |
| | | | DX=Y co-ordinate at last release | |
| 33h | 07h | | Set mouse cursor horizontal limits | 184 |
| | | *Entry:* | AX=0007h | |
| | | | CX=minimum X co-ordinate | |
| | | | DX=maximum X co-ordinate | |
| | | *Exit:* | None | |
| 33h | 08h | | Set mouse cursor vertical limits | 184 |
| | | *Entry:* | AX=0008h | |
| | | | CX=minimum Y co-ordinate | |
| | | | DX=maximum Y co-ordinate | |
| | | *Exit:* | None | |
| 33h | 09h | | Define mouse graphics cursor | 188 |
| | | *Entry:* | AX=0009h | |
| | | | BX=X co-ordinate offset | |
| | | | CX=Y co-ordinate offset | |
| | | | ES:DX=address of screen and cursor masks | |
| | | *Exit:* | None | |

| | | | | |
|---|---|---|---|---|
| 33h | 0Ah | | Define mouse text cursor | 186 |
| | | *Entry:* | AX=000Ah | |
| | | | BL= 00h (Software cursor) | |
| | | | 01h (Hardware cursor) | |
| | | | CX= Screen mask (BL=0) | |
| | | | First scan line (BL=1) | |
| | | | DX= Cursor mask (BL=0) | |
| | | | Last scan line (BL=1) | |
| | | *Exit:* | None | |
| 33h | 0Bh | | Read mouse counts | 182 |
| | | *Entry:* | AX=000Bh | |
| | | *Exit:* | CX=X count | |
| | | | DX=Y count | |
| 33h | 0Ch | | Set mouse interrupt | 191 |
| | | *Entry:* | AX=000Ch | |
| | | | CX=event mask | |
| | | | ES:DX=address of new interrupt | |
| | | *Exit:* | None | |
| 33h | 0Dh | | Turn light pen emulation on | 193 |
| | | *Entry:* | AX=000Dh | |
| | | *Exit:* | None | |
| 33h | 0Eh | | Turn light pen emulation off | 193 |
| | | *Entry:* | AX=000Eh | |
| | | *Exit:* | None | |
| 33h | 0Fh | | Set mickey:pixel ratio | 184 |
| | | *Entry:* | AX=000Fh | |
| | | | CX=X ratio (per 8 units) | |
| | | | DX=Y ratio (per 8 units) | |
| | | *Exit:* | None | |
| 33h | 10h | | Hide mouse cursor while updating | 189 |
| | | *Entry:* | AX=0010h | |
| | | | CX=top left X co-ordinate | |
| | | | DX=top left Y co-ordinate | |
| | | | SI=bottom right X co-ordinate | |
| | | | DI=bottom right Y co-ordinate | |
| | | *Exit:* | None | |
| 33h | 13h | | Set threshold for double speed | 185 |
| | | *Entry:* | AX=0013h | |
| | | | DX=threshold speed (mickeys/second) | |
| | | *Exit:* | None | |

# Index


80x86 family,11
80x87 maths co-processors, 12

## A

Adaptors, 197
Address interrupts, 85
Address marks, 269
Addressing modes, 68
Alarm, 150
Allocating memory, 87
Alt key, 161
ANSI.SYS, 366
ASCII codes, 52
ASCII files, 339
ASCIIZ, 56
Assemblers, 75
Attribute, 394

## B

Basic Input/Output System
  see BIOS
Binary, 37
  files, 76
Binary operations, 49
BIOS, 19
BIOS parameter block
  see BPB
Bits, 37
Block devices, 358
Boot record, 106
Booting, 120
BPB, 364
BUFFERS, 314
Bus Interface Unit, 28
Bytes, 39

## C

Calling programs, 86
Carry flag, 50
Central Processing Unit
  see CPU
CGA, 198
Character:
  devices, 357
  tables, 206
Characters:
  getting from keyboard, 170
  writing to screen, 229
Clearing the screen, 224
Clock, 135
  tick, 136
Code pages, 118
Cold boot, 120
COM files, 76
Command interpreter, 109
Command line:
  parsing, 347
  parameters, 80
COMMAND.COM, 109
Comma-delimited files, 339
Compatibility, 134
Configuration list, 23
CONFIG.SYS, 110
Control characters, 211
Control codes, 52
Country dependent information, 112
CPU, 28
Critical errors, 91
Ctrl-Alt-Del, 156
Ctrl-Break, 155
Current directory, 301
Current drive, 299
Cursor, 236
  functions, 237
  mask, 185
  moving, 239
  size, 237

# D


Data security, 337
Data Transfer Area see DTA
Date stamp, 293, 344
Day of week, 143
DEBUG, 77
Decimal to hexadecimal conversion, 47
Device:
  commands, 366
  drivers, 356
  header, 360
  names, 357
Dip switches, 23
Direct Memory Access see DMA
Directory structure, 288
Disk:
  buffers, 314
  compression, 283
  drives, 261
  parameter table, 262
  sectors, 275
  share modes, 329
  status, 280
  type, 309
Disk Parameter Block see DPB
Disks, 263
Display modes, 223
Display pages, 225
Displaying strings, 232
DMA, 14
DOS, 99
  loading, 124
  BIOS, 108
  error codes, 281, 319
DOS versions, 99
  changing, 106
  minimum, 103
Drive numbers, 264
DRIVPARM, 253
DTA, 313
Duplicate keys, 168


# E


Echoing characters, 172
EGA, 199
  displaying characters, 235
Ending a program, 84
End-of-file marker, 339
Environment, 111
Errors, 89
EXE files, 76
Executable files, 76
Execution Unit, 30
Expanded memory, 59
Expansion boards, 34
Expansion ROMs, 18
Extended ASCII, 56
Extended memory, 59


# F


FAT, 304
  information, 309
  structure, 306
FCB, 345
File Allocation Table see FAT
File attributes, 294
File Control Blocks see FCB
File handles, 324
  duplicating, 338
File pointer, 333
File size, 348
File specifications, 316
File types, 333
File use codes, 331
Filenames, 289
Files, 313
  closing, 336
  creating, 326
  deleting, 311, 343
  matching, 316, 346
  opening, 329
  renaming, 343
  size, 348
Filters, 354
Flags register, 63

Floppy disk controller, 15
Floppy disk drives, 261
Focal point, 187
FORMAT, 287
Formatting, 267
Fragmentation, 305
Full-sized keyboards, 163
Functions, 140

## G

Gate arrays, 197
General registers, 61
Graphics modes, 212
Grey-scale monitors, 197

## H

Hard disks, 271
Hardware cursor, 237
Hardware interrupts, 128
Hercules, 198
Hexadecimal, 41
Hexadecimal to decimal conversion, 46

## I

Indicator lights, 156
Installable device drivers, 357
Instruction flow, 31
Instructions, 72
Interleaving, 274
Internal ports, 35
Interrupt replacements, 132
Interrupt vectors, 125
Interrupts, 125
  handling, 127
IOCTL, 365

## J

Joystick, 193

## K

Kernel, 109
Key repeats, 168
Key status, 154
KEYB codes, 119
KEYB programs, 166
Keyboard, 151
Keyboard buffer, 165
  clearing, 176
Keyboard hardware, 151
Keyboard operation, 152
Keyboard status, 154
Keyboard status bytes, 153
Keyboard translation table, 161

## L

Library files, 76
Light pen, 192
Linking, 76
Logical drives, 264

## M

Maskable interrupts, 128
MCA, 32
MCGA, 189
MDA, 198
Memory, 16
  organisation, 57
  allocating, 87
  map, 17
Mickeys, 184
Midnight flag, 136
Mnemonics, 75
Modem status codes, 251
Monitor, 194
Mouse, 179
  buttons, 189
  cursor, 182
  emulation, 192
  movement, 181
  parameters, 180

MOUSE.SYS, 179
Multiplex numbers, 94
Multi-tasking, 93

## N

Networks, 315
Non-maskable interrupt, 129

## O

Offset address, 57
Operands, 74

## P

Pages, 48
Palettes, 216
Paragraphs, 48
Parallel ports, 247
Parallel printer status, 255
Parsing command line, 347
Partitions, 273
PIC, 15
Pipes, 354
PIT, 13
PIT registers, 243
Pixels, 195
  components, 201
  functions, 214
Pointer registers, 62
Pointer speed, 185
Ports, 32
  sound, 246
Print Screen function, 257
Program Segment Prefix see PSP
Programmable Interrupt Controller see PIC
Programmable Interval Timer see PIT
Protected mode, 28
Protected modes, 73
Protocol, 248
PRTSC, 257
PSP, 78

## R

RAM, 16
RAM size, detecting, 27
RAM variables, 20
Random access files, 350
Raster line, 196
Reading characters from screen, 235
Reading data, 335
Real mode, 28
Real-time clock see RTC
Receiving data, 252
Redirection, 354
Registers, 59
Reporting characters, 173
Request header, 362
Resetting drives, 283
Resolution, 195
RGB colours, 202
ROM, 19
Root directory, 288
RTC, 139
RTC functions, 144

## S

Screen:
  clearing, 224
  border, 195
  components, 194
  mask, 185
  writing to memory, 208
Sector numbers, 266
Sectors:
  reading, 274
  writing, 276
Segment address, 57
Segment registers, 61
Self-testing, 121
Sequential files, 349
Serial ports, 247

Snow, 211
Software interrupts, 130
Sound, 241
Speaker, 243
Special keys, 158
Stack, 65
  segment, 67
String input, 177
Strings, displaying, 233
Subtraction, 49
Sub-directories, 298
  creating, 302
  deleting, 303
  renaming, 304
Sub-programs, 86
Sys Req, 157
System bus, 31
System clock, 12
System ports, 33
System RAM variables, 20
System reset, 123

# T

Teletype mode, 230
Terminate and Stay Resident see TSR
Text mode, 203
Time functions, 146
Time stamp, 292, 344
Time-out errors, 257
Timing processes, 135
TSR, 96

# U

Upper Memory Area see UMA
UMA, 19, 88
User mouse interrupt, 191
User RAM, 16

# V

Verification of data, 276
Version number, 99
VGA, 199
Video DAC registers, 221
Video display, 194
Video ports, 200
Video RAM, 18, 197
Video state, 203
Volume labels, 297

# W

Warm boot, 123
Windows, 226
Words, 39
Writing data, 335

# X

XGA, 200

**Disk Offer**

In order to save you from the frustrations of having to key in listings and create your own general utilities, the author has prepared a disk containing all the source code from this book plus many other routines, both as ASCII text and as standalone programs.

The programs include: a text editor, a disk sector editor, a memory viewer/editor, and extended versions of the programs contained in the book.

Also included are A86 and D86, the symbolic debugger. Both of these are Shareware, and although no charge is made, all users should register for these. Registration gives the user a printed manual and software updates.

The price of the author's disk is £19.95 inc VAT and P&P.

To obtain your disks, send a cheque with order, stating disk format, to: